V&R

PALAESTRA

Untersuchungen zur
europäischen Literatur

Begründet von Erich Schmidt und Alois Brandl

Herausgegeben von

Wilfried Barner, Heinrich Detering,
Klaus Grubmüller, Volker Honemann,
Dieter Lamping, Gerhard Lauer

Band 331

Vandenhoeck & Ruprecht

Kristin Veel

Narrative Negotiations

Information Structures in Literary Fiction

Vandenhoeck & Ruprecht

Verantwortlicher Herausgeber:
Dieter Lamping

Bibliografische Information der Deutschen Nationalbibliothek

Die Deutsche Nationalbibliothek verzeichnet diese Publikation in der
Deutschen Nationalbibliografie; detaillierte bibliografische Daten sind
im Internet über http://dnb.d-nb.de abrufbar.

ISBN 978-3-525-20604-1

Gedruckt mit Unterstützung der Carlsberg Foundation, Kopenhagen.

Gesamtherstellung: ⊕ Hubert & Co, Göttingen

Gedruckt auf alterungsbeständigem Papier.

Contents

Acknowledgements

My interest in the field of literature and information technology has accompanied me since my second year at university when I first became engaged with the cultural implications of digital technology. This interest can be traced through most of my subsequent essays, dissertations, and articles, and some of the works of fiction discussed in this book are consequently works with which I have had a long term engagement and in which I keep finding new material and inspiration for thinking about these issues.

The research for this book has been made possible by a Carlsberg Studentship at Churchill College, University of Cambridge and the Arts and Humanities Research Council Postgraduate Award, for which I am immensely grateful. Also, Churchill College and the German Department Tiarks Fund have been generous in supporting my participation at conferences in the UK and abroad.

The number of people who have been of inspiration and encouragement to me is vast. In particular I should like to mention Dr. Christian J. Emden, who gave me the courage to pursue a Ph.D. in the first place and Dr. Isak Winkel Holm, who supported the development of the first stages of the present study. Also, I should like to thank my examiners Dr. Andrew Webber and Professor Andrew Bowie, who have both been most helpful and encouraging. Their feedback has been invaluable in the process of turning my dissertation into the present book. But most of all I would like to thank my supervisor, Dr. David Midgley, who with admirable patience and endless encouragement has given this project his indispensable support and attention through all its stages. The completion of this book is indebted to his extraordinary skill for asking critical and thought-provoking questions.

I should also like to thank Rositza Alexandrova, Kate Elswit, Dr. David Finnegan, Dr. Bettina Göbels, Dr. Nicolette Makovicky, Dora Osborne, Dr. Philip Raymont, Henriette Steiner, Uta Staiger, Dr. Inga Volmer, as well as the staff and my fellow students at the German Department and at Churchill College for their invaluable input and engaging discussions; Louise Brygger Jacobi, Lise Rovsing, Grethe Veel, Jørgen Albrechtsen and Morten Toft for unquestioning support; and finally my mother, Sidsel Veel, who sadly is not here to read these lines, but who I know would have been the proudest of all. Had she not instilled the love of literature in me from my very birth and lent her support each step of the way, this book would never have come into being.

Introduction

> There is an essential – as I see it –
> distinction between stories, on the
> one hand, which have, as their goal,
> an end, completeness, closure, and,
> on the other hand, information,
> which is always, by definition,
> partial, incomplete, fragmentary.
>
> Susan Sontag[1]

All of the texts considered in this book are characterised by a negotiation of this distinction between stories and information; they are characterised by what we shall call a *narrative negotiation* in which ways of organising information – *information structures* – are adopted, adapted, and incorporated into the narrative of cultural imagination with a particular focus on *literary fiction*.

Susan Sontag's observation was made in a posthumously published lecture from 2004, and it eloquently captures the conditions of fictional storytelling at the beginning of the twenty-first century. The amount of information that we encounter daily has increased dramatically over the last few centuries, not least due to the developments in media technology that have led to significant changes in the ability to store, access, and communicate information. Today we thus find ourselves in a world globally linked by media that provide us with continuous information from the whole world about the whole world. This has an effect on literary fiction, which can react in one of two ways. It can either reinforce the difference between fictional storytelling and the flow of information, defending fiction's ability to select what is important and exclude what is not, as Sontag argues.[2] Or it

---

1 Sontag, p. 224.

2 Sontag's distinction between »information« and »story« echoes a similar distinction which Walter Benjamin makes in the essay »Der Erzähler« (1936/37). Benjamin sees »information« as a type of communication whose content is verifiable and explainable in a way that leaves little space for the type of meaning that »story« is able to convey. For Benjamin the diminished room for »story« is linked to the way in which the material conditions of communication alter the conditions of human perception. In this and other essays (for instance »Krisis des Romans« (1930)) he draws

can aim to incorporate the overload of information into the story, thereby challenging the boundaries of what storytelling entails, but in effect creating stories that respond to what seems to be the current cultural conditions of information processing. This book explores novels that take the latter approach. These are novels that have been greeted in newspaper reviews with the common objection that they overwhelm the reader with too much information, thus failing to present the completeness that Sontag refers to as an intrinsic quality of literary fiction. However, this objection also situates these novels in a tradition which is as long as the novel genre itself; i.e. in the company of novels which, although seeking to tell a story, display a fundamental uneasiness with narrativity as a mode of representation and embody an inherent negotiation of how a story can be told that opens itself towards the inclusion of »partial, incomplete, fragmentary« information.

There are several reasons for focussing on the novel, and, in order to understand these in more depth, it is relevant to take a brief look at and consider the properties of this genre and why it facilitates an investigation into a negotiation of narrativity. From Georg Lukács and Mikhail Bakthin to Milan Kundera, most theorists of the novel seem to agree on the hybridity of the novel and its ability to include a multiplicity of linguistic registers and rhetorical codes as being the most marked characteristics of the genre. The European novel grew out of a diverse field of fictional genres. The epic tradition forms an important backdrop for the development of this type of prose writing, as does the medieval romance, as we know from Miguel de Cervantes' *Don Quixote* (1605-1615), which features a protagonist who has lost his wits from reading romances. Texts as diverse in time and scope as Petronius' *Satyricon* (1st c. AD) and Boccaccio's *Decameron* (c.1349-51) contain elements which, with hindsight, mark them out as antecedents to the novel genre. Also, looking at some of the canonical early modern novels such as Thomas More's *Utopia* (1516), Rabelais' *Gargantua* (1534) and *Pantagruel* (1534), and a century later Daniel Defoe's *Robinson Crusoe* (1719) and Laurence Sterne's *Tristram Shandy* (1759-69), effectively illustrates the large scope and heterogeneity varieties of material which the novel is able to accommodate. Even though the seventeenth and eighteenth

---

attention to the way in which material developments change the function of meaning in social life and leave their mark on modes of representation. A similar line of enquiry can be found in Theodor W. Adorno's essay »Standort des Erzählers im zeitgenössischen Roman« (1954) in which he considers the conditions for the novel in the twentieth century. The type of approach found in theorists such as Benjamin and Adorno highlights the intricate and mutually dependent relationship between the developments of society, technology, and modes of representation. The present study aims to explore contemporary fiction's negotiation between information and story as it takes shape in an information society, adopting a perspective which does not regard information as necessarily threatening to story-telling.

centuries witnessed a consolidation of the genre and a marked increase in its popularity, in particular among the reading bourgeoisie, the genre remains hybrid as it continues to divide into subgenres such as the adventure novel, the epistolary novel, the Bildungsroman, the comic novel, the realist and the naturalist novel. Entering the twentieth century the notion of a crisis of the novel begins to be heard. In his essays on Alfred Döblin and Nikolai Lesskow, Walter Benjamin contrasts the old art of storytelling with the novel and laments the erosion of the epic.[3] His main objection to the novel, which has much in common with the critiques of Lukács and Adorno, has to do with the close connection between the emergence of the novel and that of modern, introspective subjectivity. The novel and its medium (the book, which encourages silent reading as a private occupation) seem to lend themselves to an articulation of the individual and his or her inner thoughts and feelings. In *Die Theorie des Romans* Lukács describes the form of the novel as: »die Wanderung des problematischen Individuums zu sich selbst«,[4] and indeed the genre seems to have come of age in the same period as this form of subjectivity.

We here touch upon a marked difference in thinking about the novel's historical character. For Lukács as well as Adorno the advent of the novel genre is intricately linked to modernity and what is called the bourgeois age.[5] The formal crisis for the novel consequently has to do with the crisis of bourgeois subjectivity and individuality. Mikhail Bakthin, on the other hand, bestows on the novel genre the ability to renew itself over and over; as a subversive genre he argues that it is new in whatever age it emerges.[6] Indeed, it seems today that, although the death of the novel has been proclaimed repeatedly, it remains a very robust genre, not least due to its ability to adapt and constantly transgress itself. Also, the preoccupation with investigating the human subject is something which remains a topic for the novel and which is explored and contested in the twentieth and twenty-first centuries too. It is precisely this ability to adapt, along with its continued interest in human existence and its representation, which facilitates the creation of a space that allows for the present book's exploration of narrativity. The close relationship between the novel genre and subjectivity makes it particularly well suited to address the adequacy of narrativity for representing human life and subjectivity. Although narrative negotiations can be found in narrative genres other than the novel, the novel's heterogeneous form and ongoing interest in the representation of human existence makes it

---

3 Benjamin, Krisis des Romans; Benjamin, Der Erzähler.
4 Lukács, p. 70.
5 Adorno, p. 61.
6 Bakthin, p. 7.

especially useful for this type of investigation and helps to emphasise the historical perspective in which contemporary narrative negotiations should be seen.

The aim of the present study is to broaden the understanding of the conditions of literary fiction in an information age by regarding the narrative negotiation, which we shall trace, from a double perspective: one that concerns *the impact of information technology[7] on the development of literary forms and modes of representation*, and another which relates the discussion to a more fundamental questioning of the *relationship between narrative and human perception and representation inherent in the novel genre.* These two aspects of the enquiry are brought together through Ernst Cassirer's notion of *symbolic form*, which provides a theoretical framework for approaching the cultural impact of information technology. This introduction will outline the nature of this double perspective, which also determines the overall structure of the book, and will then move on to illustrate the usefulness of the concept of symbolic form for this approach. The first section situates the enquiry in the theoretical field of information technology and cultural studies, establishing the relevance of speaking of an impact of information technology on culture in the twenty-first century. The second section goes on to look at the reasons why it may be argued that the narrative negotiation between stories and information is intrinsic to the novel genre, or indeed something fundamentally human. This brings us to the third section, which shows how the concept of symbolic form provides a relevant theoretical framework for approaching the cultural impact of information technology that allows for equal acknowledgement of each of the two perspectives accounted for in the two previous sections.

1.1 Information Overload

Looking firstly at the impact of information technology, regard must be had to the extensive academic field to which this study relates. The extent of the impact of information technology on human life has inevitably caused it to generate interest in nearly every academic field, with the matter having been approached from sociological, economic, legal, psychological, philosophical, and aesthetic perspectives, as well as causing new disciplines to arise. In this context we shall not attempt a survey of the wide range of work done on the impact of the computer since the first prototypes were de-

---

7 The term »information technology«, as it is used in this book, refers to computer-based information and communication systems (often also referred to as ICT - »Information and Communication Technology«).

veloped in the 1930s and 1940s, but merely point out that our relationship to digital information technology has been dominated by two opposing sentiments. Firstly, the hope that this technology would make our world a better and easier place to live – that it would help us reach erstwhile unattainable goals.[8] And secondly, the fear that something fundamentally human could be lost, that the advent of digital technology could mean that human communication would become mere mathematical calculation where everything is turned into numbers – imageless, soundless, and wordless entities. 0's and 1's.[9] Although both this optimism and scepticism are still at the heart of much of what is said and thought about information technology today, we are now moving slowly away from these conceptions of information technology and are beginning to see it as part of our everyday lives. When information technology is no longer a foreign object which threatens or promises to change everything we know and believe, it is time to start contemplating how it influences the way in which we experience and represent the world. This is what is important for many media theorists today.[10]

---

8 See, for instance, Donna Haraway's »A Cyborg Manifesto: Science, Technology, and Socialist-Feminism in the Late Twentieth Century« from 1985. Haraway sees possibilities for breaking down the Western traditions' dualisms in the melting of man and machine: »High-tech culture challenges these dualisms in intriguing ways. It is not clear who makes and who is made in the relation between human and machine.« (Haraway, p. 532). The same kind of optimism has dominated theories on the internet and its perceived opportunities to break down geographical, social, political and cultural borders by giving all (or at least all who have access to the internet) a medium for reaching a large audience. The American frontier myth has been transposed to the internet, where one hopes to bring about a change in the political and social geography of power and contribute to the creation of a more democratic world in which minorities are heard (Eubanks). When it comes to the aesthetics of information technology, this discourse was initially governed by a belief in the new medium to realize the aspirations of the avant-garde movements (Lovejoy; Bolter) or poststructuralist theory (Landow, Hypertext; Landow, Hypertext 2.0; Landow, Hyper/Text/Theory; or Landow and Delany).

9 A »high« versus »low« culture divide is transposed to the computer field, and the computer comes to embody an unwanted levelling of culture. Sven Birkerts' *The Gutenberg Elegies* (1994) is exemplary in this respect: »Next to the new technologies, the scheme of things represented by print and the snail-paced linearity of the reading act looks stodgy and dull. Many educators say that our students are less and less able to read, or analyze, or write with clarity and purpose. Who can blame the students? Everything they meet with in the world around them gives the signal: That was then, and electronic communications are now.« (Birkerts, p. 119). The scepticism can also be found in science fiction which characterises the computer as a potential threat, which will eventually acquire a life of its own and attempt to take over the world. See, for instance, Stanley Kubrick's *2001: A Space Odyssey* (1968) or the Terminator movies (1984-2003).

10 Although different in their aim and scope, several theorists fit this description, for example Marie-Laure Ryan, who deals with questions of narrativity in digital media; Lev Manovich, who looks at new media aesthetics especially in relation to visual culture and cinema; Espen Aarseth, whose focus is on game studies; Mark B.N. Hansen, whose interest lies in the implications for human perception and consciousness; and N. Katherine Hayles, who approaches questions of subjectivity, the body, literature, and information technologies. They are among the people who dominate the field of digital aesthetics today and promise to go beyond the dichotomies of earlier

In the essay »Flesh and Metal. Reconfiguring the Mindbody in Virtual Environments« N. Katherine Hayles argues that:

Living in a technologically engineered and information-rich environment brings with it associated shifts in habits, postures, enactments, perceptions – in short, changes in the experiences that constitute the dynamic lifeworld we inhabit as embodied creatures.[11]

One of the premises of this study is that information technology, and the changes it brings about, have an impact on our experience of the world and the way in which we represent it, and that looking at how this impact works its way into the narrative construction of contemporary fiction gives us an insight into the nature of this effect. The focus of this book is not on where »human logic« and »machine logic« differ, but on how human imagination deals with and incorporates the effects of information technology in the way in which narrative structures are formed. When talking about information technology and its impact, it is thus important to regard this in the larger field of social experience to which it belongs.

1.2 Narrative Negotiations

The other premise from which we shall work is that this negation of narrativity also forms part of a long literary tradition of uneasiness with narrativity as a mode of representing human life and experience. In this section the foundation is laid for the adoption of such an approach in the rest of the book. We shall explore the nature of uneasiness about narrativity by looking firstly at the importance which narrativity has recently acquired across a wide number of academic fields, and contrast this with the resistance towards narativity that can also be found in postmodern fiction and contemporary theory. This necessitates a more precise identification of the nature of this uneasiness about narrativity, which will be obtained by looking at Roman Jakobson's theory of language and David Lodge's exploration of the relationship between language and literary tendencies from the nineteenth century onwards. We shall thus be able to establish the resistance towards narrativity as being simultaneously related to fundamental linguistic qualities and reflected in the development of literary history, which prepares us for the exploration of the position of contemporary literature.

---

discourses. In the development of the argument we shall return to their individual approaches. However, the theoretical shift is also reflected in contemporary printed literature: the computer no longer mainly occurs in science fiction; it has become an everyday object, and we can now begin to see how it has left its mark on ways of representing and narrating.

11 Hayles, Flesh and Metal, p. 299.

In chapter 2 we shall take a closer look at three canonical German novels which are representative of the hybridity and problematisation of narrative which we discussed above as general features of the history of the novel: Goethe's *Wilhelm Meisters Wanderjahre* (1829), Robert Musil's *Der Mann ohne Eigenschaften* (1930-42), and Arno Schmidt's *Zettels Traum* (1970) all stand out in German literary history (as well as in literary history more generally) as challenging novel experiments which push the boundaries of the genre. In their own way, each of these works address the issue of narration, resist it, and yet also make it possible. They all explore the relationship between narrativity and the perception and representation of human existence by developing narrative structures that make use of figures such as the archive, the network, and the game to suggest a transgression of the narrative. They are therefore interesting as historical reference points which embody an early formulation of the same issues that will be seen in the more recent novels that incorporate the figures of information technology in their articulation of a negotiation of narrativity.[12]

The correspondences which we shall see between the canonical novels and the more recent examples point towards an ongoing negotiation of narrativity intrinsic to the novel genre. This is worth exploring further, not least because narrativity has within recent years become almost universally acknowledged as representing a way of understanding human life and experience across a large number of academic disciplines. The so-called »narrative turn« spread from the development of structuralist theories of narrative in France in the mid to late 1960s. In 1969 Tzvetan Todorov coined the term »la narratologie« to describe the theory and study of narrative structures as they can be found in the work of French structuralists such as Roland Barthes, Claude Bremond, Gérard Genette, and Algirdas Julien Greimas. In subsequent decades narration has come to be seen as a fundamental condition of our representation of experience and an explanatory mode for our ways of representing experience within a wide range of academic disciplines. More recently, cognitive semantic theorists such as Mark Turner have sought to describe the operations of the mind as essentially narrative, arguing that: »Story is a basic principle of mind. Most of our experience, our knowledge, and our thinking is organized as stories«.[13]

---

12 As can be seen from the selection of texts, this study takes a Germanic context as its starting point. This allows for the recognition of thematic correspondences and intertextual references between the selected texts. However, the issues dealt with are not done justice when they are regarded as limited to a specific linguistic area, and Scandinavian, English, and French examples are thus included in order to indicate the scope of the argument.

13 Turner, p. i.

This cognitive side of the argument for narrativity also has an existential equivalent. A key figure in this approach has been Paul Ricœur, who points to narrative as the dominating cultural form enabling humans to understand time, the world, and their own identity. When we construct a narrative we establish a model for understanding ourselves as subjects placed in time in the shape of a sequential plot. Narration transforms the surrounding heterogeneous world into a plot, a construction of a whole which Ricœur describes as »concordance discordante«[14] – an incoherent coherency. In his book *Narrative and the Self* (1991) Anthony Kerby eloquently sums up the breadth of the use of narrative as a model for human conceptualisation:

> Narratives are a primary embodiment of our understanding of the world, of experience, and ultimately of ourselves. Narrative emplotment appears to yield a form of understanding of human experience, both individual and collective, that is not directly amenable to other forms of exposition or analysis.[15]

However, alongside this increasing trust in narrativity as the fundamentally human way of understanding ourselves and our presence in time, literary works from the same period by writers such as Jorge Luis Borges and Italo Calvino display an accentuated uneasiness with narrativity. In the introduction to *Narrative across Media. The Languages of Storytelling* (2004), Marie-Laure Ryan comments on this ambiguity towards narrativity, which can be found especially in what might be termed postmodern texts:

> Many postmodern texts present themselves as bits of pieces of a narrative image but prevent the reader from ever achieving the reconstruction of a stable and complete narrative script. This may explain why narrative theory has never been comfortable with either including or excluding postmodern literature.[16]

The present study aims to show that this discomfort was present long before the emergence of the postmodern texts, although it seemed to intensify throughout the twentieth century alongside the increase in the amounts of information available in our lifeworld. As a narrative form par excellence, which furthermore is closely linked to modern subjectivity, the novel genre provides a particularly fruitful focus area for studying this development. The resistance to the narrative mode of representation appears to be an inseparable companion – an inherent reaction or challenge – which makes its presence felt to a greater or lesser extent whenever we have a narrative. In the article »Against Narrativity« (2004), Galen Strawson goes so far as to set forth the argument that:

---

14 Ricœur, p. 13.
15 Kerby, p. 3.
16 Ryan, Narrative across Media, p. 10.

It's just not true that there is only one good way for human beings to experience their being in time. There are deeply non-Narrative people and there are good ways to live that are deeply non-Narrative.[17]

Strawson argues against the conception of narrativity as equivalent to human nature. He theorizes the possibility of an *episodic* self-experience alongside a *diachronic* self-experience. In contrast to a diachronic self-experience, an episodic self-experience implies that »one does not figure oneself, considered as a self, as something that was there in the (further) past and will be there in the (further) future«.[18] In making this claim Strawson distinguishes between a human being taken as a whole and the experience of oneself as a self. I can thus be aware that I have a past as a human being, but therefore not conceive of this past as a narrative, because I do not relate to this past as the past of the self I conceive myself to be in the present. People who are what Strawson calls episodics are likely to have no particular inclination to conceive of their life in narrative terms, whereas many diachronics do. Narrative is here taken to mean: »a certain sort of *developmental* and hence temporal *unity* or *coherence* to the things to which it is standardly applied – lives, parts of lives, pieces of writing«.[19] Considering your life as a narrative, however, entails more than having a diachronic outlook on life – it also entails some tendency towards *form-finding*.[20]

In *Narrative across Media*, Marie-Laure Ryan comments on the difficulty of defining the opposite of narrative:

Since we have a clearer intuitive idea of what narrative is than of what it contrasts to, the Saussurean program of defining the units of language differentially fails in this case for a lack of neighbouring elements.[21]

In order to understand the nature of an opposition to narrativity in a larger framework, let us, as a starting point, look at Roman Jakobson's classic essay »Two« Aspects of Language and Two Types of Aphasic Disturbances« from 1956 and the way in which he addresses what he regards as the dual nature of language. For Jakobson it is axiomatic that »Speech implies a SE-

---

17 Strawson, p. 429.
18 Ibid. p. 430.
19 Ibid. p. 439.
20 Ibid. p. 441. What is at stake here is, to a certain degree, a question of definition. Strawson is not willing to regard »random or radically unconnected sequences of events even when they are sequentially and indeed contiguously temporally ordered« (Strawson, pp. 439-40) as narrative. A more inclusive definition of narrative might do so and venture to see narrative in literally everything. Because human beings live in time, sequence is essentiality impossible to avoid. So on the one hand we are dealing with a question of definitions, and on the other Strawson's article reflects an inclination in theory and contemporary art which seeks beyond narrative and tries to identify its opposites.
21 Ryan, Narrative across Media, p. 8.

LECTION of certain linguistic entities and their COMBINATION into linguistic units of a higher degree of complexity«.[22] He draws on Ferdinand Saussure's conception of language as consisting of a *syntagmatic axis* (concerning positioning) and a *paradigmatic axis* (concerning substitution). The paradigmatic relation describes what Saussure calls »associative relations«,[23] i.e. the possibility of exchanging words in a sentence, whereas the syntagm describes a larger entity that contains a meaning in itself. Language is thus characterised by two complementary yet radically opposed operations: *selection* and *combination*. A sentence is constructed by selecting certain linguistic entities and combining them into a linguistic unit. In the sentence »The cat watched the bird«, the word »watched« is selected from the range of words that would fill the same function, i.e. it has to be a verb and taken from the same semantic field (other options could be »looked at«, »stared at«, »gazed at«). The axis of selection thus has to do with the paradigmatic relation between words (the associative possibilities of exchanging words in a sentence). Elements in the paradigmatic dimension are represented by *not* being there – they are the words not chosen. The axis of combination on the other hand is related to the syntagm, i.e. the actual combination of the words which *were* chosen and which in combination make up a larger linguistic unit that contains a meaning in itself. This underlying conception of language might be represented schematically as follows:

Selection (Paradigm, Metaphor, Similarity)

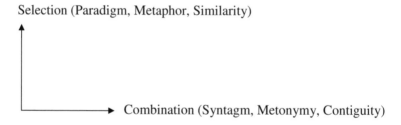

Combination (Syntagm, Metonymy, Contiguity)

Jakobson relates these two characteristics of language to the stylistic phenomena of metonymy and metaphor, and proposes a theory of language as oscillating between a metaphoric and a metonymic pole. Selection has to do with perceiving *similarity* and is therefore the process by which metaphor is generated, whereas metonymy involves combination because it has to do with relations between things that stand in a *contiguous* relation to one another. The context of the word thus becomes highly important.

---

22 Jakobson, p. 58.
23 Saussure, p. 121.

In addition to the well-known link he establishes between metaphoric and metonymic language and two types of aphasia, Jakobson also relates the distinction between the metaphoric and the metonymic pole of language to art and culture more generally:

In normal verbal behaviour both processes are continually operative, but careful observation will reveal that under the influence of a cultural pattern, personality, and verbal style, preference is given to one of the two processes over the other.[24]

According to Jakobson's theory, poetry, lyrics, and periods such as Romanticism and Symbolism thus belong to the metaphoric axis, whereas prose, epics, and realism belong to the metonymic axis. This gives us a starting point for relating Jakobson's distinction to the uneasiness with narrativity which we are tracing. A helping hand is given in *The Modes of Modern Writing. Metaphor, Metonymy, and the Typology of Modern Literature* (1977) by David Lodge, in which he relates Jakobson's thesis that all discourse tends towards either the metaphoric or the metonymic pole to the oscillation Lodge identifies in modern literature between the belief that art mimics life on the one hand and the belief that life mimics art on the other.[25] The intriguing achievement of Lodge's book is to relate these two diverging views on the relationship between art and life to Roman Jakobson's theory of the polarity between metaphor and metonymy. This provides a theoretical framework for analysing modern literature, and Lodge proceeds to map out the oscillation between realism and modernism throughout the twentieth century as an alternation between a metaphoric and a metonymic preference in the mode of representation. According to Lodge the implications of Jakobson's theory can be summed up as follows:

The theory (crudely summarized) states that all discourse connects one topic with another, either because they are in some sense similar to each other, or because they are in some sense contiguous with each other; and implies that if you attempt to group topics according to some other principle, or absence of principle, the human mind will nevertheless persist in trying to make sense of the text thus produced by looking

---

24 Jakobson, p. 90.

25 The notion that art should mimic life is, generally speaking, the classical definition of Western aesthetics, which prevailed until the beginning of the nineteenth century, and stimulated an ongoing debate about the manner of imitation. However, Romantic theories of imagination mark a change in thinking about the relationship between art and life which became more and more outspoken during the nineteenth century. It can be summed up in Oscar Wilde's famous dictum that »life imitates art«, meaning that the reality we perceive is constructed by culturally determined mental structures, and that it is art which contributes to renewing these mental structures. As a consequence art does not imitate life, but other art. Art in a sense hereby presents itself as an autonomous loop that feeds on itself (Lodge, p. 70).

in it for relationships of similarity and/or contiguity; and insofar as a text succeeds in defeating such interpretation, it defeats itself.[26]

As Lodge sees it, realist texts subscribe to a metonymic order, while modernistic texts oppose this and aim to find alternative ways of organising a story through a practice of metaphoric order or radical use of metonomy. What is interesting for our purpose here is Lodge's observation that an emphasis on metaphorical or paradigmatic relationships in the discourse leads to a weakening of metonymic or syntagmatic relationships such as contiguity in time and space and cause and effect.[27] These are exactly the categories that we shall observe becoming problematic in the novels we shall be looking at, and which serve to problematize a narrative conception of human existence and the novel genre.

The link between realism and metonymy that Jakobson proposes and Lodge develops could be taken further by looking at the link between metonymy and narrative more specifically, rather than between metonymy and realism as Lodge does. Realist fiction most often takes the form of a narrative, but a narrative need not be realistic in order to be a narrative. Realism often entails a recognisable world and most often also a certain degree of reference to the prevailing social and political situation. A narrative, on the contrary, is still a narrative even if the world to which it refers does not stand in a mimetic relation to our own world (the examples of science fiction and fairy tales appear to prove this point). What interests us in this context is not the correspondence between fiction and the »real world«, but rather the features of narrativity and »its neighbouring elements«. It is part of Lodge's argument that modernism organises narrative in non-linear ways, and it is from this description of the characteristics of modernist fiction that we shall take the cue:

Modernist fiction eschews the straight chronological ordering of its material, and the use of a reliable, omniscient and intrusive narrator. It employs, instead, either a single, limited point of view, or a method of multiple points of view, all more or less limited and fallible: and it tends towards a fluid or complex handling of time, involving much cross-reference backwards and forwards across the chronological span of the action.[28]

Rather than focussing mainly on realist and modernist representation, it seems for this purpose more appropriate to shift the centre of attention and relate the polarity between metonymy and metaphor to the distinction between narrative and its neighbouring elements. The metonymic characteris-

---

26 Lodge, p. 228.
27 Ibid. p. 104f.
28 Ibid. p. 46.

tics that Jakobson identifies (combination, contiguity, and context), which he relates to prose and epic, make sense as descriptive factors of what distinguishes a narrative, according to Marie-Laure Ryan's definition:

A narrative text is one that brings a world to the mind (setting) and populates it with intelligent agents (characters). These agents participate in actions and happenings (events, plot), which cause global changes in the narrative world. Narrative is thus a mental representation of causally connected states and events that captures a segment in the history of a world and of its members.[29]

Likewise, the metaphoric pole (selection, similarity, substitution) seems to lend itself to the aim of transgressing narratives, which we shall see in the figures of the archive, the network, and the game, and subsequently the database, the hyperlink, and the computer game. The distinction between metaphor and metonymy thus gives us a point of reference in the definition of the characteristics of narrative's »neighbouring elements«, which will become more concrete when we turn to specific works of fiction. In the analysis of the construction of the narrative, the thinking behind the metaphor/metonymy distinction will become useful as a framework for identifying the elements that support the narrative and those that disrupt it.

This rather lengthy excursion via Jakobson and Lodge helps us to answer the central question of whether non-narrative traits should be regarded as representative of certain movements in modern literary history or whether we are in fact dealing with two fundamental yet diverging ways of perceiving and representing experience and human existence in modernity. Our analysis of narrative and its neighbouring elements in relation to Roman Jakobson's positing of metaphoric and metonymic poles of language seems to underscore the assumption that the opposition is not merely a literary fad but has roots in fundamentally different ways of connecting one topic with another in language. However, Lodge's analysis has shown us that modern literary history seems to oscillate between these two poles. When read with these two points in mind, the fluctuation between narrative and the transgression of narrative indeed presents itself as something fundamentally human, though it is possible that different literary periods might privilege one over the other.

The question that now remains is where to situate those works of contemporary fiction that work with ways of organising information that relate

---

29 Ryan, Narrative across Media, p. 337. The anthology *Narrative across Media*, from which this definition is taken, gives an insight into the dominant positions on narrative within the areas of face-to-face narration, still pictures, moving pictures, music, and digital media, operating from the viewpoint that narrative is non-media specific. The narrative definition found here is thus useful for capturing essential characteristics of narrative which can be found across cultures and across media.

to information technology. In chapter 3 an attempt will be made to tackle the way in which narrativity is addressed in novels of the last two decades, some of which may well fall under the heading »postmodern«, and others which consciously aim to transgress what is commonly conceived of as the postmodern. In *The Modes of Modern Writing*, Lodge discusses postmodernist fiction, referring to works by John Vladimir Nabokov, Alain Robbe-Grillet, and Thomas Pynchon among others. Lodge's claim is that postmodern literature should not be considered as either subscribing to a metonymic or a metaphoric order. Rather, postmodern literature distinguishes itself by defying the obligation to choose between the two principles of connecting one topic with another and rejecting order altogether through various strategies of mediation, which Lodge terms contradiction, permutation, discontinuity, randomness, excess, and short circuit. Through this rejection of order, postmodern literature essentially threatens to abolish itself by destroying the norms against which it can be measured.[30]

However, a recent argument for the continued validity of the two types of ordering principles in contemporary culture can be found in Lev Manovich's discussion of narrativity in relation to what he terms a database logic in *The Language of New Media* (2001). His theories will be discussed in more detail in chapter 3.1, which focuses specifically on the database, but in this context it is relevant to point to the way in which he conceptualises the distinction between narrative and »its neighbouring elements«. His starting point is the following:

Many new media objects do not tell stories; they do not have a beginning or end; in fact, they do not have any development, thematically, formally, or otherwise that would organize their elements into a sequence.[31]

Instead he describes their structure as that of a »database« and sees the logic of this as opposing a narrative logic: »Database and narrative are natural enemies. Competing for the same territory of human culture, each claims an exclusive right to make meaning out of the world.«[32] Although Manovich's conceptualisations of the database can be qualified, as we shall see in chapter 3.1, the database seems to be characterised by another type of ordering principle than that of narrativity. Manovich defines the relationship between the database and narrative by using Saussure's terms syntagm and paradigm. He applies to the database the paradigmatic relation (the associative possibility of exchanging words in a sentence) that we found on the metaphoric pole, whereas he applies to the narrative the syntagm (a larger entity

---

30 Lodge, p. 145.
31 Manovich, The Language of New Media, p. 218.
32 Ibid. p. 225.

that contains a meaning in itself) that we found on the metonymic pole. The syntagmatic elements are present (they are what we see), whereas the paradigmatic elements are present only in their absence (we can imagine the words not chosen). According to Manovich this relationship between presence and absence is turned upside down by digital media. Whereas in the novel it is the paradigm (all the potential words the writer did not choose) which is implicit, in the computer it is the syntagm (the concise structure which makes the sentence a unified whole) which is only potentially present.[33] Translated into the dichotomy between narrative and non-narrative, we thus see a continuation into contemporary times of the fluctuation between the two, where the elements challenging narrativity nonetheless seem to have acquired modern-day support from the logic of information technology.

This allows us to formulate one of the central questions of this study: how does the novel react to the encounter with the pervasiveness of information technology, which apparently accentuates modes of representation that have a different ordering principle than that of a causal, linear narration? Manovich describes the exchange between information technology and other parts of human culture as a two-way barter: whereas the interfaces of the computer were originally built so as to mimic familiar physical interfaces such as a filing cabinet, a trash can and a control panel, today we see the logic of the computer percolating back into other parts of human culture. It can be argued that this is the case for the mode of representation to be found in contemporary novels, which, through information technology, acquire figures that influence the construction of narrative structures and aid them in articulating an ongoing negotiation of narrativity inherent in the novel genre. Apart from the database we shall look at the hyperlink and the computer game as examples of information structures that each highlight different characteristic elements of the way in which information technology organizes information and represents the world. What we are in need of is a methodology for articulating this relationship between the figures of information technology and their cultural impact.

1.3 Information Technology as Symbolic Form

We have now been introduced to the two different contexts in which we shall explore literary fiction in an information age: firstly, the impact of information technology on the development of literary forms and modes of

---

33 Ibid. p. 231.

representation, and secondly, a more fundamental questioning of the relationship between narrative and human perception and representation. In the present section these two strands are brought together by approaching information technology in terms of Ernst Cassirer's notion of *symbolic forms*. The present study sets out to show that information technology can be regarded as a symbolic form in our present-day lives. This approach allows us to take both the contemporary influence of information technology and an ongoing negotiation of narrativity into consideration when dealing with the close analyses of recent fiction.

In *The Language of New Media*, Lev Manovich uses the term symbolic form to describe the database as a way of structuring our conception of the world:

> A literary or cinematic narrative, an architectural plan, and a database each present a different model of what a world is like. It is this sense of a database as a cultural form of its own that I want to address here. Following art historian Erwin Panofsky's analysis of the linear perspective as a ›symbolic form‹ of the modern age, we may even call database a new symbolic form of the computer age [...] a new way to structure our experience of ourselves and of the world.[34]

Although Manovich does not elaborate further on the way in which he uses the term symbolic form, and even if it seems to have become absorbed into more or less general usage, I believe that Manovich's choice of the term indicates the need for developing specific concepts with which to reflect on the cultural significance of the forms of digital media. Art historian Erwin Panofsky's (1892-1968) use of the term symbolic form, which Manovich refers to here, was inspired by the German philosopher Ernst Cassirer (1874-1945), who developed an extensive philosophy of human culture on the basis of the notion of symbolic forms. Let us consider therefore the way in which Cassirer envisages the symbolic form before we come back to why the concept is useful for thinking about the impact of information technology on contemporary culture.

In »Der Begriff der symbolischen Form im Aufbau der Geisteswissenschaften« (1921-22) Cassirer defines a symbolic form in the following manner:

> Unter einer ›symbolischen Form‹ soll jede Energie des Geistes verstanden werden, durch welche ein geistiger Bedeutungsgehalt an ein konkretes sinnliches Zeichen geknüpft und diesem Zeichen innerlich zugeeignet wird.[35]

---

34 Ibid. p. 219.
35 Cassirer, Der Begriff der symbolischen Form, p. 175.

However vague this definition seems at first, it captures the essential features of what Cassirer has in mind when he speaks about symbolic forms. A symbolic form consists of three elements: a sensory sign, a spiritual meaning, and a spiritual energy which describes the way in which the other two are connected. Echoing Kant's concept of the *schema*, a symbolic form is characterized by the interaction of the transformative energy of the spirit and the concrete sign that can be perceived.[36] The concrete presents itself to the senses and can be perceived, but it is simultaneously interlinked with a spiritual meaning which determines its form and the way in which it is perceived. What Cassirer calls spirit may only be experienced when it manifests itself in something concrete. Likewise, something concrete can only be experienced and recognized when it is structured and has a meaning.[37] The term »Energie«, used by Cassirer when talking about the symbolic form, points back to Wilhelm von Humboldt's distinction between language as *ergon*, meaning finished work, and language as *energia*, which describes a process in which something is being formed or transformed.[38] A symbolic form is consequently a way in which to form and thereby transform the world, because it aims to encompass reality and in that way determine the way in which the world is perceived and represented.

A symbolic form can thus be understood as a framework which makes certain experiences possible, gives human beings certain means of expressing themselves, and thereby also determines the content which is communicated through the symbolic form. In other words the schemata or symbolic forms which we have at our disposal determine what makes up reality for

---

36 Although the degree to which Cassirer can be labelled a neo-Kantian can be discussed (Krois, p. 6), it is commonly acknowledged that Cassirer's thinking as a whole is imbued with the optimistic spirit of Enlightenment and a genuine hope for man's progressive self-liberation (see, for instance, Foucault, Une histoire restée muette). Kant's concept of the schema lies at the core of Cassirer's notion of symbolic forms. To Kant the schema is something that mediates between, on the one hand, the principles that reason makes use of in its cognition of the world (the categories), and on the other, what appears to the senses. Whereas the schema for Kant is a sort of »helping function«, Cassirer extends and elaborates this function and allows for it to be historically founded, rather than subject to concepts of reason that exist before experience. Within recent years the importance of the relationship between Goethe's concept of the symbol (as something that mediates between the general and the specific) and Cassirer's notion of the symbolic has likewise been brought out (Naumann; Stephenson).

37 As opposed to a notion of representation as imitation of an already existing reality, Cassirer's concept of symbolic form implies that representation is an active cognitive process by which a certain conception of the world obtains a sensory expression. A sign or a symbol does not create meaning, but it fixates and completes what is already inherent in perception in a not yet articulated form, so that we are able to comprehend it. In other words representation is already part of the sensory experience. It is this intricate relationship between perception and representation, in which one cannot exist without the other, that the term symbolic form aims to capture.

38 Krois, p. 151.

us. Cassirer himself points to myth, the arts, language, religion, technology, and science as different symbolic forms that operate as autonomous entities and compete with one another. However, the concept has subsequently been applied to more specific examples: Panofsky has defined the linear perspective as a symbolic form, and Franco Moretti has described the »Bildungsroman« as a symbolic form in which »youth« is the »material sign« that represents the »spiritual content« of modernity. In the following we shall consider what an understanding of information technology as a symbolic form contributes to the analysis of contemporary culture.

Instead of regarding the database as the symbolic form of the computer age, as Manovich does, we shall consider information technology as the symbolic form and the database as only one »concrete material sign«[39] of this symbolic form. We thereby expand the inquiry to include those characteristics of information technology that are not included in the connotations generated by the database (such as network, navigation, immersion, and emergence, which influences the construction of the narrative of the works of fiction considered in chapter 3).

To regard information technology as a symbolic form implies recognition of the fact that it represents a certain image and embodies a certain way of perceiving contemporary society. The worldview that information technology represents (its »Energie des Geistes«) is on the one hand made up of specific material signs (in this study we identify the database, the hyperlink, and the computer game as three such signs). On the other hand we find the cultural significance of the information society (which translated into Cassirer's terms would be what he calls »ein geistiger Bedeutungsgehalt«). The conception of information technology as a symbolic form thus works as a theoretical framework for exploring contemporary fiction that not only alludes to information technology as a feature of contemporary life, but also makes use of particular dimensions of information technology in the way in which it organises information and represents experiences. Simultaneously, the fact that we can recognise the concrete material signs of the database, the hyperlink, and the computer game in contemporary fiction substantiates the claim that information technology carries a wider cultural significance, and that it is in fact appropriate to regard it as a symbolic form.

However, the concept of symbolic form and its applicability necessarily needs some qualification, which takes into account the limitations of the notion, in order to be useful for our present purpose. In the essay »The Missing Core of Cassirer's Philosophy. Homo Faber in Thin Air« (2004) Gideon

---

39 Cassirer's use of »sinnlich« might equally be translated as »sensory«. The translation as »material« in the formulations used henceforth in this book should be understood as meaning »perceptible to the senses« (following Panofsky, pp. 40-41).

Freudenthal criticizes Cassirer's philosophy of symbolic forms for lacking materiality. Freudenthal argues, with technology as his example (because technology by having to do with human tools most clearly calls for a focus on materiality), that, whereas Cassirer in his theory of the symbolic form emphasizes the importance of the unity of the material and the spiritual, »he avoids all examples and discussion of some real piece of technology, let alone references to technological innovations of his time«.[40] Materiality is indeed heavily underplayed in Cassirer's actual development of his philosophy, although it is there in the more general definition of the symbolic form. This lack of concretisation is what Panofsky and Moretti seem to have overcome when they talk about the linear perspective and the Bildungsroman respectively as symbolic forms. It is with this added layer of concretisation that the concept becomes useful for thinking about information technology. However, even then the notion of symbolic form does not lend itself to an exploration of the affective influence of technology on society and individuals, which often comes with a focus on materiality, and which we find in the considerations of the development of storytelling by thinkers such as Benjamin and Adorno. When looking at information technology as a symbolic form and its reflection in narrative structures it is thus necessary to bear in mind that the possibilities which technology creates are intricately interwoven with the needs generated by the social experience of actual human beings living in a society and responding affectively to their environment. An important point in Cassirer's philosophy of symbolic forms is that the world cannot be understood solely through the perspective of one symbolic form. On the contrary, our world is constituted by the multiplicity of symbolic forms active within it. When in this study the focus is centred on information technology, this is not to say that there are not other factors – other symbolic forms – determining our experience of the world and the narrative structures with which we surround ourselves. The argument here is merely that information technology can and should be regarded as a symbolic form, because it has come to play such a dominant part in the reality of modern societies.

Let us now turn to explore the reason for regarding information technology as a symbolic form on its own terms and not just as a phase in the development of technology or media. Cassirer explains how each symbolic form goes through a *mimetic*, an *analogue* and a pure *symbolic* phase. The description of this development is, as John Michael Krois clarifies, not an empirical theory, but an ideal of the history of human culture that Cassirer envisions.[41] Cassirer uses language as an example of this process in »Der

---

40 Freudenthal, pp. 218-19.
41 Krois, p. 80.

Begriff der symbolischen Form im Aufbau der Geisteswissenschaften«, but the development from the concrete to the more abstract can be extended to all of the symbolic forms that he identifies. The development from a mimetic to a symbolic phase is a development from the particular to the general in which man's relation to reality becomes more and more indirect. In primitive languages the use of onomatopoeia marks a mimetic phase in which there is a connection between sound and meaning – comprehension is connected to the objective world. In the analogue phase the connection between sound and meaning is not merely related to a certain quality of the object, but is linked to subjective thought and feeling. Finally, the pure symbolic phase occurs when language no longer aims at mimicking the surrounding world, but is freed from physiological and psychological influences and is anchored only in its own medium.[42]

These various dimensions and phases become important when we want to understand information technology as a symbolic form. If we compare Cassirer's theory of the three phases (which goes towards a more and more indirect relation to the world) to Friedrich A. Kittler's account of the development of media over the last 200 years, we see an interesting correspondence. According to Kittler, the development from pen and paper to typewriter, gramophone, film and photography, and eventually the computer represents a development in which communication is replaced by calculation:

In computers everything becomes number: imageless, soundless, and wordless quantity. And if the optical fiber network reduces all formerly separate data flows to one standardized digital series of numbers, any medium can be translated into another. With numbers nothing is impossible. Modulation, transformation, synchronization; delay, memory, transposition; scrambling, scanning, mapping – a total connection of all media on a digital base erases the notion of the medium itself. Instead of hooking up technologies to people, absolute knowledge can run as an endless loop.[43]

This dystopian vision of communication as transcending human awareness resembles to a certain degree the development within a symbolic form from the mimetic phase (in which there is a close proximity between the sign and what it signifies) to the pure symbolic phase (in which the signs do not express anything in themselves). However, the analogy is not adequate – or,

---

42 Cassirer, Der Begriff der symbolischen Form, p. 182. This theory can be qualified and further developed in the light of neuroscientific research today which indicates that even patterns of mathematical abstraction are related to the way in which our brain and visual perception functions (Stafford, p. 114). This seems to indicate that the phases of symbolic forming might not only be the result of the development of culture, but has its roots in the way in which our sensory mechanism works; a point to which we shall return in the conclusion.

43 Kittler, Literature, Media, Information Systems, p. 32.

put in another way, it draws attention to the way in which dystopian conceptualisations of the future of communication, such as Kittler's notion of
the computer, neglect to see the computer as a sophisticated machine that
makes use of all three dimensions of the symbolic form.

The central argument here is that we can regard information technology
as a symbolic form in itself, not merely a phase in the development of technology or media as symbolic forms. As a symbolic form, information technology accentuates concrete material signs such as the database, the hyperlink, and the computer game in contemporary culture. These are all in contact with several of the phases of symbolic forming: the webpage's mimetic
imitation of a printed page and the abstract, binary world of computer code
are both equally part of the cultural impact of information technology. By
taking into account that a symbolic form operates with all these different
phases, it becomes clear how the notion of the symbolic form allows us to
analyse the many different aspects of information technology without limit-
ing it to a reductive view of the computer as an abstract machine that is essentially foreign to other modes of cultural production. In this way we also
become able to explain why the logic of the computer appears to be so fruitful for the development of human imagination for a number of contemporary novelists. In the following quotation Cassirer talks about art as a symbolic form. However, the same powerful argument can be raised with regards to information technology as a symbolic form:

The forms of art [...] are not empty forms. They perform a definite task in the construction and organization of human experience. To live in the realm of forms does
not signify an evasion of the issues of life; it represents, on the contrary, the realization of one of the highest energies of life itself. We cannot speak of art as ›extra-
human‹ or ›superhuman‹ without overlooking one of its fundamental features, its con-
structive power in the framing of our human universe.[44]

The forms of information technology are also not empty, and they should
not be seen as foreign to human nature. Even though they appear to emphasise a non-narrative approach to combining and representing information,
they are – with Galen Strawson's argument about deeply non-narrative
people in mind – just as fundamentally human. In this respect, it is important to stress that the fundamental interest in this study is in how the cultural
imagination reacts to and incorporates technology rather than in the determination of the properties of technology in and of itself. The dialectic between narrative and non-narrative is consequently not regarded as being
that between the human and the non-human.

---

44 Cassirer, An Essay on Man, p. 167.

If we are to move beyond the apocalyptic and utopian conceptions of information technology as something essentially transformative of our world and our imagination found in much of the early scholarship, then it is fruitful to regard information technology as a symbolic form. This approach resolves methodological problems regarding how to analyse the impact of information technology on our contemporary world, because it allows us to see both the contemporary significance and the more fundamental relation to human perception and representation. In *My Mother was a Computer* (2005) Hayles remarks that:

> At issue is whether computation should be understood as a metaphor pervasive in our culture and therefore indicative of a certain ›climate of opinion‹ (in Raymond Williams's phrase) at the turn of the millennium, or whether it has ontological status as the mechanism generating the complexities of physical reality.[45]

She goes on to argue that we are currently at a time in history when this is not possible to determine, because we are »at a cultural moment when the question remains undecidable – a moment, that is, when computation as means and as metaphor are inextricably entwined as a generative cultural dynamic«.[46] However, by regarding information technology as a symbolic form we can argue that there is nothing particularly extraordinary about the cultural moment in which we find ourselves. As a symbolic form, information technology is inextricable from the way in which we perceive the world. Regarding information technology as a symbolic form allows us to conceive of it both as a prevailing cultural metaphor connected to a specific period in time, and at the same time as something founded in fundamental human ways of perceiving and representing information. It is also no surprise that the concrete material signs on which we shall focus (the database, the hyperlink, and the computer game) have antecedents in the figures of the archive, the network, and the game. These remain engaged in dialogue with the imaginative vocabulary of previous periods.

In their famous encounter in Davos in 1929, Heidegger dismissed Cassirer's philosophy of symbolic forms as a neo-Kantian approach which is more interested in what takes place at the level of culture than that of »Being«.[47] However, to Cassirer these two dimensions are inextricable; culture is not merely a superficial phenomenon, it is intimately linked to human existence. Presentation and representation cannot be separated. This is also the reason why the concept of symbolic form is more useful for our present purpose than, for instance, a related term like »cultural metaphor«

---

45 Hayles, My Mother was a Computer, p. 20.
46 Ibid. p. 20.
47 Gründer.

which is more exposed to the kind of criticism Heidegger raised towards Cassirer. As will become apparent from our reading of specific texts, the term cultural metaphor thus designates a different level of enquiry (mainly concerned with concrete textual references to information technology) than that of symbolic form (which takes into account the more indirect modes of influence on narrative structures).

The aim of this book is to uncover the ways in which the logic of new media feeds back into the novel's ongoing debate about narrativity. In chapter 2 we shall therefore trace a negotiation of narrativity as a representational mode in canonical works by Goethe, Musil, and Schmidt in order to uncover historical reference points for the enquiries made in chapter 3. We shall consequently be looking at the function of the archive in *Wilhelm Meisters Wanderjahre*, the network in *Der Mann ohne Eigenschaften*, and the game in *Zettels Traum*. Each of the three sections of chapter 2 corresponds to one of the three sections in chapter 3, which consider the database, the hyperlink, and the computer game respectively. Chapter 3 aims to explore how these concrete material signs manifest themselves and are used in relation to narrativity and the representation of human existence in contemporary European fiction. We shall look at works by Jan Kjærstad, Thomas Hettche, Botho Strauß, Svend Åge Madsen, Reinhard Jirgl, David Mitchell, Günter Grass, and Guy Tournaye, all of which not only allude to information technology as a feature of contemporary life, but also make use of particular dimensions of information technology in the way in which they organise information and represent experiences. All of the selected texts thus share the common trait that, in their reflection on human existence, they display an uneasiness with narrativity that makes them grapple for other modes of representation. The concept of symbolic form works as a conceptual framework for the analyses, which helps to identify the impact of information technology on these examples of contemporary fiction. But simultaneously the analyses of these particular works of fiction provide the evidence that information technology can indeed be regarded as a symbolic form.

1.4 Writing Novels Today

At the end of his essay Data Visualisation as New Abstraction and Anti-Sublime, written in 2002, Lev Manovich formulates the present challenge to theorists and artists in the following way:

For me, the real challenge of data art is <u>not</u> about how to map some abstract and impersonal data into something meaningful and beautiful – economists, graphic designers, and scientists are already doing this quite well. The more interesting and at the end maybe more important challenge is how to represent the personal subjective experience of a person living in a data society. If daily interaction with volumes of data and numerous messages is part of our new ›data-subjectivity‹, how can we represent this experience in new ways? How new media can represent the ambiguity, the otherness, the multi-dimensionality of our experience, going beyond already familiar and ›normalized‹ modernist techniques of montage, surrealism, absurd, etc.? In short, rather than trying hard to pursue the anti-sublime ideal, data visualization artists should also not forget that art has the unique license to portray human subjectivity – including its fundamental new dimension of being ›immersed in data‹.[48]

The aim of this study is to probe this experience of an information society in order to understand further how information technology affects contemporary culture, its narrative structures, and modes of representation. But rather than looking at the artworks produced in and of the medium itself, we shall look at the genre of the printed novel and how it adjusts and reacts to a contemporary culture heavily influenced by information technology. It is in the force field between the printed novel and information technology that arises when information technology works its way into the narrative structures of the stories told that we are able to gain insights not only into contemporary culture but also into the dynamics of human perception and representation more generally. As the investigation of the novels *Wilhelm Meisters Wanderjahre*, *Der Mann ohne Eigenschaften*, and *Zettels Traum* will show, narrative negotiations, which turn to other forms and figures than the linear narrative do not arise with the invention of information technology. However, information technology as a symbolic form provides us with a new set of concrete material signs to articulate this narrative negotiation. Exploring the characteristics of these allows us to broaden our understanding of the impact of information technology upon contemporary culture and the conditions for literary fiction in an information age.

---

48 Manovich, Datavisualisation as New Abstraction and Anti-Sublime.

1. Narrative Negotiations

2.1 Re-presenting the Archive:
Goethe's *Wilhelm Meisters Wanderjahre*

Let us start by considering the implications of the *archive* as a figure in narrative fiction. The archive is a good place to start when looking at the negotiation between story and information, because archival theory is preoccupied with the essence of what the present study is about: how do we organize information? The archive and the shifting archival practices embody changing views on this issue. In the last few decades we have witnessed an increased interest in the archive as a theoretical principle and art metaphor, not least due to the challenges and increased possibilities that the organisation of information faces with the advent of digital databases. In this chapter we shall see how Goethe's *Wilhelm Meisters Wanderjahre oder Die Entsagenden*[1], written in the early nineteenth century, makes use of the archive in its negotiation of narrativity. The aim is to shed light on the relationship between the connotations that the archive carries, the narrative structures of the novel, and its representation of the conditions of human existence. Reading *Wanderjahre* through the figure of the archive instigates our investigation of novels which present a negotiation of narrativity. However, it is also a means of establishing ways in which the archive is present as a figure in literary fiction before the prevalence of digital databases. The present chapter thus also aims to provide a conceptual background to chapter 3 which identifies the figure of the database in recent fiction.

Wanderjahre stands out in comparison with Goethe's early work and with other nineteenth-century novels. It was not until the latter half of the twentieth century that it attracted serious scholarly interest. The novel appears on the one hand as a throwback to early modern novels such as *Don Quixote* and *Tristram Shandy*, which were characterised by the same form of disparate material that characterises *Wanderjahre*. On the other hand the renewed interest in *Wanderjahre* in recent years has brought into prominence the characteristics that link this work to twentieth-century novel-experiments which challenged narrativity and the developmental

---

1 First published in 1821. A revised version came out in 1829. This is now considered the standard version. Henceforth referred to as *Wanderjahre*.

structure of the »Bildungsroman«, of which Goethe himself had been one of the founding fathers. By commencing our enquiry of narrative negotiations with this work, which seems to evade categorisation and point simultaneously backwards and forwards, the porosity of the delimitations of this study becomes apparent. However, an argument can be made for beginning precisely here in the early nineteenth century when the modern subject is coming into being; the century which saw Romanticism's painful awareness of totality as a utopia whose realisation is only possible through the fragment, but also the large epic narratives of Dickens, Tolstoy, and Flaubert, which provided the narrative structures of Realism against which the novel-experiments of the twentieth century would revolt. By carving out its own place in literary history, *Wanderjahre* becomes powerful evidence for the contention that a negotiation of narrativity is intrinsically linked to the novel genre itself, although a desire to challenge narrativity was certainly more characteristic of some periods than it was of others. For *Wanderjahre* the figure which embodies this negotiation is the archive and it will therefore be the pivotal point of our exploration.

2.1.1 *Wanderjahre* and the Archive

Wanderjahre presents itself as a sequel to *Wilhelm Meisters Lehrjahre*, which Goethe had published in 1795-96. It begins as a story of the travels of Wilhelm and his son Felix. Wilhelm is under a journeyman's oath and is therefore not allowed to stay more than three nights under the same roof. Eventually he leaves his son at a school for a pedagogical upbringing and decides to become a surgeon, which, towards the end of the novel, enables him to join a group of emigrants who have assembled before their departure to North America. However, out of this basic plot a convoluted structure of nested stories shoots out. Each of Wilhelm's encounters initiates a new tale. Either he is told a story by someone, given a written tale, a diary or letters to read, or he himself becomes entangled in an adventure through the people he meets. Both Books Two and Three end with a collection of aphorisms and a poem for which there is no immediate explanation. The novel as a whole appears to be assembled by an editor who describes his undertaking as »die Pflicht des Mitteilens, Darstellens, Ausführens und Zusammenziehens«.[2] He thus takes on the responsibility for selecting and connecting the texts, but not the content of each story.

---

2 Goethe, p. 471.

The novel was not well received by the critics when it first came out. The aphorisms and poems were removed from several editions due to claims by Goethe's secretary Eckermann that they were originally added only to make the novel fill out three volumes, and their removal was regarded as making the novel more coherent. Not until well into the twentieth century did the later Goethe receive seriuos critical interest, and in 1949 the poems and aphorisms were reinserted into the novel. Hermann Broch was one of the first to appreciate *Wanderjahre* as a forerunner of the modernist novel in the essay »James Joyce und die Gegenwart« (1936):

> Und es ist [die] Totalität des Daseins, die [Goethe] zu ganz neuen Ausdrucksformen drängte, und die in den ›Wanderjahren‹ den Grundstein der neuen Dichtung, des neuen Romans, legte.[3]

In 1968 Volker Neuhaus published an article which emphasised the disparate form and the significance of the archive as a deliberate composition. This decisive article initiated the interpretation of *Wanderjahre* as an »Archivroman«. Neuhaus places the notion of archival fiction at the centre of his analysis, thereby giving up on the idea of an omniscient narrator:

> Alle Teile des Romans werden so in Eigenverantwortung der verschiedenste Personen erzählt, ohne eine übergeordnete auktoriale Verantwortung. Die einzelnen Perspektiven ergänzen sich, verstärken sich oder heben sie auf. Aus allen spricht der Autor, und in keiner seiner Figuren bekommen wir ihn zu fassen, daß wir sagen können: Das ist die Meinung Goethes.[4]

Neuhaus thus challenged the interpretation given by Erich Trunz in 1950 in the Hamburger Ausgabe. Trunz seperated the narrative frame of Wilhelm's travels from the novellas, whereas Neuhaus emphasized that all of the disparate elements in the novel stem from a larger body of archive material which the editor organizes and presents to the reader, thereby constructing the novel. The novel consequently lacks an authoritative narrator who organizes its statements and modes of expression. The editor is the closest thing we have to an organizing authority, but he repeatedly reveals his own lack of control over the incongruent material that he presents.

In *The Novel as Archive. The Genesis, Reception, and Criticism of Goethe's* Wilhelm Meisters Wanderjahre (1998), Ehrhard Bahr develops this conception further. He uses the idea of the archive as the structuring component of the novel to argue that *Wanderjahre* is a decisive text for the »death of the author«, an idea that Michel Foucault identified as first occurring in the writings of the French poet Stéphane Mallarmé (1842-1898). In

---

3 Broch, p. 206.
4 Neuhaus, p. 25.

the mixture of letters, diaries, novellas, fairy tales, songs, poems, and aphorisms of which *Wanderjahre* consists, Bahr identifies the disappearing act
of the author:

> The author disappears behind this plurality of discourses by abandoning his point of
> view and avoiding any commitment. Instead of a plot, a number of different texts (or
> discourses) from various archives are presented that are to be integrated into a whole
> by the reader.[5]

However, in order to avoid putting the novel into a context that has more to
do with the archival techniques of the late twentieth century, applying a
Foucauldian interpretation to the concept of the archive in *Wanderjahre* requires a heightened awareness of the connotations carried by the archive in
the nineteenth century.[6] Before we go any further, let us therefore briefly try
to define an archive and consider the connotations ascribed to the figure of
the archive in the early nineteenth century. This will make it easier to determine and use conceptions of the archive that belong to a different cultural context in our subsequent reading of the novel.

The records of an archive can be distinguished from other forms of information dissemination, in so far as they are removed from the original
context of meaning in which they were created and intended to operate. An
important function for an archive is therefore to create the necessary knowledge about the context from which the records have been taken, in order to
enable the reader to interpret them. A central way of doing this in modern
archival theory is to use the so-called *principle of provenance*, under which:
»Records/archives of the same provenance (agency, corporate body, person,
family) must not be intermingled with records of other provenances«.[7]

Closely linked to this principle is the notion of respect for the original
order. During the nineteenth century the principle of provenance replaced
the earlier *principle of pertinence* according to which archives were arranged by their subject content regardless of their provenance and original
order. There are varying opinions on precisely when the principle of provenance was implemented, and different European countries differ on whether
the principle of provenance also includes respect for the original order. Archival scientist Peter Horsman states that these archiving ideas were applied
in Germany as early as 1816,[8] and it can therefore be surmised that they

---

5 Bahr, p. 99.

6 The archive became an appealing figure to the visual art scene, especially after the 1960s,
and much of the conceptualisation of this figure stems from this period onwards. An intriguing
glimpse into the significance of the archive for modern visual art is given in the anthology *The Archive*, which brings together key twentieth-century writings by theorists and artists (Merewether).

7 Gränström, p. 13.

8 Horsman, p. 53.

were discussed and possibly even practised at the time Goethe wrote *Wanderjahre*.

Archival scientist Claes Gränström relates the development of the principle of provenance to the development of historical science in the nineteenth century and the historicism of the German historian Leopold Ranke (1795-1886), who sought to reconstruct the periods of the past »wie es eigentlich gewesen ist« by focussing on primary sources and thereby obtain objectivity in the writing of history. A principle of provenance in which the original order of an archive is maintained concurs with this focus on original source material. However, it can also be seen as a response to the rapid growth in the amount of material that had to be archived. For the archivists, the principle of provenance meant that they could manage the records handed over to them as aggregated material and thereby »limit their arrangement activities to the preservation, and if necessary reconstruction, of the original order and stop describing and ›cataloguing‹ records in their ›collections‹ at the item level«.[9] Interpretation of the records becomes a job for the reader of the archive rather than the archivist.

In *Wanderjahre* we encounter an archivist at work, namely Angela, who keeps Makarie's archive:

Unser Freund ward sodann in ein Zimmer geführt, wo er in Schränken ringsum viele wohlgeordnete Papiere zu sehen hatte. Rubriken mancher Art deuteten auf den verschiedensten Inhalt, Einsicht und Ordnung leuchtete hervor.[10]

It is explicitly stated that the aphorisms at the end of Book Three come from this archive, which seems to be ordered according to the principle of provenance, in so far as they are not grouped by subject, but often occur in conjunction with other aphorisms, whose statements seem to stem from the same conversation. However, as Neuhaus has observed, we also encounter the archive in another more general sense: the editor appears to be dealing with a larger archive that stems from many different origins. Some are Angela's transcriptions of conversations, others accounts of events and tales from the hand of Friedrich, not to speak of the large amount of letters and diaries from other sources. Origin is, however, most often carefully commented upon by the editor. The novel with which we, as readers, are presented can thus be regarded as the result of the editor's attempt to read and make sense of material from an archive organized according to the principle of provenance. He attempts to piece together a consistent story, which necessarily results in omissions and a restructuring of the material, but it is nonetheless clear that he is dealing with records of whose origin he is well

---

9 Erlandsson, p. 33.
10 Goethe, p. 139.

aware, and which he most often confides to the reader. In fact the assembled form of the novel seems to derive precisely from his constant attempts to remain faithful to some notion of original order.[11]

2.1.2 Narrative and Archive

Having thus identified the move from non-recognition to acknowledgement of the archive in *Wanderjahre* scholarship, as well as the technicalities of the early nineteenth-century archive, we are now in a position to take a closer look at the archive as a motif as well as a narrative structure in the novel. Starting from what the novel itself defines as an archive, we shall look in more detail at the collections of aphorisms, »Betrachtungen im Sinne der Wanderer. Kunst, Ethisches, Natur« and »Aus Makariens Archiv«[12], in order to show how the reader is drawn into the process of interpretation through the oscillation between the multiplicity of small narratives and the narrative resistance provided by the aphorisms.

Rather than condensing and drawing the significance of the narrative events together, the aphorisms seem to differentiate the content by pointing out correspondences throughout the novel. This function might be further understood by drawing on Michel Foucault's conceptualisation of the figure of the archive in *The Archaeology of Knowledge* (1972). To Foucault, an archive is not to be regarded as a collection of actual documents, but should be approached in terms of the conditions and relations that define statements and discourses. An archive consists not of a static collection of texts, but exists rather as a set of relations and institutions that enable statements to continue to exist:

> Instead of seeing, on the great mythical book of history, lines of words that translate in visible characters thoughts that were formed in some other time and place, we have, in the density of discursive practices, systems that establish statements as events (with their own conditions and domain of appearance) and things (with their own possibility and field of use). They are all these systems of statements (whether events or things) that I propose to call *archive.*[13]

To Foucault, the archive is more a set of relations than a set of objects, and the archive can thus be seen as a vibrant system that lingers between what can possibly be said and what has already been said. The archive is »the

---

11 When the original order is broken, as with Leonardo's diary which we read in several instalments, it is explained by the fact that the material has only later become available to the editor.

12 The aphorisms will be referred to as »MA« and »BW« respectively.

13 Foucault, The Archaeology of Knowledge, p. 128.

general system of the formation and transformation of statements«.[14] However, Foucault rejects the interpretation of an archive as consisting of a multitude of statements that in unison reveal one single historical totality. Rather he focuses on the rareness of each statement:

Far from being that which unifies everything that has been said in the great confused murmur of a discourse, far from being only that which ensures that we exist in the midst of preserved discourse, it is that which differentiates discourses in their multiple existence and specifies them in their own duration.[15]

This understanding of the archive is useful for appreciating the function of the aphorisms in *Wanderjahre*, because, rather than condensing the meaning of the novel, the aphorisms behave somewhat like the statements in Foucault's notion of the archive and »differentiate the discourses in their multiple existences« by pointing out contradictory correspondences within the novel and emphasising the individual statement.

This effect is underscored by the aphorisms' origination, of which we learn in the following conversation between Wilhelm and Angela:

Meine Herrin‹, fuhr sie fort, ›ist von der Wichtigkeit des augenblicklichen Gesprächs höchlich überzeugt; dabei gehe vorüber, sagt sie, was kein Buch enthält, und doch wieder das Beste, was Bücher jemals enthalten haben. Deshalb machte sie mir's zur Pflicht, einzelne gute Gedanken aufzubewahren, die aus einem geistreichen Gespräch, wie Samenkörner aus einer vielästigen Pflanze, hervorspringen. ›Ist man treu‹, sagt sie, ›das Gegenwärtige festzuhalten, so wird man erst Freude an der Überlieferung haben, indem wir den besten Gedanken schon ausgedrückt finden. Hiedurch kommen wir zum Anschauen jener Übereinstimmung, wozu der Mensch berufen ist, wozu er sich oft wider seinen Willen finden muß, da er sich gar zu gern einbildet, die Welt fange mit ihm von vorne an.‹ Angela fuhr fort, dem Gaste weiter zu vertrauen, daß dadurch ein bedeutendes Archiv entstanden sei.[16]

The aphorisms seem to be the product of an individual's participation in a conversation, and are kept in a secret archive in order to preserve a historical consciousness. The order in which the aphorisms appear seems mostly random. In so far as they are grouped only vaguely by subject, their order does not appear to obey the principle of pertinence. As already indicated, the principle of provenance seems to have been applied, given that many of the aphorisms can be grouped in sections of two or three that appear to stem from the same conversation, given that they either agree or conflict with one another.

---

14 Ibid. p. 130.
15 Ibid. p. 129.
16 Goethe, p. 138.

Turning to the question of how the aphorisms should be read as part of the whole novel, a discussion about the Uncle's inscriptions between Hersilie, Juliette, their uncle, and Wilhelm gives us an indication. Wilhelm comments:»Kurzgefaßte Sprüche jeder Art weiß ich zu ehren, besonders wenn sie mich anregen, das Entgegengesetzte zu überschauen und in Übereinstimmung zu bringen«.[17] Aphorism 177 »BW« states something similar:

Man sagt: zwischen zwei entgegengesetzten Meinungen liege die Wahrheit mitteninne. Keineswegs! Das Problem liegt dazwischen, das Unschaubare, das ewig tätige Leben in Ruhe gedacht.[18]

This oscillating reading of internal contradictions is also the interpretation which the novel as a whole seems to encourage, in that the aphorisms circle around the same issues as the novellas, letters, and poems. The juxtaposition of novel and aphorisms thus establishes a dialogue between statements and examples that provide mutual tools for interpretation. Johannes John formulates this observation in the following precise manner:

[...] die Aphorismen als Probe aufs Exempel, als Prüfstein [...] an dem der Leser im aktiven Nachvollzug der Maximen – was sich als Übersetzung des Postulats des Wanderns in ›geistige Beweglichkeit‹ ebenso symbolisch deuten läßt – sich gleichsam den Schlüssel zum Verständnis des Romans erarbeiten mußte.[19]

The first two aphorisms in »Betrachtungen im Sinne der Wanderer« seem to allude to this correspondence. The first reads: »Alles Gescheite ist schon gedacht worden, man muß nur versuchen, es noch einmal zu denken«,[20] and the second continues: »Wie kann man sich selbst kennenlernen? Durch Betrachten niemals, wohl aber durch Handeln. Versuche deine Pflicht zu tun, und du weißt gleich, was an dir ist«.[21] Here, »Betrachtung« and »Handeln« are juxtaposed in a way that seems to undermine the authority of the aphorisms in an ironic manner, since »Betrachtung« refers back to the title of the aphorisms (»Betrachtungen im Sinne der Wanderer«), whereas the narrative that we have just left undoubtedly contains more »Handeln« than the aphorisms. What is at stake is an interaction between the narrative parts of the novel that involve actual agents and events and the aphorisms that encourage the reader to become an interpreter, because they do not fit into a narrative sequence that explains their intention. The narrative and the aphorisms thus seem to have an interrelated grip on each other which leads them into

---

17 Ibid. p. 82.
18 Ibid. p. 336.
19 John, p. 180.
20 Goethe, p. 309. See also John, p. 145f. for in-depth discussion of the reception of this aphorism.
21 Goethe, p. 309.

an ongoing dialogue. Mapping out this relation is the job of the reader of the novel. It is a job that resembles that of a reader of a nineteenth-century archive that has been organized according to the principle of provenance. Such an archive would consist of several different archives whose origin and internal order have been respected, and therefore appears all the more disintegrated to the reader who has to use it, than if it had been organized according to subject. Had we only been given the aphorisms, we would have had to conjure up ilustrative material to explain the statements in our own minds. However, *Wanderjahre* provides this material in the form of the narrative. The novel as a whole can thus be read as illustrating the mental process of reading an archive in that it provides both disparate data material and a suggestion for connecting these into a larger narrative framework. As Aphorism 12 »BW« states: »Es steht manches Schöne isoliert in der Welt, doch der Geist ist es, der Verknüpfungen zu entdecken und dadurch Kunstwerke hervorzubringen hat.«[22]

Let us take Aphorism 29 »BW« as an example and try to map out some of the possible correspondences it creates within the rest of the novel:

Der zur Vernunft geborene Mensch bedarf noch großer Bildung, sie mag sich ihm nun durch Sorgfalt der Eltern und Erzieher, durch friedliches Beispiel oder durch strenge Erfahrung nach und nach offenbaren. Ebenso wird zwar der *angehende* Künstler, aber nicht der *vollendete* geboren; sein Auge komme frisch auf die Welt, er habe glücklichen Blick für Gestalt, Proportion, Bewegung; aber für höhere Komposition, für Haltung, Licht, Schatten, Farben kann ihm die natürliche Anlage fehlen, ohne daß er es gewahr wird. [23]

This aphorism seems to correspond to the scene in Book Two, chapter seven situated at Lago Maggiore, where the dilettante Hilarie learns to paint and thus refines her innate abilities. However, there are also echoes of Wilhelm's encounter with the principles of the Pedagogic Province. Reading the aphorism thus sets off a chain reaction of associations which makes the reader remember the many characters who go through an education in the course of the novel. The opinion put forward in Aphorism 29, and in the scene at Lago Maggiore, seems to contradict the inclination to master one trade that governs Wilhelm's choice to become a surgeon. However, read in conjunction with Wilhelm's statement about wanting to take the opposite position when reading the uncle's proverbs, Aphorism 29 is not just a comment on what goes on in the novel; it makes the reader aware of the ongoing discussion between the individual parts of the novel. What this particular aphorism adds is the comparison between becoming an artist and be-

---

22 Ibid. p. 310.
23 Ibid. p. 313.

coming a human being, a comparison which makes it possible to interpret the process of becoming a human being as an artwork that has to be learned. For some, the learning process is more necessary than for others, and a parallel is established between the incomplete artist and the incomplete human being – the wandering soul of the *Wanderjahre*.

Another example of how the aphorisms make the reader aware of the correspondences within the novel can be found in Aphorism 106 »MA«:

Etwas Mönchisch-Hagestolzenartiges hat die Kristallographie und ist daher sich selbst genug. Von praktischer Lebenseinwirkung ist sie nicht; denn die köstlichsten Erzeugnisse ihres Gebiets, die kristallinischen Edelsteine müssen erst zugeschliffen werden, ehe wir unsere Frauen damit schmücken können.[24]

This juxtaposition of stone and life, celibacy and women, echoes a discussion Wilhelm has in Book One, chapter three with Jarno, whom the reader knows as a misanthropic character from *Lehrjahre*. He has now taken on the name Montan and lives in the mountains, where he studies geology. He explains this new interest as being a result of his wish to get away from people and describes the attraction of the cliffs as rooted in the fact that they cannot be comprehended. Unlike letters, the rocks do not convey the obvious and are therefore of interest:

Hier darf ich nicht fürchten, wie wohl geschieht, wenn ich mich lange und liebevoll mit einem Pergament abgegeben habe, daß ein scharfer Kritikus kommt und mir versichert, das alles sei nur untergeschoben.‹ – Lächelnd versetzte der Freund: ›Und doch wird man auch hier deine Lesarten streitig machen‹.[25]

Wilhelm does not agree with Jarno's take on life, and his life has indeed shown another »Lesart«. Jarno's view, however, is linked to Aphorism 62 »BW«: »Wir würden gar vieles besser kennen, wenn wir es nicht zu genau erkennen wollten. Wird uns doch ein Gegenstand unter einem Winkel von fünfundvierzig Graden erst faßlich«;[26] this statement seems also to reflect on the aphorisms themselves since ambiguity is praised. Nonetheless, the narrative shows that even the indecipherable and cold Jarno can be cut as a gem for a lovely lady; we learn of his love for Lydie towards the end of the novel, and the aphorism thus makes us aware of the ongoing discussion within the novel.[27]

---

24 Ibid. p. 514.
25 Ibid. pp. 43-44.
26 Ibid. p. 319.
27 Furthermore, it can be argued that Aphorism 106 »MA« comments on the theme of renunciation (also indicated by the subtitle »Die Entsagenden«) which applies to many of the characters of the inserted novellas, as well as to Wilhelm himself.

The connections we have observed in these two examples would, of course, still exist without the aphorisms, and it can be argued that the constant disruption of the narratives and shift of narrator and perspective likewise work towards encouraging the reader to engage in the process of mapping out correspondences. However, while the narratives evoke *identification* on the part of the reader due to the fact that they feature agents who go through a form of development, they do not trigger the same degree of direct involvement in the reading as do the aphorisms. The aphorisms *engage* the reader by alienating her from the progression of the plot and by encouraging her to relate actively to the correspondences within the text, since otherwise the aphorisms will remain irrelevant appendices to the novel as a whole and not add to the reading in the way we have seen in the two examples above.

2.1.3 The Reader of the Archive

Alongside the tendency in *Wanderjahre* scholarship to emphasize the significance of the archive there exists an inclination to stress the role of the reader. The aphorisms are often a key point in this discussion, because, as we have seen, they bestow responsibility for the interpretation on the reader in a more direct manner than the narrative, and thus direct attention to the function of the reader in the interpretational act. Erhard Bahr uses this point to underpin his claim that *Wanderjahre* stages a disappearance of the author in a Foucauldian sense:

The aphorisms do not fix meaning but open it up, contributing to the ambiguity of the novel and its ironic texture. They have the function of activating the reader as interpreter and of providing instructions on how to read the world and its representation in the novel.[28]

Bahr does not comment on Foucault's concept of the archive, but it appears reasonable on these grounds to recall Foucault's redefinition of the archive as a more general discursive entity. This also implies a conception of the subject as »a particular, vacant place that may in fact be filled by different individuals«[29] – different readers, one might add.

We have seen that the juxtaposition of narrative and aphorisms in the novel can be regarded as illustrating the mental process of reading an archive, providing us with both the disparate archive material and the narratives it evokes. Let us now try to further understand the nature of this »im-

---

28 Bahr, p. 48.
29 Foucault, The Archaeology of Knowledge, p. 95.

plied reader«. In *The Role of the Reader. Explorations in the Semiotics of Texts* (1981), Umberto Eco addresses the process of reading by introducing the concept of the *model reader*. According to Eco, every text has to envisage a model of a possible reader that is able to deal with the expressions of the text, for instance through a specific linguistic code, certain literary style, or by indicating specialized knowledge that the reader is presumed to hold. Eco distinguishes between, on the one hand, an open text which actively involves its reader in its production and is designed to be read in multiple ways, and, on the other hand, a closed text which aims at pulling the reader along a predetermined path. The freedom of an open text's reader consists in deciding how to activate the various textual levels.[30] The notion of a model reader is interesting in this context, because it provides a framework for thinking about *Wanderjahre* as a novel that emphasizes the importance of the reader by using the archive as a reference point. However, Eco's methodology forces us to consider how actively an archive determines its reader compared to the fictional texts that Eco deals with. Eco operates with a very wide notion of narrative and argues that most texts can be considered to contain a narrative – even Peirce's chemical description of the production of lithium. However, Eco deals only with texts that can be ascribed to one origin. An archive, by contrast, will most often include material from various origins and contexts, and thus bring together several different sets of textual levels. and codes. This enlarges the possible interpretations of the model reader considerably, and allows us to question whether an archive can have a model reader at all.

To answer this question and at the same time understand more deeply the complicated role of the editor in *Wanderjahre*, let us turn to a point Derrida makes in his conceptualisation of the archive.[31] In *Archive Fever. A Freudian Impression* (1995), Derrida refers to the archive as an authority that marks out a border which defines that which is non-archive. Archiving consequently represents an attempt both to preserve something to be remem-

---

30 Eco, p. 39.
31 For Derrida, a theory of the archive is closely connected to psychoanalysis and memory. The notion of archive fever is a reference to Freud's concept of the death drive, which is linked to repetition compulsion. Derrida argues that the archive is working against itself, because its own destruction (forgetting) is inherent in its preconditions for existing (memory and repetition). Archive fever is thus to have a need for archives that borders on the self-destructive: »It is to have a compulsive, repetitive, and nostalgic desire for the archive, an irrepressible desire to return to the origin, a homesickness, a nostalgia for the return to the most archaic place of absolute commencement« (Derrida, Archive Fever, p. 91). However, since the psychoanalytic connotations that the archive's function carries are not the key concern for our consideration of the archive's function in *Wanderjahre*, we shall not explore in detail the psychoanalytical implications of the archive figure. This has received much attention in art and theory throughout the twentieth century, especially in relation to Holocaust research. See, for instance, Agamben.

bered and to leave out something to be forgotten. The archive is never closed, but can be regarded as an ongoing process that has a tacit connection to the future, in the sense that every new interpretation of the archive extends and enriches it: »The archivist produces more archive, and that is why the archive is never closed. It opens out of the future«.[32] The process of appraisal and selection is a continual one and not just something that takes place only when the archive is founded. On this basis, the editor can himself be regarded as being part of the enrichment and extension of the archive by virtue of the fact that the archive passes through his hands and mind. He might not, after all, be quite as disempowered as previous scholarship has claimed. In fact with this notion of the archive it becomes possible to argue that an archive may indeed have a model reader.

Throughout the entirety of *Wanderjahre*, the editor functions as a link between us, as readers, and the archival material we access. The responsibility of assembling the various novellas, letters, poems, and aphorisms told by different people is bestowed upon him. Embedded in the fiction itself, we thus gain a very explicit image of a model reader who works to activate the various textual levels and codes from the archives with which he has been trusted. When reproducing the novella »Nicht zu weit«, which he has access to from Friedrich's transcription of the main character's own account, he must sheepishly admit that he has usurped »die Rechte des epischen Dichters« and »einen geneigten Leser nur allzu schnell in die Mitte leidenschaftlicher Darstellungen gerissen«.[33] In other words, he has been caught by the impetus for narrative that disparate data material evokes. Rather than regard the editor as an example of the disappearance of the author, as Bahr does, it is thus possible to regard him as a reflection of the reader – the model reader of an archive organised after the principle of provenance. He attempts to find correspondences in the material he is given, but he also maintains the disparate origins of the texts and their individual textual codes and structures, so we as readers of *Wanderjahre* get the sensation of encountering material joined together from a larger archive. This effect is produced because the editor does *not* take on the role of an omniscient narrator with a privileged overview of the material.

The editor's own statement (from the passage in which we first encounter him) highlights his function as a mirror for the reading process of the *Wanderjahre* itself. He has just explained how Wilhelm gains access to the archive of Makarie and continues:

---

32 Derrida, Archive Fever, p. 68.
33 Goethe, p. 427.

Besonders achtete er die Hefte kurzer, kaum zusammenhängender Sätze höchst schät-
zenswert. Resultate waren es, die, wenn wir nicht ihre Veranlassung wissen, als paradox erschienen, uns aber nötigen, vermittelst eines umgekehrten Findens und Erfin-
dens rückwärtszugehen und uns die Filiation solcher Gedanken von weit her, von un-
ten herauf womöglich zu vergegenwärtigen.
   Auch dergleichen dürfen wir aus oben angeführten Ursachen keinen Platz einräu-
men. Jedoch werden wir die erste sich darbietende Gelegenheit nicht versäumen und
am schicklichen Orte auch das hier Gewonnene mit Auswahl darzubringen wissen.[34]

What seems to be alluded to here is the selection of aphorisms entitled »Aus
Makariens Archiv«. However, it also seems to reflect back on the editor's
own practice. His errand is that of »vergegenwärtigen« – a process that relies on an »umgekehrte[s] Finden[s] und Erfinden[s]«. He is not constructing but reconstructing – the process he undertakes is »umgekehrt« – because he deals with material that is already there, introducing coherence to
disparate material of the past and thereby aiming to understand the material's origins.

2.1.4 Human Existence as Narrative Construction

Most *Wanderjahre* scholarship has highlighted the focus on the individual's
role in society as a central theme. In *Individualität in Goethes* Wanderjahre
(1997), Claudia Schwamborn explores the thesis that *Wanderjahre* prob-
lematizes and discusses individuality caught between tradition and freedom:

Individualität erscheint in diesem Roman einerseits in der Perspektive der Tradition,
in der das Individuum in einen von Gott geschaffenen Kosmos eingebettet war. Andererseits werden die Entwicklungslinien des neuzeitlichen Individualitätsbegriff ausge-
zogen, der sowohl die Chance von Freiheit und Entfaltung in sich birgt als auch die
Gefahr des bloßen Utilitarismus, der Funktionalisierung.[35]

In the article »*Wanderjahre* im Hypertext« (2001), Wolfram Malte Fues
links the novel's representation of the human subject to the question of the
narrative construction of the novel. He uses the concept of hypertext as a
metaphor for understanding *Wanderjahre* as a novel that presents parallel
texts and constantly asks its reader what she wants to hear.

Im ›fortlaufenden Vortrag‹ im *Mann von funfzig Jahren* wie im Gang der *Wanderjahre* überhaupt wird das Verhältnis zwischen Totalität und Individualität, deren simul-
tane Geltung allem Verlauf schlechthin zugrundeliegt, an den Aussichts- und Wende-
punkten von diesem Grund auf erwogen und bestimmt, so als käme ein Computer-

---

34 Ibid. pp. 139-40.
35 Schwamborn, p. 167.

Programm an jeder seiner Schnittstellen auf seine eigentümliche Grammatik erwägend und überlegend zurück.[36]

Fues thereby challenges what he calls Friedrich Kittler's »Epochalisierung der Moderne«.[37] In *Aufschreibesysteme 1800/1900* (1985) Kittler presents the early nineteenth century as the time when the human subject was a symbolic entity that would bind everything together. The pen and the characters on the page (which were the »Aufschreibesysteme« of the early nineteenth century) contain and distribute information, whereas the analogue media of the late nineteenth and early twentieth centuries, such as photography, film, and the gramophone signify that the subject has become one of the functions of the discourse rather than the pivotal point. As a result of his reading of the novella »Der Mann von funfzig Jahren« in particular, Fues claims that *Wanderjahre* shows how the human subject had already been transgressed as the centre of interpretation in the nineteenth century:

Die Signifikanz des Human-Subjekts weist dann nämlich bereits auf ihrem Höhepunkt über sich selbst hinaus, ihre kontingente Transzendenz zu ihrer Abweichung von sich überdeterminierend, dezentrierend, entstellend.[38]

By interpreting *Wanderjahre* as a novel that consists of parallel texts, Fues is able to regard it as signifying a transgression of the human subject, which is traditionally seen as characteristic of modernity. On the basis of our investigation of the significance of the archive for the novel, it should by now be clear that it is not necessary to look to hypertext for a cognitive template for the form of *Wanderjahre*; the nineteenth-century archive organised by the principle of provenance carries the necessary connotations. We shall see presently how the archive and the narrative negotiation it embodies also provide significant insights into the conception of the human subject displayed in this novel, and allows us to see the formation of an intricate relation between human existence, narrative construction, and the organisation of the text which will become central to our reading of Robert Musil's *Der Mann ohne Eigenschaften* in chapter 2.2.

A historical, sociological view of *Wanderjahre* would emphasize that Wilhelm's shift from wanderer to surgeon signifies the necessity of taking on one specific role in life and society. This is what Schwamborn emphasizes in the quotation above. Early on in the novel Wilhelm has a conversation with Jarno in which Jarno advocates the importance of knowing one trade – having one purpose in life. Later on, Wilhelm decides to become a surgeon and leave behind the rootless existence of the traveller who picks

---

36 Fues, p. 154.
37 Ibid. p. 144.
38 Ibid. p. 144.

up random knowledge along the way. This reflects a development in society in the nineteenth century. Goethe's epoch saw the nobility, who could afford to travel around Europe to acquire a general education, losing power to the commoners who made their way in the world through the skills that their trade gave them. It is thus the interpretation of the term »Bildung« that is at stake. Whereas it traditionally had connoted a general knowledge about the world – »Kunst, Ethisches, Natur« as the subtitle of the first set of aphorisms goes – specific education became increasingly important in the nineteenth century, not least as early industrialisation set in with an increased division of labour.

However, on another level – that of the construction of the narrative with which Fues deals and which we have tried to map out in relation to the figure of the archive in this chapter – the novel presents another view on the philosophical and psychological implications of human existence in the nineteenth century. This claims that the human subject cannot be understood as one function or one identity. The shift in narrative strategy that occured from when Goethe wrote *Wilhelm Meisters Lehrjahre* until he published *Wanderjahre* rests first and foremost, as Stefan Blessin has pointed out, on the fact that: »Die Mittelpunktsfigur ist nicht mehr das Organisationsprinzip«.[39] We are now dealing with several equal strains of narrative that are not organized around one person and his horizon: »Es findet eine Verselbständigung in lauter autonome Welten statt«.[40] As we have seen, the layers of textual codes and structures are increased due to the many diverse pieces of text which are bound together, not by an omniscient narrator, but by an editor with a limited point of view. If it is not possible to regard the human subject as an organizing entity around which the narration can revolve in *Wanderjahre*, then what are we in fact told about the conditions of human existence? Let us once again look at the function of the aphorisms. The juxtaposition of the narrative and the aphorisms has revealed the contrast between action and reflection (»Handeln« and »Betrachten«) to be a recurring theme on a thematic as well as on a structural level. Aphorism 142 »MA« elaborates on this dichotomy:

Ich denke, Wissenschaft könnte man die Kenntnis des Allgemeinen nennen, das abgezogene Wissen; Kunst dagegen wäre Wissenschaft zur Tat verwendet; Wissenschaft wäre Vernunft, und Kunst ihr Mechanismus, deshalb man sie auch praktische Wissenschaft nennen könnte. Und so wäre denn endlich Wissenschaft das Theorem, Kunst das Problem.[41]

---

39 Blessin, p. 240.
40 Ibid. p. 240.
41 Goethe, pp. 519-20.

Extending the dichotomies which this aphorism displays in relation to the two parts of the novel with which we have dealt – the abstract aphorisms and the illustrative action of the novellas – we see how the two central sets of reasoning and representation with which the novel works are played out in diverse thematic forms throughout the novel, creating between them a mediation which Volker Neuhaus termed »Archivroman« – a novel negotiating its narrativity through the figure of the archive. Furthermore, we can begin to see that we find the representation of human existence as mediation between these dichotomies.

The overall metaphor for human existence in *Wanderjahre* is the wanderer. The wanderer embodies the many diverse dimensions of life that a human being encounters over a lifetime. Jarno describes Wilhelm as: »einen Wanderstab, der die wunderliche Eigenschaft hat, in jeder Ecke zu grünen, wo man ihn hinstellt, nirgends aber Wurzel zu fassen«.[42] Most of the other characters of the novel appear to be searching for a purpose for their existence. For the majority, this purpose is not something fixed or already given, but is something at which they gradually arrive. This is where the correspondence between the form of the »archive novel« and its representation of human existence becomes apparent. An archive may also lack a given purpose at the start. It may be infused with intentions in so far as something is left out and other things remembered, as Derrida points out, but on the whole the archive is a text in its becoming, waiting for a reader, just as *Wanderjahre* represents human existence as a process of becoming, lingering between »Betrachten« and »Handeln«, reflection and narrative. The barber's tale »Die Neue Melusine« represents such an undertaking. The barber's renunciation consists of silence. He is only allowed to tell fairy tales, and he therefore transforms the various experiences of his life into coherent stories. Human existence for him consequently appears as incongruent data material, imbued with an impetus to construct narrative plots. Aphorism 132 »BW« condenses this view of human existence as something simultaneously dispersed and united, particular and universal:

Grundeigenschaft der lebendigen Einheit; sich zu trennen, sich zu vereinen, sich ins Allgemeine zu ergehen, im Besondern zu verharren, sich zu verwandeln, sich zu spezifizieren und wie das Lebendige unter tausend Bedingungen sich dartun mag, hervorzutreten und zu verschwinden, zu solideszieren und zu schmelzen, zu erstarren und zu fließen, sich auszudehnen und sich zusammenzuziehen. Weil nun alle diese Wirkungen im gleichen Zeitmoment zugleich vorgehen, so kann alles und jedes zu gleicher Zeit eintreten. Entstehen und Vergehen, Schaffen und Vernichten, Geburt und Tod, Freud und Leid, alles wirkt durcheinander, in gleichem Sinn und gleicher

---

42 Ibid. p. 50.

Maße, deswegen denn auch das Besonderste, das sich ereignet, immer als Bild und Gleichnis des Allgemeinsten auftritt.[43]

Here, life is described as a liquid material that constantly changes form and vibrates from the energy generated by all these ongoing processes. The novel deals with its material in a similar way, since the archive material with which we are presented is disparate and constantly pointing towards new correspondences. It is in need of a reader to structure it, because it is not arranged according to subject (i.e. ascribed a fixed place and function in the development of the plot; the editor shows us the *process* of doing this, not a fixed, consistent result), instead most of the individual novellas, letters, and poems maintain their original form, and therefore the archival novel as a whole takes on an assembled form in constant dialogue with itself. This means that the lives portrayed in the novel likewise appear assembled. The inherent paradox of the principle of provenance is thus transferred to the novel's representation of human existence. On the one hand, we have an increased focus on the individual that this way of organizing according to origin implies, and, on the other hand, we see a disparate form that requires the interpretative participation of the reader to make sense of it. What is at play is a clash between the wish for soothing storytelling and the disturbing impetus to regard the meaning of the narrative as an ongoing process of negotiation that requires participation in order to make sense. The reader of the novel has to mediate between identification with the narrative at hand and an active participation in the construction of the correspondences of the text, in the same way as human existence is played out between filling out a set role in society and being in a continuous process of becoming.

2.2 Wie komme ich zum Erzählen:
Robert Musil's *Der Mann ohne Eigenschaften*

In the previous chapter we explored the figure of the archive in Goethe's *Wanderjahre*. We saw how, by embodying a different way of organising information, the archive facilitates a problematisation of the narrative of the novel that portrays the process of reading as a practice of negotiation between the narrative plot (with which we identify) and the aphorisms (which encourage us to see the multiplicity of opposing viewpoints) at work in the

---

43 Ibid. p. 329.

text. In Robert Musil's *Der Mann ohne Eigenschaften* (1921-1942)[44], written some hundred years later, we find a similar problematisation of the way in which information is organised, this time articulated not in the shape of an archive organised by a principle of provenance, but in the structure of the *network*.

Semantically, an interesting development in the meaning of the word »network« takes place in the early twentieth century. In the English language, »network« is used from 1560 to describe a »net-like arrangement of threads, wires, etc.«, which derives from the noun »net« plus »work«. The extended sense of »any complex, interlocking system« dates from 1839 (originally in reference to transport by rivers, canals, and railways). The meaning »broadcasting system of multiple transmitters« dates from 1914, while the sense »interconnected group of people« is not reported until 1947. We thus see a transition from a concrete, object-related structure to a more social interpretation and use of the word in the course of the first half of the twentieth century.[45] This chapter will explore the problematisation of causal narrativity and the novel genre in *MoE* through the figure of the network. *MoE* is historically situated precisely in this period of semantic transition, in which it becomes increasingly common to use the figure as part of a social analysis. The foundation for the network figure as we recognize it today[46] is thus laid in this period which Musil aims to capture. This is significant, because it explains and underlines *why* it makes sense to go back and look at a novel like *MoE* through the figure of the network in order to understand more fully how the figure of the hyperlink is used in contemporary novels, as we shall do in chapter 3.2.

MoE is often grouped with works like Marcel Proust's *À la Recherche du Temps perdu* (1913-1927), James Joyce's *Ulysses* (1922), and Virginia Woolf's *To the Lighthouse* (1927), each of which in different ways opposes

---

44 Musil began writing in 1921 and the novel remained unfinished when he died in 1942. In 1930 Book One was published, in late 1932 Book Two, and in 1943 his wife published some chapters from his posthumous papers. Henceforth referred to as *MoE*.

45 In the entry »Netz« in *Wörterbuch der philosophischen Metaphern* Christian Emden describes the figure of the net as a philosophical metaphor occurring since antiquity. The net is inherent in both the organic spider's web and the crafted fisherman's net. Its connotations have varied from, on the one hand, being evoked as a thing that hides something – a web of illusions which covers the true facts of the case – to, on the other hand, embodying order and providing a starting point for knowledge and cognition. Emden traces the social interpretation of the figure back to the writings of Georg Simmel and Max Weber. See also Böhme's article »Netzwerke« for further conceptualisation of the network figure.

46 Like the figure of the archive, the network has in recent years been significantly accentuated in contemporary theory, art, and literature. Today it is used to describe a wide variety of systems of interconnected components – neural, transport, computer, communication, economic, as well as social networks. See, for instance, urban theorist Manuel Castells who describes contemporary society as a »network society« or Mark C. Taylor who refers to a contemporary »network culture«.

nineteenth-century realism and its indebtedness to the paradigms of evolution and linear causality in science and intellectual life. Explaining and exploring causal connections as a relationship in which cause and effect are bound together in a linear progression was a mode of representation that was challenged by several early modernist writers.[47] However, in a letter to the Berlin critic Walther Petry from March 1931 Musil resists Petry's description of *MoE* as aiming to dissolve the novel genre in the same way as Proust and Joyce: »Daß Joyce, Proust usw. die Form auflösen, ist soweit ich Einblick habe, auch meine Meinung, nur würde ich es gern anders gemacht haben.«[48] Here Musil appears – at the same time as he realizes the contemporary pressure on the form of the novel – to resist this dissolution. When reading *MoE* one strongly senses the way in which the novel is pervaded by a deeply founded wish to tell a story at the same time as it renders narrative coherency problematic.[49] This is the inner struggle that leads to *MoE*'s attempt at finding alternative ways of telling its story. This chapter will explore three ways in which the novel embodies a *struggle*. Firstly, the main character, Ulrich, struggles to come to terms with his own life and identity; secondly, we see a struggle in coming to terms with narrativity as an adequate way of representing life; and finally we see a struggle in the way in which the text itself is organized. This chapter aims to show that it is the figure of the network with its inherent resistance towards causal linearity, which articulates these three instances of struggle.

2.2.1 »Wenn dieses Buch gelingt, wird es Gestalt sein«

MoE tells the story of Ulrich, who has trained in the army, as an engineer, and as a mathematician. None of these three vocations has brought him any fulfilment, and he decides to take a »holiday from his life« in the crucial years of 1913-1914, shortly before Europe is cast into the First World War. However, he becomes involved in a committee preparing the celebration in honour of the Austrian Emperor's seventy year reign in 1918, and through Ulrich's social life we encounter a gallery of characters moving in and around the city of Vienna. When Ulrich reencounters his sister Agathe, whom he has not known since their childhood, he withdraws from life to engage in a symbiotic relationship with incestuous undertones – in pursuit

---

47 On modernist narrative and the realist paradigm see, for instance, Lodge; Midgley, The German Novel in the Twentieth Century; or Kontje. For *MoE*'s relation to the realistic novel see Eisele.

48 Musil, Briefe-Nachlese, p. 14.

49 See Rasch, pp. 78-80; Moser; Eisele; Nusser; or Pfeiffer.

of a quasi-mystical awareness of the world, which he refers to as »der andere Zustand«. This is where the published material ends. In the posthumously published fragments, diverging versions of Musil's intentions for the rest of the novel can be found, but the work remains unfinished, and a substantial part of Musil scholarship has been engaged in the question of whether »der andere Zustand« should be regarded as a viable utopia or whether disillusion is unavoidable as the progression of time inevitably leads into the First World War.

However, *MoE* consists just as much of philosophical reflections on the conditions of human existence put forward by Ulrich, the narrator, or in the dialogues between the characters. As in *Wanderjahre*, action and reflection are intricately interwoven.[50] The question which remains is how the connections are made – not only those between the plot and the essays within the text, but also those in Ulrich's life and in the modern world; in this sense what is at issue on several different levels is the concept of *causality*.

In the early twentieth century, when *MoE* was conceived, causality had become a highly debated issue.[51] This was true not only in physics, with the emergence of quantum physics and Einstein's theory of relativity, but also in areas such as philosophy and psychology – not least in the evolving discipline of Gestalt psychology. According to Gestalt psychology, we actively construct meaning when we perceive. Its main principle is that the whole is more than the sum of the parts. The classic example is that a melody is more than the sum of the individual notes. Referring to the Austrian physicist and philosopher Ernst Mach (1838-1916), Silvia Bonacchi gives the following precise definition in *Die Gestalt der Dichtung. Der Einfluss der Gestalttheorie auf das Werk Robert Musils* (1998):

Die Wirklichkeit kommt uns in Gestalten entgegen. Es ist sehr schwer, diese fundamentale Erfahrung zu widerlegen. Wir hören Melodien, und nicht einzelne Töne, wir hören sinnvolle Worte und nicht Geräusche, wir sehen Dinge und nicht eine indifferente Masse von Punkten. Schon ein Kind unterscheidet ein böses Gesicht von einem guten. Der Maler muß eine mühsame Ausbildung durchmachen, um etwa die Farben, die Linien eines Gesichtes unterscheiden zu können. Unverbundenheit ist keineswegs eine natürliche Leistung. [52]

What is interesting about Bonacchi's description of Gestalt theory is this emphasis on connectivity. In the quotation she establishes a dichtonomy between disconnected parts and integrated wholes which, as we shall see, is central to Musil's way of thinking about the novel. We also see that the fig-

---

50 The oscillation between plot and essay has been much discussed in Musil scholarship, see, for instance, Rasch, p. 82ff; Eisele, p. 171f; Moser, p. 175f; and Pfeiffer.
51 See, for instance, Kern.
52 Bonacchi, p. 241.

ure of the network and the concept of Gestalt appear to have fundamental
similarities in their way of conceiving connectivity and the relation between
the part and the whole. Significantly, Musil wrote his doctoral thesis on
Ernst Mach's problematization of causality, which works from the point of
view that science establishes functional relations between facts, not causal
connections. To Musil, Gestalt theory shared with art an interest in understanding human experience, and it is thus no surprise that the relation between part and whole, and an interest in how these are connected, can be
found throughout *MoE*.[53] In fact, Musil's notebooks reveal that he wished
his novel to present itself as a »Gestalt« – an integrated whole that is more
than the sum of its parts and in which inner and outer are indistinguishable:

> Gedanken dürfen nicht um ihrer selbst willen darin stehen. Sie können darin, was eine
> besondere Schwierigkeit ist, auch nicht so ausgeführt werden, wie es ein Denker täte;
> sie sind ›Teile‹ einer Gestalt. Und wenn dieses Buch gelingt, wird es Gestalt sein.[54]

Having established the importance of how elements are connected, and the
resemblances between the figure of the network and the concept of Gestalt,
let us now move on to have a closer look at how this is articulated at three
levels in the text: the level of Ulrich's life, the discussion of narration as a
theme in the text, and the level of the organisation of the text as a whole.

2.2.2 Human Existence as Network

The first level we shall look at concerns Ulrich's view on the conditions of
modern existence, which he describes with the two terms *Seinesgleichen*
and *Eigenschaftslosigkeit*, and the possibility he sees for surviving under
these conditions through the faculty of *Möglichkeitssinn*. As we shall see,
all three concepts have the figure of the network imbedded in them. Our
comprehension of the dynamics of the text relies to a large degree on a sensation of the nature of the text itself; the aim of this section is thus to create
a textual mosaic by extracting central quotations that convey not only an
understanding of the central concepts of the text, but also their actual execu-
tion in the text.

The concept of *Eigenschaftslosigkeit* describes the fact that human identity does not equate to a certain quality that encapsulates all of a human being's identity. To Ulrich, identity is blurred, plastic, and multi-faceted:

---

53 In »Brief an G.«, dated 26.01.31, Musil describes how he envisioned the *MoE* project: »es
hätte einen neuen Erzählungsstil gegeben, worin das äußerlich Kausale zu Gunsten phänomenaler
und motivischer Zusammenhänge ganz aufgelöst worden wäre.« (Musil, Briefe 1901-1942, p.
497).
54 Musil, MoE, p. 1942.

Denn ein Landesbewohner hat mindestens neun Charaktere, einen Berufs-, einen Na-
tional-, einen Staats-, einen Klassen-, einen geographischen, einen Geschlechts-, ei-
nen bewußten-, einen unbewußten und vielleicht auch noch einen privaten Charakter;
er vereinigt sie in sich, aber sie lösen ihn auf, und er ist eigentlich nichts als eine klei-
ne, von diesen vielen Rinnsalen ausgewaschene Mulde, in die sie hineinsickern und
aus der sie wieder austreten, um mit andern Bächlein eine andre Mulde zu füllen.
Deshalb hat jeder Erdbewohner auch noch einen zehnten Charakter, und dieser ist
nichts als die passive Phantasie unausgefüllter Räume; er gestattet dem Menschen alles, nur nicht das eine: das ernst zu nehmen, was seine mindestens neun andern Charaktere tun und was mit ihnen geschieht.[55]

The world Ulrich encounters thus appears to him as if it has extracted itself
from the human being and operates as an independent system of interrelated
connections that render the human obsolete as the centre of things:

Heute dagegen hat die Verantwortung ihren Schwerpunkt nicht im Menschen, sondern in den Sachzusammenhängen. Hat man nicht bemerkt, daß sich die Erlebnisse
vom Menschen unabhängig gemacht haben? […] Es ist eine Welt von Eigenschaften
ohne Mann entstanden, von Erlebnissen ohne den, der sie erlebt, und es sieht beinahe
aus, als ob im Idealfall der Mensch überhaupt nichts mehr privat erleben werde und
die freundliche Schwere der persönlichen Verantwortung sich in ein Formelsystem
von möglichen Bedeutungen auflösen solle.[56]

This conflicting relation between the world and personal experience is captured in the concept of *Seinesgleichen*. Seinesgleichen is part of the subtitle
of the first book »Seinesgleichen geschieht«; the word expresses sameness,
as in the notion of »his kind« or of a »peer«. However, by referring to this
sameness as an event, the term comes to describe the process of sameness
occurring and arising:

Oder wenn man unter dem Eindruck steht, daß nur *Seinesgleichen geschieht*, weil das
Leben – zum Platzen voll Einbildung auf sein Hier und Jetzt, letzten Endes aber ein
sehr ungewisser, ja ausgesprochen unwirklicher Zustand! – sich in die paar Dutzend
Kuchenformen stürzt, aus denen die Wirklichkeit besteht.[57] [My emphasis]

Seinesgleichen is a process that causes things to resemble each other – by
being channelled through prefabricated compartments or »cake molds«.
Cognition, according to Ulrich, is thus always only a re-cognition of the
same.[58] If we now turn to look at the occurrence of the figure of the network

---

55 Ibid. p. 34.
56 Ibid. p. 150.
57 Ibid. p. 591.
58 In Musil scholarship Seinesgleichen has been linked to Musil's rhetorical use of allegory
and repetition. Jörg Kühne argues that »Gleichnis« works on both the formal and the content levels
of the novel. Seinesgleichen and allegory, with their duplication of form, are thus related to the

in *MoE,* we see that the network and the connotations this figure carries in the novel assist in developing an image of modern existence as characterised by Eigenschaftlosigkeit and Seinesgleichen:

Man kann weder auf die Straße treten, noch ein Glas Wasser trinken oder die Elektrische besteigen, ohne die ausgewogenen Hebel eines riesigen Apparats von Gesetzen und Beziehungen zu berühren, sie in Bewegung zu setzen oder sich von ihnen in der Ruhe seines Daseins erhalten zu lassen; man kennt die wenigsten von ihnen, die tief ins Innere greifen, während sie auf der anderen Seite *sich in ein Netzwerk verlieren, dessen ganze Zusammensetzung überhaupt noch kein Mensch entwirrt hat;* man leugnet sie deshalb, so wie der Staatsbürger die Luft leugnet und von ihr behauptet, daß die Leere sei, aber scheinbar liegt gerade darin, daß alles Geleugnete, alles Farb-, Geruch-, Geschmack-, Gewicht und Sittenlose wie Wasser, Luft, Raum, Geld und Dahingehn der Zeit in Wahrheit das Wichtigste ist, eine gewisse Geisterhaftigkeit des Lebens; es kann den Menschen zuweilen eine Panik erfassen wie im willenlosen Traum, ein Bewegungssturm tollen Umsichschlagens *wie ein Tier, das in den unverständlichen Mechanismus eines Netzes geraten ist.*[59] [My emphasis]

The network here referred to is that of law and order and it is characterized by being invisible, beyond the senses and therefore incomprehensible. Nonetheless, it is also described as all-pervasive and likened to things which are unavoidable in human life – such as water, air, space, money, and the passing of time. In this chapter Ulrich tries to influence the mechanisms of the network by defending a drunken worker who is being arrested, but ends up being arrested himself. He is thus ultimately identified by the state and enrolled as the secretary of the Parallel Action. In this way Ulrich is disciplined and assigned a place in the network. The references to network structures in *MoE*[60] thus seem to convey a picture of human existence in the modern world as being made up of interrelated dynamics in which man has to learn to manoeuvre so as not to be caught as a helpless fly. However, the

---

lack of action in the novel and dominate especially in the first part, whereas the second part of the novel is to a larger degree dominated by what Ulrich calls Möglichkeitssinn (Kühne, p. 85).

59 Musil, MoE, pp. 156-57.

60 Other examples of direct use of the network figure: »*In dem ungeheuren Netz von Schienen, Weichen und Signalen,* das sich um den ganzen Erdball zieht, verlieren wir alle die Kraft des Gewissens. Denn wenn wir die Stärke hätten, uns noch einmal zu prüfen und noch einmal unsere Aufgabe zu beachten, so würden wir immer das Nötige tun und das Unglück vermeiden.« (Musil, MoE, p. 713). Or: »Die äußerst eindringliche Vorstellung eines braven, liebevollen, klugen kleinen Jungen, die man sich von ihm gemacht hatte; Hoffnungen, die ganz und gar noch nicht seine eigenen waren; ungewisse Erwartungen einer ehrenvollen erwünschten Zukunft, die wie die offenen Flügel *eines goldenen Netzes nach ihm langten.*« (Ibid. p. 648). However, the examples of a conception of the world as being made up of numerous interrelated connections without a centre are multiple, even when the words »Netz« / »Netzwerk« are not explicitly mentioned: »Es war das […] die bekannte Zusammenhanglosigkeit der Einfälle und ihre Ausbreitung ohne Mittelpunkt, die für die Gegenwart kennzeichnend ist und deren merkwürdige Arithmetik ausmacht, die vom Hundertsten ins Tausendste kommt, ohne eine Einheit zu haben.« (Ibid. p. 20). [My emphasis].

description of private, as well as public, life evokes the figure of the network. Ulrich repeatedly comments on the way in which the self is composed of connections:

Das Ich erfaßt ja seine Eindrücke und Hervorbringungen niemals einzeln, sondern immer in Zusammenhängen, in wirklicher oder gedachter, ähnlicher oder unähnlicher Übereinstimmung mit anderem; so lehnt alles, was Namen hat, aneinander in Hinsichten, in Fluchten, als Glied von großen und unüberblickbaren Gesamtheiten, eins auf das andere gestützt und von gemeinsamen Spannungen durchzogen. Aber darum steht man auch‹, fuhr er plötzlich anders fort ›wenn aus irgendeinem Anlaß diese Zusammenhänge versagen und keine der inneren Ordnungsreihen anspricht, allsogleich wieder vor der unbeschreiblichen und unmenschlichen, ja vor der widerrufenen und formlosen Schöpfung![61]

The oscillation between, on the one hand, being connected and thus being kept together by an outer structure that keeps things in their place, and, on the other hand, a sense of internal lack of form, is in this way described in terms that bring to mind the structure of a network that simultaneously embodies order and disorder.

Turning now to look at how *Möglichkeitssinn* – Ulrich's solution to the modern condition of life – is described, it is interesting to observe that, once again, the figure of the net is evoked. Möglichkeitssinn becomes a method of survival for Ulrich in this world of Eigenschaftlosigkeit and Seinesgleichen, and it shapes especially the second part of the novel and the posthumous notes:

Wenn es aber Wirklichkeitssinn gibt, und niemand wird bezweifeln, daß er seine Daseinsberechtigung hat, dann muß es auch etwas geben, das man Möglichkeitssinn nennen kann. [...] So ließe sich der Möglichkeitssinn geradezu als die Fähigkeit definieren, alles, was ebensogut sein könnte, zu denken und das, was ist, nicht wichtiger zu nehmen als das, was nicht ist.[62]

This flair for possibility is both a consequence and a method of handling the condition of Eigenschaftslosigkeit and Seinesgleichen in modern society. Living hypothetically opens the possibility of manoeuvring in a world which is experienced as overly deterministic and thus as excluding human agency. Repetition is transformed into co-existing versions of the world which, rather than merely repeat, expand the field in which the human being can manoeuvre. Also in the description of the condition of Möglichkeitssinn we recognize the figure of the network: »Solche Möglichkeitsmenschen leben, wie man sagt, in einem feineren Gespinst, in einem Ge-

---

61 Musil, MoE, p. 1090.
62 Ibid. p. 16.

spinst von Dunst, Einbildung, Träumerei und Konjunktiven.«[63] Here we see two sides of network connotations at play: on the one hand, the network is something which should be dissolved in order to penetrate illusion and deception, and, on the other hand, there is an acknowledgement of the fact that the complexity that the network embodies is a precondition for knowledge and cognition. In this quotation Möglichkeitsmenschen are described from the point of view of people who do not understand the advantages of Möglichkeitssinn and therefore regard their world as a web of illusions. However, as is shown in the larger context from which this quotation is taken, Möglichkeitssinn is an advantage if used in the right way; in fact, possibly the only way of manoeuvring in a world of Eigenschaftslosigkeit.

Ulrich's struggle in life involves looking for a way of being accurate about the way we live now, and the figure of the network gives him a tool for articulating this. However, by looking at the way networks are referred to in *MoE* we realise that the network figure is ambiguous. On the one hand, the connotations are those of a fisherman's net, or a spider's web, in which the human being is caught and has little room for agency. The ability of the »handlungsfähige« characters of the novel to act rather than reflect relies on the fact that they know and obey the rules of this network. On the other hand, there is a different set of connotations at work when the novel describes Möglichkeitssinn as having network characteristics. Möglichkeitssinn entails envisioning the world in another way than that in which it meets you, and it therefore brings with it the potential ability to understand the shape, texture, and complexity of the network. In the words of Christian Emden: »Netze schaffen Ordnung, können allerdings bei zunehmender Komplexität auch Metaphern für die Unordnung begrifflichen Denkens werden.«[64] This is the doublesidedness of the network connotations which come to the fore in *MoE*'s description of society and the conditions of human existence.

2.2.3 Narrative Networks

Möglichkeitssinn is, thus, as much a symptom as a solution, since the constant consciousness of other options is part of rendering traditional ways of experiencing and representing events problematic. In the following lengthy quotation Ulrich's life-problem reveals itself as intricately interwoven with the question of epic representation, and we can thus begin to see how Ul-

---

63 Ibid. p. 16.
64 Emden, p. 249.

rich's probing of modern existence is related to the negotiation of narrativity in the novel:

Es ist die einfache Reihenfolge, die Abbildung der überwältigenden Mannigfaltigkeit des Lebens in einer eindimensionalen, wie ein Mathematiker sagen würde, was uns beruhigt; die Aufreihung alles dessen, was in Raum und Zeit geschehen ist, auf einen Faden, eben jenen berühmten ›Faden der Erzählung‹, aus dem nun also auch der Lebensfaden besteht. Wohl dem, der sagen kann ›als‹, ›ehe‹ und ›nachdem‹! Es mag ihm Schlechtes widerfahren sein, oder er mag sich in Schmerzen gewunden haben: sobald er imstande ist, die Ereignisse in der Reihenfolge ihres zeitlichen Ablaufes wiederzugeben, wird ihm so wohl, als schiene ihm die Sonne auf den Magen. Das ist es, was sich der Roman künstlich zunutze gemacht hat [...] Die meisten Menschen sind im Grundverhältnis zu sich selbst Erzähler. Sie lieben nicht die Lyrik, oder nur für Augenblicke, und wenn in den Faden des Lebens auch ein wenig ›weil‹ und ›damit‹ hineingeknüpft wird, so verabscheuen sie doch alle Besinnung, die darüber hinausgreift: sie lieben das ordentliche Nacheinander von Tatsachen, weil es einer Notwendigkeit gleichsieht, und fühlen sich durch den Eindruck, daß ihr Leben einen ›Lauf‹ habe, irgendwie im Chaos geborgen. Und Ulrich bemerkte nun, daß ihm dieses primitiv Epische abhanden gekommen sei, woran das private Leben noch festhält, obgleich öffentlich alles schon unerzählerisch geworden ist und nicht einem ›Faden‹ mehr folgt, sondern sich in einer unendlich verwobenen Fläche ausbreitet.[65]

This passage, which thematizes the relationship between causality, narration and human life, is a classic statement of what makes the conventional form of the novel problematic for the representation of human experience in the post-industrial social world.[66] Ulrich here exposes the fundamental appeal of narrative as a way of understanding oneself and putting one's life into perspective by placing the events of life in a causal chain where everything is tied together in a plot-like development. We have seen how,

---

65 Musil, MoE, p. 650.

66 The passage occurs in the chapter »Heimweg« at the end of Book One after Ulrich has been offered a chance to join the industrial magnate Arnheim in his business and become a man of action rather than contemplation. On his way home he strolls through town remembering a childhood photo of himself and his mother, evoking images of a village and idyllic country-life as opposed to city-life. He is also on his way home in another sense, because when he reaches his house he finds a telegram announcing the death of his father, resulting in his departure to his childhood home the following day. On many different levels this chapter thus thematizes the experience of returning home as we know it from epic narration: The hero has been exposed to life, learned his lessons, come to terms with himself, and is now ready to return home and fulfil his role in life. However, this does not happen to Ulrich in the material available to us, and we do not know if it was Musil's intention that Ulrich would ever reach such closure. The traditional structure of a story about personal development is thus mockingly inverted. Even the modernist artist myth – in which the hero at odds with society comes to terms with life by narrating it – is drawn into question when Ulrich contemplates that this year leaves him with two options: either to kill himself or write a book. For a discussion of the role of the protagonist in *MoE* in relation to the realist tradition see Eisele, p. 167f.

through the concept of Seinesgleichen, he describes a world which has become »unerzählerisch«. In this quotation he admits that his own personal life, too, has become unfit for narration. We thus realise how Ulrich's diagnosis of modern society and his own life-problem are linked to questions of narrative representation.

Galen Strawson's contention that there are people who do not necessarily conceive of their lives as narratives, people he describes as »episodics«, has already been mentioned. The implications of this claim are interesting when seen in the light of Ulrich's problems with narrativity as a mode of representing and understanding life. Whereas Ulrich believes that he has lost contact with the epic, Strawson suggests that not all people experience the world as a narrative and that an understanding of our lives as an unfolding story is not necessary in order to lead a good life. Various questions follow from this: Is Ulrich essentially a non-narrative person caught up in an environment that traditionally employs a narrative outlook upon the world, and is this the cause of his struggle? And, if narrativity is not essential for a good life for Ulrich, then what sort of form responds to an episodic outlook upon life?

In the chapter »Auch die Erde, namentlich aber Ulrich, huldigt der Utopie des Essayismus« Ulrich explains the advantages of the form of the essay to describe human existence:

Ungefähr wie ein Essay in der Folge seiner Abschnitte ein Ding von vielen Seiten nimmt, ohne es ganz zu erfassen, – denn ein ganz erfaßtes Ding verliert mit einem Male seinen Umfang und schmilzt zu einem Begriff ein – glaubte er, Welt und eigenes Leben am richtigsten ansehen und behandeln zu können. Der Wert einer Handlung oder einer Eigenschaft, ja sogar deren Wesen und Natur erschienen ihm abhängig von den Umständen, die sie umgaben, von den Zielen, denen sie dienten, mit einem Wort, von dem bald so, bald anders beschaffenen Ganzen, dem sie angehörten.[67]

Interestingly, we see the figure of the network at play in both the description of Ulrich's discomfort with narrativity and in the description of the essay form: life is »eine verwobene Fläche«, which does not concur with the simplifying narrative embodied by the thread (Faden), and the form of the essay consequently seems much more adequate as a mode of description. However, narrativity is not discharged without hesitancy. In a conversation with Diotima, Ulrich argues that life should be led as characters in a book:

Versuchen wir einander zu lieben, als ob Sie und ich die Figuren eines Dichters wären, die sich auf den Seiten eines Buchs begegnen. Lassen wir also jedenfalls das ganze Fettgerüst fort, das die Wirklichkeit rund macht.[68]

---

67 Musil, MoE, p. 250.
68 Ibid. p. 573.

Here Ulrich expresses a wish to leave reality, with all its nuances, behind. Reality contains all that which is not necessary, whereas a book leaves things out and mainly communicates what is important for the progression of the story. This quotation points to the ambivalence with which Ulrich gives up on narrativity. On the one hand, Ulrich wishes to live his life narratively – this would entail that he could exclude the unnecessary. On the other hand, his Möglichkeitssinn urges him to expand the possible ways of living rather than narrow them to those that are necessary. We thus begin to see the way in which narrativity is simultaneuously longed for and resisted in the text. To explore further this ambiguous relationship to narrativity, let us turn to a passage in which Ulrich reflects on whether emotion is a condition or a process. Ulrich's reflections link up with Gestalt psychological considerations, as well as contemporary ideas in physics such as Werner Heisenberg's *uncertainty principle* from 1927 (which states that the simultaneous determination of both the position and momentum of a particle each has an inherent uncertainty), and Niels Bohr's notion of *complementarity* (by which a photon can be regarded as both a wave and a particle, depending on how one looks at it). However, it can also be read as an elaboration on the way in which Ulrich's notion of human existence is inscribed in a debate about the adequacy of narrativity as a mode of representation:

Von der gewohnten Vorstellung ausgehend, das Gefühl sei ein Zustand, der von einer Ursache kommt und Folgen bewirkt, bin ich in der Ausführung zu einer Beschreibung geführt worden, die zweifellos einen Vorgang darstellt, wenn das Ergebnis über längere Strecken betrachtet wird. Gehe ich aber dann von dem Gesamteindruck eines Vorgangs aus und will diese Vorstellung festhalten, so sehe ich ebenso deutlich, daß zwischen benachbarten Stücken allenthalben das Nacheinander fehlt, das Eins-hinter-dem-anderen, das doch zu einem Vorgang gehört, ja sogar jede Andeutung eines Ablaufs in bestimmter Richtung. Im Gegenteil, es deutet sich zwischen den einzelnen Schritten eine wechselseitige Abhängigkeit und Voraussetzung an, ja sogar das Bild von Wirkungen, die ihren Ursachen voranzugehen scheinen. Auch Zeitverhältnisse kommen nirgends in der Beschreibung vor, und alles das weist aus verschiedenen Gründen nun wieder auf einen Zustand hin.

Ich kann also streng genommen vom Gefühl bloß sagen, daß es sowohl ein Zustand als auch ein Vorgang zu sein scheint, ebenso wie es weder ein Zustand noch ein Vorgang zu sein scheint; und eines von beiden will so berechtigt erscheinen wie das andere.[69]

Ulrich juxtaposes an experience of emotion as, respectively, a process and a condition. What is emphasised as characteristic of emotion as a process is causality (»von einer Ursache kommt und Folgen bewirkt«) and sequence

---

69 Ibid. p. 1159.

in a certain direction (»Ablauf in bestimmter Richtung«). By contrast, emotion as a condition is described in terms that resemble that of a network structure (»eine wechselseitige Abhängigkeit und Voraussetzung an, ja sogar das Bild von Wirkungen, die ihren Ursachen voranzugehen scheinen«). The description of these two conditions thus resembles the juxtaposition between the sequence of narration (»Faden der Erzählung«) and the experience of life as an interwoven field (»eine verwobene Fläche«), which we saw in Ulrich's thoughts on epic representation in the »Heimweg« chapter. Reading the quotation above as also reflecting on the relationship between narrative sequence and essayistic contemplation, we can begin to understand their complementary nature. Neither of them is dispensable; they each provide different ways of looking at human existence that give different insights. As in *Wanderjahre* the challenge consists in mediating between process and condition, »handeln und denken«, plot and essay. In *MoE* these conflicts find a way of coexisting, and we shall have a closer look at the manner in which they do so in the following section.

2.2.4 Reading Networks

Previous scholarship has dealt extensively with the correspondence between the representation of Ulrich's struggle with the conditions of human life and the form of the novel. Different readings have regarded cause and effect differently: Wolfdietrisch Rasch noted in 1967 that »Das Existenzproblem Ulrichs wird unmittelbar zum Formproblem des Romans«[70], whereas Ulf Eisele argued in 1979 that:

Nicht ›das Existenzproblem Ulrichs wird unmittelbar zum Formproblem des Romans‹, es verhält sich genau umgekehrt: Die dem MoE als Roman zugrunde liegende literarische Problematik ist verantwortlich zu machen für die prekäre Situation Ulrichs als Romanhauptfigur.[71]

Ulrich's attitude towards life makes a traditional »Bildungsroman« with a coherent linear narrative impossible, in the same way as the distorted form of the novel obstructs rather than helps Ulrich to reach closure in his existential probing. In *Aphorismus und Romanstruktur. Zu Robert Musils* Der Mann ohne Eigenschaften (1990), Peter C. Pfeiffer compares Musil's use of aphorisms and essay with Goethe's *Wanderjahre* and Marie von Ebner-Eschenbach's *Božena* and *Unsühnbar*, concluding that:

---

70 Rasch, p. 79.
71 Eisele, p. 167.

Das lineare Erzählen destruiert Musil im *Mann ohne Eigenschaften* durch zahlreiche essayistische Einschübe und Aphoristische Elemente und verweist so auf den anomischen Gesellschaftszustand, der allgemeingültiger Orientierungen entbehrt.[72]

Pfeiffer identifies a difference between Book One and Two of *MoE* in that the use of aphorisms in Book One resembles that of *Wanderjahre*, in which the aphorisms maintain an authority of their own, whereas in Book Two the aphorisms are more woven into the text. He also argues that in the unpublished sections of the novel conceived after 1933, Musil returns to the more autonomous insertion of aphorisms. His argument is that that which is radically modern in *MoE* is in dialogue with *Wanderjahre*. However, there is a significant difference between the positioning of the aphorisms in *MoE* and *Wanderjahre*. In *Wanderjahre* the aphorisms are grouped in closed sections referred to as archives. This is the reason why they could be excluded from the print editions up until 1949. Although the extent to which the essay sections are integrated into the narrative in *MoE* varies, they nowhere exist so separately that exclusion could be considered. This means that, while the reading of the archive sections in *Wanderjahre* encourages the reader to go back over the narrative material and realise the correspondences, in *MoE* one is constantly trying to follow the theoretical reflections and the plot development simultaneously. In his notebooks to *MoE* Musil makes the following comment on this twin-faceted nature of the novel:

Meine Meinung ist, daß erzählte Episoden überflüssig sein dürfen und nur um ihrer selbst willen vorhanden, Gedanken aber nicht. Ich stelle bei einer Komposition die Schlichtheit über denn sog. Gedankenreichtum, u. im Falle dieses Buches sollte nichts überflüssig sein. Die Ausführungen über die Zusammenfügung von Gedanken und Gefühlen, die dieser Teilband enthält, gestatten mir, das so zu begründen: die Hauptwirkung eines Romans soll auf das Gefühl gehen. Gedanken dürfen nicht um ihrer selbst willen darin stehen. Sie können darin, was eine besondere Schwierigkeit ist, auch nicht so ausgeführt werden, wie es ein Denker täte; sie sind ›Teile‹ einer Gestalt. Und wenn dieses Buch gelingt, wird es Gestalt sein, und die Einwände, daß es einer Abhandlung ähnele u. dgl. werden dann unverständig sein. Der Gedankenreichtum ist ein Teil des Reichtums des Gefühls.[73]

What we see here is the significance of the concept of Gestalt for Musil's thinking. By aiming to make *MoE* a Gestalt, Musil creates a whole that consists of an intricate balance between thoughts and emotions, between reflection and action. The challenge is to set up the connections between part and whole in a fruitful way. Ulrich claims that »Wirklichkeitsmenschen« have too vivid a cognition of the parts but a carelessness towards the whole,[74]

---

72 Pfeiffer, p. 55.
73 Musil, MoE, p. 1942.
74 Ibid. p. 40.

which Bonacchi interprets as a: »Mangel an Verbindungskraft«.[75] From this
it follows that Möglichkeitsmenschen must have a larger appreciation for
the whole – the Gestalt – and thus a more developed »Verbindungskraft«.
We must, however, ask ourselves what kind of whole we are dealing with?
What shape does it take?

The figure that appears to do justice to *MoE* is to envision the whole of
the novel as a network,[76] and, as we have seen, Musil's conception of Gestalt bears a strong resemblance to this figure. Plot and reflection can be regarded as nodes and gaps respectively: without either of them the network
structure would collapse and the story as a whole could move forward only
through small changes in the different nodes. A node in the novel could, for
instance, be Walter and Clarisse, Rachel and Soliman, or Moosbrugger.[77]
When a change occurs in each of these subplots the story as a whole moves
forward. However, each little change is followed by a stabilizing period of
contemplation, in which the network that has been disturbed by a change
finds its balance in the manner of a large, rather slow organism. Rather than
engaging the reader in finding correspondences and playing on the reader's
urge to construct narratives from disparate material as in *Wanderjahre*,
MoE encourages the reader to regard linear sequence as only one of many
ways of comprehending and representing the world. Ulrich's inclination to
think rather than act (»denken« rather than »handeln« as Arnheim quotes
from *Wanderjahre*)[78] can be regarded as an indirect consequence of the

---

75 Bonacchi, p. 323.

76 Jan Kjærstad uses the figure of the web to describe *MoE* in the essay »Menneskets Nett«.

77 This reading seem to correspond to Moser's description of the characters: »Die Erzählfigu-
ren befinden sich an der Überschneidung verschiedener Diskursarten, die einerseits durch sie hin-
durchgehen und durch deren Zusammenwirken sie andererseits konstituiert werden. Sie sind also
nicht mehr Träger einer Mission, einer Handlung, eines Schicksals, deren Sinn sie verkörpern
würden und deren Vollendung ihnen auf Grund ihres Charakters und ihrer Eigenschaften als Individuum anvertraut wäre, sondern vielmehr Knotenpunkte in einem Netz überpersönlicher Beziehungen.« (Moser, p. 183). It also bears resemblance to the conceptualisation of *MoE* found in
Hoffmann and Kümmel who, in different ways, focus on the discursive formations which have
made the novel possible, not as the product of one writer, but as »programmed« by the existing
discourses.

78 Musil, MoE, p. 541. In the light of the link between *Wanderjahre* and *MoE*, which we are
exploring, it is interesting to note that Arnheim chooses to quote *Wanderjahre*. However, the Goethe that Arnheim quotes is not the Goethe of the experimental approach to narrative, which we saw
in the previous chapter of this study, but Goethe as an established cultural figure in Germany. The
fact that Arnheim refers to Goethe is thus part of a parody which aims to characterise Arnheim as
conservative and unimaginative. Nonetheless, in this context (dealing with the juxtaposition of
»handeln« and »denken«) it is worth noting that a reference to Wilhelm Meister also occurs in
Musil's notebooks in conjunction with a discussion of Ulrich's inability to act and the political and
social usefulness of the novel: »Die praktische (polit. soziale) Brauchbarkeit eines solchen Buchs.
(Avantgarde) / Auch Wilh. Meister ist wohlhabend gewesen / Die Leute verlangen, daß U. etwas
tut. Ich habe es aber mit dem Sinn der Tat zu tun. Heutige Verwechslung. Natürlich muß zb. Bols-

network formation. Action demands an acting subject and creates a sequence because there is a »before« and an »after« the action, whereas the full range of possibilities can only be maintained by refraining from action. The novel consequently presents itself as a field which is made up of a plot-world consisting of character-nodes and the vast surrounding field of possibilities that lie between the nodes and determine how they can be connected. The time of the novel is thereby stretched into a continuum that makes the text appear as a flickering field of simultaneity and possibility. This sensation becomes especially prevalent in the sections with Ulrich and Agathe in the part entitled »Ins Tausendjährige Reich (Die Verbrecher)«. When Agathe goes to visit Lindner or when General Stumm von Bordwehr comes to give an account on the progression of the Parallel Action, it seems to be a crude interference of reality, not only in »the other condition« of the siblings, but also in the almost meditative progression of their discussions and thoughts. The theoretical reflections lend the text a sense of an organic sprawling flux, which the nodes of plot-related action bring to a halt and redirect forward. The experience of *Wanderjahre* is thus inverted, so that it is the narrative progression of the plot, rather than the non-narrative theoretical reflections, which breaks up the reading experience.

This conception of the novel as a network consisting of the connections between plot-nodes and reflection-spaces leads to the question of what it entails to read a network. In his investigation of the experience of the modern city in *The Practice of Everyday Life* (1988), Michel de Certeau makes a distinction between »to see« and »to do«. Viewed from a distance the city becomes a map that can be read, understood, and interpreted as a whole. Encountering the city in this way bestows power upon the viewer, because she is at a distance and does not risk being dragged into and absorbed by the city. At street level, however, the walker is at the mercy of the city. You move through space, making use of it, but you are only able to encounter it in parts and cannot see the entire structure, because you are a part of the creation of this space. If we disregard the bias towards the perspective of the walker inherent in de Certeau's distinction, a comparison with this double mode of reading a city is fruitful as an illustration of how *MoE* presents itself to the reader. On the one hand you are inclined to immerse yourself in the progression of the plot – the narrative development which revolves around the actions of the fictional characters, but also limits the perspective to the immediate part of the action. On the other hand the reflective strands stretching out in between the plot-related events enable the reader to acquire

---

ch. geschehn; aber a) nicht durch Bücher b) haben Bücher noch andere Aufgaben. Ähnlichkeit mit Kriegssituation u KPQ« (Musil, MoE, p. 1940). Musil seems here to indicate kinship between Ulrich and Wilhelm.

a more encompassing view of the multiple perspectives which the novel of-fers.[79] It is a way of reading that makes the reader mediate between the per-spective of a Wirklichkeitsmensch (who sees only the parts) and a Möglichkeitsmensch (who is able to see the whole); both perspectives being necessary. Musil seems to imply something similar when he remarks in his notebooks: »ich bitte mich zweimal zu lesen, im Teil u. im Ganzen«.[80]

2.2.5 »Wie komme ich zum Erzählen«

In a letter to Bernard Guillemin, Musil describes the intricate relationship between the story of Ulrich and the narrative negotiation going on in the text: »Das Problem: wie komme ich zum Erzählen, ist sowohl mein stilis-tisches wie das Lebensproblem der Hauptfigur, und die Lösung ist natürlich nicht einfach.«[81] *MoE* is a work that simultaneously addresses, resists, and makes narration possible and thus essentially questions the relationship be-tween narrativity and the perception and representation of human life. In his article »Against Narrativity«, Strawson tries to settle accounts with the con-ception that »a richly Narrative outlook is essential to a well-lived life, to true or full personhood«.[82] Likewise it can be argued that *MoE* tries to go beyond the belief that a richly narrative outlook is essential to a novel. *MoE* challenges narration as the only form of representation that renders meaning to human existence and probes other ways of telling a story by employing the figure of the network in the characterisation of human existence in the modern world, the discussion of narrativity as representational mode, and in the organisation of the text itself. As we shall see in chapter 3.2, the network-image in contemporary novels is often linked to information technology imagery. However, by looking at the network at work in *MoE* we are reminded that the network as a figure should be seen in a larger literary and socio-cultural context. The foundation for the enormous emphasis that this image acquires with poststructuralism and information technology is laid much earlier. *MoE* captures a time of unrest and upheaval in the history of the network-figure when the social application of the

---

79 As Barbara Maria Stafford makes clear in her discussion of Romantic art, recent neurosci-ence shows that the simultaneity of capturing experience »in discrete units and as a dream of en-gulfing immersion« stems from the way in which our brain works: »The brain is simultaneously an externally directed, selectionist mechanism – dynamically framing its environment through vari-ance in the populations of neurons and an internally organizing system – solipsistically occupied with itself in the regulation of its diverging and overlapping dendritic arbors.« (Stafford, p. 35).

80 Musil, MoE, p. 1941.

81 Musil, Briefe 1901-1942, p. 498.

82 Strawson, p. 428.

network-image gains ground, paving the way for its engagement as part of a narrative negotiation of human perception and representation.

2.3 Shuffling Text:
Arno Schmidt's *Zettels Traum*

1334 pages. Over ten million characters in a format of 12.8 x 12.3 inches. These are the physical dimensions of Arno Schmidt's *Zettels Traum*[83] (1970). Inside the book we find typewritten pages, parallel columns, advertising materials, photographs, and footnotes. We also encounter the fictitious characters Daniel Pagenstecher, Paul Jacobi, his wife Wilma, and their teenage daughter Franziska. Through the course of the novel we follow their discussion of the life and works of Edgar Allan Poe, their attempts to interpret and translate his writings, and the playing out of the relationships between these four figures.

However, *ZT* is a book with a strong emphasis on its physical manifestation. The format and layout of the novel is what first strikes you, while the narrative – the story – is almost overpowered. Written in 1970, the work is situated in a period characterised by experimentation with literary forms. The Oulipo movement, concrete poetry, and the neo-avant-garde all emphasise the physical layout of the written text, and within the coming decade Jean-François Lyotard would verbalize a suspicion of grand meta-narratives and privilege precisely the type of micro-narratives and language games we find in *ZT*. However, Arno Schmidt's place in literary tradition has been a matter of debate, not least because he himself insisted on a position secluded from the literary scene, and it is only with difficulty that he can be associated with specific trends in post-war German literature. Brian Lennon has commented that Schmidt's writings display »all the familiar hallmarks (disjunction, interiority, linguistic ›play‹, pastiche, parody etc., etc,) of both modernist and postmodernist works of fiction [...] with such inventive extremity as would be difficult to surpass on the printed page«,[84] whereas Michael Minden notes that Schmidt distinguishes himself from most modernist and postmodern experimental writing by not questioning the reliability of fiction and language as modes of representation:

In theory at least, Schmidt avoids the notion of literature as a self-justifying artefact, of a game, a pattern, a prolonged and ultimately desolate flirtation with its own

---

83 Henceforth referred to as *ZT*.
84 Lennon, p. 170.

meaninglessness – the glimpse of the void beyond confessed artificiality of which Alter speaks as characteristic of much modern fiction. And, however much, in practise, Schmidt extends the function of language beyond a transparent representational medium, his conception of language is always pronouncedly anthropocentric; man uses language, language does not use man.[85]

Instead Minden emphasises Schmidt's affinities with the playful pre-modern novel of the eighteenth century, such as those by Sterne, Smolett, Fielding, and Wieland. Other characteristics of Schmidt's writing that go beyond the modernist and postmodern traits are pointed out by people such as Rüdiger Zymner, who traces Schmidt's literary antecedents back to the tradition of mannerism and the baroque writer Johann Fischart (1546-90), and by Volker Langbehn, who refers to Schmidt's indebtedness to the Jena Romantics and their notion of the fragment. Schmidt thus holds an ambiguous position by virtue of both launching probably one of the most stylistically and formally challenging undertakings in modern German fiction (which has even caused *ZT* to be denounced as non-art and nonsense)[86] and maintaining an opinion on the nature of literature and representation which has it own take on the twentieth century's fundamental questioning of the reliability of language's representation of the world.

David Hayman has described *ZT* as a »work-in-progress«.[87] In these terms *ZT* can be read as a novel in the making, which on both a thematic and a formal level foregrounds a discussion of the conscious and unconscious material that goes into the creation of a literary work. But it also provides the basis for approaching the procedural nature of *ZT* as a discussion of narrativity, which will be the focus of this chapter. Firstly, however, let us try to get to grips with the scope of the novel and identify possible modes of reading it by drawing on the figures of the archive and the network which have been discussed in the previous two chapters.

2.3.1 Reading *Zettels Traum*

The text is divided into in three columns. The centre column is where the actual action takes place. Here we encounter Daniel Pagenstecher, the main protagonist of the story, who aids Paul Jacobi and his wife Wilma in their translation of Edgar Allan Poe's work from English into German. The discussions of the writings are situated in the left column, while the right

---

85 Minden, pp. 6-7.
86 Bock, p. 194.
87 Hayman, p. 21.

column is made up of quotations from literature, myth, recipe books, dictionaries, newspapers, radio and TV news. These commentaries provide additional information and often re-contextualise the information in the centre column. However, this tripartite structure is not an absolute one, but instead is something which is frequently adapted and broken. The columns thus interact and metamorphose as we read.

This conglomeration of material – the piling up of information and encyclopaedic monstrosity which battles with the progression of the narrative plot in *ZT* – harks back to what we found in *Wanderjahre* in the figure of the archive. Over the course of more than ten years Schmidt filled 130,000 index cards (Zettel) with content, and subsequently spent four years transforming this archival material into *ZT*. It is consequently not unjust when Karl Riha describes it as a »wild gewordener Zettelkasten«[88] or Podak and Vollmann characterises it as »ein gewaltiges Bezugssystem«[89]. In the text itself Daniel Pagenstecher states: »nach Großn Dichtungn, sei das=Höchsde auf der Welt ?:Große NachschlageWerke zu liefern«[90], a quotation which seems to point to the encyclopaedic form of *ZT*. As Volker Langbehn comments:

In *Zettel's Traum*, the multiple insertions of various disciplines and quotations from other literary texts signify ruptures and jolts that evade the comprehension of historic events as progressive linear development in time. For Schmidt, recollection turns into collection and production; the recovery of old and forgotten texts from the vaults of our memory banks becomes textual archaeology.[91]

This quotation indicates the Benjaminian scope of *ZT* by highlighting the vast archive of intertextual references from which the novel seems to draw its material. The already massive volume of the work is thus magnified: not only do we as readers have to take in the 1334 folio size pages, we also have to recognize that the work in our hands presents itself as only that which has reached the surface; beneath we sense an enormous archive made up of world literature, radio news, TV news, recipes, photographs, and drawings.

The figure of the archive (as described in chapter 2.1) is thus highly appropriate as a mode of reading this text. However, insights can also be gained from applying the figure of the network (as described in chapter 2.2). The non-linear mode of reading across the folio page, which arises from the interaction of the three columns of text, evokes an accentuated

---

88 Riha, p. 102.
89 Podak and Vollmann, p. 219.
90 Schmidt, ZT, p. 1047.
91 Langbehn, p. 43.

version of the figure of the network, which we saw in *MoE*. The understanding of the text is not found in one or the other column, but in the relation between the three which arises in the mind of the reader, who thus becomes a conscious player in making sense of the text. Text is »Textgewebe – aus Worten«[92] as it is said in *ZT*. In the following quotation we see how Langbehn uses the image of the network in order to describe the reading process of *ZT*:

> Instead of providing a text that has a beginning and an end, Schmidt defies the tradition by creating a text as a node within a network of references [...] Schmidt's *Zettel's Traum* is nodal by way of its systems of interrelated passages (scenes, images, or topics), which defy the idea of a coherent and generalized narrative development. Various strands of information break through the narrative surface, allowing the reader to decipher nodes or clusters of signification.[93]

A network of connotations arises in the interaction between the columns, and the insertion of visual material in the form of photos and drawings add to the montage-like style of the book and inevitably leads one to ask oneself whether there is a centre to this labyrinthine textual web. The narrative negation which goes on in the text is closely tied to the way in which the text reflects back on itself and exposes the way in which meaning is created and negotiated: »Ein Kunstwerk, das man nur 1 Mal zu sehen=hören braucht, um es erschöpfend erfaßt zu habm : das wäre kein KunstWerk!«[94]

ZT thus poses anew the question raised by both *Wanderjahre* and *MoE* about what the genre of the novel entails. In the words of Gert Ueding:

> Roman? – Nur schwer läßt sich dieses opus in die üblichen Gattungsgrenzen einfügen; auch die seit JOYCE, DÖBLIN UND MUSIL üblich gewordenen Vokabeln wie Antiroman, Roman eines Romans oder ähnliche tragen nur wenig Kennzeichnung bei: sind es doch Etiketten, geboren aus der Verlegenheit von Literaturwissenschaftlern und Rezensenten solchen literarischen Werken gegenüber.[95]

ZT seems to push the limits of the novel genre even further than the early modernists did, because it turns the network of signification inside out so explicitly, and, like the Pompidou Centre in Paris (1971-1977) exposes its own internal workings to the viewer. It encapsulates its encyclopaedic ambition in a way resembling that of the German Romantics, but it also opens itself up to its readers and invites them to be part of the text in a manner much more radical than we have seen in both *Wanderjahre* and *MoE*. We thus have to look further for a figure that captures the open

---

92 Schmidt, ZT, p. 26.
93 Langbehn, p. 189.
94 Schmidt, ZT, p. 112.
95 Ueding, p. 227.

dynamics of this text. Although giving us valuable points of reference for engaging with this text, neither the archive nor the network provide us with a framework which allows us to fully grasp what makes this text stand out. The optic through which we shall attempt to approach *ZT* in this chapter is that of the *game* – not merely in terms of linguistic play, but also as a way of approaching the dynamics at the heart of the novel's discussion of narrativity and consciousness.

2.3.2 The Game

Ueding has described *ZT* as a »gigantisches Bilderrätsel«,[96] and it is the game qualities of *ZT* that we shall now explore further. Firstly, however, we need to establish how and why we might employ the game as a framework for interpreting the negotiation of narrativity in *ZT*. By looking at the figure of the game, we are also tracing an antecedent to the figure of the computer game as a concrete material sign of information technology as a symbolic form, which we shall explore further in chapter 3.3. Using the figure of the game to interpret *ZT* is thus a way not only of getting to grips with the negotiation of narrativity in this novel, but also of establishing ways in which the game as a figure is present in literary theory before the wide dissemination of information technology. It thereby provides a background to the identification of the figure of the computer game in recent fiction. *ZT* is chosen because it raises issues of the game-like qualities of language and representation that became so prevalent in critical discourse following poststructuralism and deconstructivism in the 1970s and 1980s, thereby completing our journey through the history of modern novels with a precarious relationship to narrativity. Despite the fact that *ZT* is so »sui generis« in German literature that it is hard to group with general tendencies, it is equally hard to exclude it when tracing novels which display and thematize an uneasiness with narrativity.

Although the conceptualisation of the game became a particular focus of attention in the course of the second half of the twentieth century, it is a phenomenon which has generated interest throughout Western philosophy. Two main trends can be identified: a figurative use of the concept of the game relating it to language and aesthetics, and a performative emphasis dealing with the game as an actual physical event, which is found especially in anthropological and sociological approaches. This distinction originates from Kocher and Böhler's article »Über den ästetischen Begriff des Spiels

---

96 Ibid. p. 229.

als Link zwischen traditioneller Texthermeneutik, Hyperfiction und Computerspielen« (2001). Kocher and Böhler distinguish between a figurative understanding of the game (whose occurrence they date to the eighteenth century) and a performative-communicative understanding of the game which they argue was prevalent before the eighteenth century and which they see revived in the computer game. The aim in chapter 3.3 will be to test whether this revival of a notion of the game as an actual physical event is reflected in the way in which the recent novels at which we shall be looking deal with the figure of the game. For now, let us briefly point out a few significant lines of enquiry in the conceptualisation of the game until the advent of the computer game. The aim is to get a conception of the theoretical framework in which the figure of the game is embedded in 1970 when Schmidt published *ZT,* and to suggest how it might be fruitful as a mode of reading *ZT*'s negotiation of narrativity.[97]

Going back to Aristotle's *Ethics,* play is first and foremost equated with leisure and contrasted with labour:

The maxim of Anacharsis, ›Play to work harder‹, seems to be on the right lines, because amusement is a form of relaxation, and people need relaxation because they cannot exert themselves continuously.[98]

This denotes the more concrete notion of a game as an actual physical occurrence. However, if we read Aristotle's conception of mimesis as also applying to play and games, the more figurative interpretation can likewise be traced in his writings.[99] Stefan Matuscheck has shown how different conceptualisations of the game can be traced from Petrarca in fourteenth-century Italy, Erasmus and Rabelais in the fifteenth century, sixteenth-century mannerism, through to the seventeenth and eighteenth century, and Mihai Spariosu has illuminated the function of play in, among other works, Cervantes' *Don Quixote*. It is consequently possible to argue that the game as a vehicle for philosophical thinking and literary production is present well before the eighteenth century. However, it is especially the works of Kant and Schiller in the eighteenth century that generally mark an accentuated emphasis on the aesthetic dimension of the notion of play which foregrounds a figurative use of the term. For Immanuel Kant (1724-1804) play is explicitly associated with imagination and art (although still contrasted with work). In *Kritik der Urteilskraft* he writes:

---

97 For a fuller exposition of the figure of the game in Western thinking see, for instance, Avedon and Sutton-Smith; Sutton-Smith; Matuscheck; and Spariosu.

98 Aristotle, p. 327 [1176b 39].

99 See, for instance, chapter four of his *Poetics* where mimesis is related to children's games: »First, there is man's natural propensity, from childhood onwards, to engage in mimetic activity« (Halliwell, p. 34).

Wird auch Kunst vom Handwerke unterschieden; die erste heißt freie, die andere kann auch Lohnkunst heißen. Man sieht die erste so an, als ob sie nur als Spiel, d. i. Beschäftigung, die für sich selbst angenehm ist, zweckmäßig ausfallen (gelingen) könne.[100]

Play is consequently something which is agreeable on its own account and has no direct purpose. However, even art as play needs constraints:

Daß aber in allen freien Künsten dennoch etwas Zwangsmäßiges oder, wie man es nennt, ein Mechanismus erforderlich sei, ohne welchen der Geist, der in der Kunst frei sein muß und allein das Werk belebt, gar keinen Körper haben und gänzlich verdunsten würde: ist nicht unrathsam zu erinnern (z.B. in der Dichtkunst die Sprachrichtigkeit und der Sprachreichthum, imgleichen die Prosodie und das Silbenmaß), da manche neuere Erzieher eine freie Kunst am besten zu befördern glauben, wenn sie allen Zwang von ihr wegnehmen und sie aus Arbeit in bloßes Spiel verwandeln.[101]

It is this dichotomy between constraint and free play which Friedrich Schiller (1759-1805) further develops in *Über die ästhetische Erziehung des Menschen*, especially in the Fifteenth Letter. Play for Schiller is all that is not internally or externally contingent or constrained. He establishes the notion of »Spieltrieb«, which functions as a mediator between the form-drive (»Formtriebes«) and the sense-drive (»sinnlichen Triebe«, whose object is life and which describes all material being that is present to the senses). The sense-drive and the form-drive are dialectically opposed and are brought together only by the play-drive (»Spieltriebes«). Beauty which equalises art and play is thus neither mere life nor mere form, but living form – »lebende Gestalt«[102]. These distinctions will become useful when, in relation to *ZT,* we return to Galen Strawson's notion of human form-finding as not being inherently narrative.

In Kant and Schiller we see a use of play which aligns it with aesthetics and art in a more direct manner than had been the case up until the eighteenth century. Play becomes more of a conceptual tool associated with aesthetics and language, and less of an actual physical event. This line of enquiry can be followed into the twentieth century in the philosophy of thinkers like Nietzsche, Heidegger, Wittgenstein and Eugen Fink, for whom the concept of play or game becomes a conceptual tool for understanding language, being, and the human world. However, not until the second half of the twentieth century in the wake of poststructuralism and decontructivism does the figure of the game become the dominant cultural figure we know today. The figure of the game seems to embody much of the postmodern

---

100 Kant, p. 156 [§43].
101 Ibid. p. 157 [§43].
102 Schiller, p. 100.

experience of the world as a playground for a multiplicity of alternate identities and linguistic play. For Derrida (and with him de Man) the concept of the game is used to describe the dissolution of linguistic meaning and the endless postponement of the signifier: »L'avènement de l'écriture est l'avènement du jeu«.[103] As we shall see, the figurative interpretation of the game, which reaches its most extreme expression in deconstructivism, is definitely at work in *ZT*, especially in the way in which it plays with intertextual references and develops its own psychoanalytical mode of reading.

However, it is also worth bearing in mind the more concrete, performative conceptualisation of the game which we find in the twentieth century in studies with an anthropological, psychological, cultural or sociological aim.[104] Elliot M. Avedon and Brian Sutton-Smith's *The Study of Games* provides extensive bibliographies for the numerous fields in which games have been studied and gives a glimpse into the diversity of disciplines which have occupied themselves with the concept of games. Avedon and Sutton-Smith point to the study of children's games, recreational games, military games, business and industrial games, games in education, games in diagnostic and treatment procedures, games in social science, and mathematical game theory.[105] Although it is beyond the scope of the present study to explore all of these further, they do bring attention to the multiplicity of angles from which games may be approached and emphasises the vast field from which the figure of the game draws its connotations in the twentieth century – many of which entail more concrete performative notions of game than the linguistic-aesthetic conceptualisations mentioned above. However, even though the anthropological and sociological approach has a broader aim and interest than the aesthetic use of the concept of the game outlined above, the two approaches overlap and intermingle and are therefore sometimes difficult to separate. A particularly striking example of the ongoing fuel for aesthetic conceptualisations which the concrete notion of the game

---

103 Derrida, De la Grammatologie, p. 16.

104 Psychological anthropologist Frederik Jacobus Johannes Buytendijk's *Wesen und Sinn des Spiels* (1933) and cultural historian Johan Huizinga's *Homo Ludens* (1938) being some of the earliest and most influential.

105 This reminder of the complexity of the figure the game is further developed by Sutton-Smith in *The Ambiguity of Play* (1997) in which he categories the study of games into seven rhetorics: rhetorics of progress, rhetorics of fate, rhetorics of power, rhetorics of identity, rhetorics of the imaginary, rhetorics of self, rhetorics of frivolity. However, as Jesper Juul has shown it is indeed possible to identify what makes a game. In *Half-real: Video Games between Real Rules and Fictional Words* he outlines what he calls »the classic game model« according to which a game is: »1. a rule-base formal system; 2. with variable and quantifiable outcomes; 3. where different outcomes are assigned different values; 4. where the player exerts effort in order to influence the outcome; 5. the player feels emotionally attached to the outcome; 6. and the consequences of the activity are optional and negotiable« (Juul, Half-real, p. 7).

seems to hold is found in the use literary theorist Wolfgang Iser makes of sociologist, philosopher, and literary critic Roger Caillois' conceptualisation of the game. In the seminal *Les Jeux et les Hommes* (1958), Caillois divides play into four main categories depending on whether the role of competition (agon), chance (alea), simulation (mimicry), or vertigo (ilinx) is dominant. These categories are picked up by Iser in *Das Fiktive und das Imaginäre* (1991) and used in his attempt to construct a literary theory around the concept of game which aims to tease out something positive from decontructivism's view of language as game and establish this quality not as loss of meaning, but rather as potential meaning. The distinction between a figurative use of the concept of game, relating it to language and aesthetics, and a performative emphasis dealing with the game as an actual physical event may consequently seem a little too rigid to describe what is actually at work in the figure of the game. The understanding of the concept of game that we are working towards here, and which will prove fruitful as a manner of reading *ZT,* should consequently be situated in the field between the figurative and concrete notions of the game. As we shall see, the figure of the game in *ZT* occurs in a very abstract manner relating to language games and the workings of consciousness. Even in its most abstract interpretation, however, it is important to keep in mind the concrete physical action from which this figure stems in order to understand its connotations. As will become apparent, the thematic content, as well as the composition and physical layout, of *ZT* make the figure of the game an adequate framework for approaching this enigmatic work and penetrating its negotiation of narrativity.[106]

2.3.3 Reading *ZT* through the Figure of the Game

The enormous scope of *ZT* in format, as well as content, inevitably and obviously limits the extent to which it may be analysed in this chapter. For that reason, the aim here will be to identify issues regarding the negotiation of narrativity found in *ZT* and the way in which these can be read through the figure of the game. In the following we shall therefore focus on the way

---

106 We hereby align ourselves with modes of reading found for instance in Peter Hutchinson's *Games Authors Play* (1980), Ruth E. Burke's *The Games of Poetics: Ludic Criticism and Postmodern Fiction* (1994), and Warren Motte's *Playtexts: Ludics in Contemporary Literature* (1995), just to mention a few who have undertaken to analyse especially postmodern fiction from the viewpoint of literature as a game, and also regard specific literary works as reflecting explicitly on qualities of the game.

in which the discussions of narrativity and consciousness in the text reveal a fictional world resembling that of the game.

The first concept introduced in *ZT* on which we shall focus is the so-called *Etym theory*. Schmidt had originally formulated this idea in a series of essays on James Joyce. Here he explains the dual nature of language: the language of consciousness comprising words, and the language of the unconscious consisting of etyms. The etyms allow what is supposedly really meant to come to the surface: »dann wär hier eine schöne Gelegenheit für die Etym=Methode, den Wahrheits=Kern zu ermitteln«.[107] The etym theory is linked to Freud's notion of word association, and in *ZT* the etym theory becomes a mode of interpretation set out by the main protagonist Pagenstecher in his aim to uncover hidden meaning in Edgar Allan Poe's formulations, usually with sexual connotations. The etym theory is therefore a pivotal point for *ZT* in so far as the majority of the text is made up of analyses of the etyms in Poe's works showing the subconscious sexual references present in the texts. But the etyms are also present in *ZT* itself – thereby opening itself up towards the reader and enabling a potential »Etymanalyse« to be carried out on *ZT* itself. As we shall see, the underlying etym theory presented in the text, and forming the conceptual framework for the dialogue about Poe's texts, is central for the challenge of narrativity at work in this text, turning the progression of the text into an endless loop of possible interpretations and potential meaning. An implicit consequence of the play with etyms is that the author loses some control over the text, because his unconscious becomes part of the text – something which Schmidt tries to counter by introducing the »4te Instanz«, a faculty which develops in some authors in the second half of their lives and makes them able to master and balance the subconscious and the super-ego.[108] What we see at work here is thus, on the one hand, an attempt to open the text and allow the reader into the process of signification in a way that turns the reader into a player, and, on the other hand, a hesitation towards giving up the author's privilege of knowing what his own text contains.

We see the same oscillation between opening the text up as a playground and setting up rules to guide the movements of the reader in the intertextual references and visual layout which forms the texture of *ZT*. The three columns interact with and comment on each other, thus creating a text which requires the reader to work hard to be able to decipher the allusions and connotations. The unique spelling and typography, which is heavily based on oral speech and makes use of punctuation as a pictographic means of expression, also participates in transforming the text into a vibrating play with

---

107 Schmidt, ZT, p. 235.
108 Ibid. p. 914f.

words and connotations that aims to dissolve the boundaries between writing, speaking, and thinking. However, in comparison with the archive sections in *Wanderjahre*, which, as we saw, encourage the reader to take an active role and seek out the correspondences between the narrative and the aphorisms, the reader of *ZT*, in his attempt to decipher the potential meaning of the text, has to accept the text as a fragmentary insight into the workings of consciousness, thereby acknowledging that only a fraction of the connotations and textual references can be identified. Compared to *Wanderjahre,* the amount of narrative is reduced to a bare minimum in *ZT,* and the narrative strands that can be identified do not necessarily give the reader reliable clues to the meaning of the quotations and visual material. In *Sitara und der Weg dorthin. Eine Studie über Wesen, Werk & Wirkung Karl Mays* (1963) Schmidt comments on the method of using quotations and appropriated material:

Denn auch Exzerpte werden schließlich individuell gemacht; vor allem erfolgt die Neu-Gruppierung des so gewonnenen, angeeigneten Materials in recht persönlicher ›spielräumlicher‹ Weise, und das Meiste hat eben doch schwerlich eine andere Autorität als des Verfassers Fantasie.[109]

The textual mosaic arises from bits and pieces of material drawn from elsewhere, but they are interwoven into a highly idiosyncratic text which uses dialect, punctuation and alternative spelling as the means of creating a new text, rather than aiding the reader in tracing the origins of the text. The text therefore becomes a permutation of material – drawn from other texts in what Schmidt, with reference to Karl May, calls a »spielräumlicher Weise«, thereby emphasising play less as a participatory act and more in the technical sense of leeway and flexibility. The text thus becomes a space for the play of multiple meanings and begins to challenge notions such as author, originality, and plagiarism. This alliance between play and plagiarism becomes quite tangible in the following play with words: »Also ›play=Dscherism‹ Wilma; ›to play‹ = Sich dran spielen ▮▮▮▮; mit andern Worten: ›ipsieren‹«.[110] In a game, as well as in *ZT,* we find a framework of rules into which the player puts his or her own consciousness and all the material within that consciousness in order to understand the references given by the authoring consciousness. However, in order for this to work an amount of elbowroom which allows for the aggregated parts to play with one another (ein Spielraum) is needed.

In order to understand further how the fictional world of *ZT* is linked up with the figure of the game we consequently have to turn to the theory of

---

109 Schmidt, Sitara und der Weg dorthin, p. 56.
110 Schmidt, ZT, p. 942.

consciousness presented in *ZT* and in Schmidt's œuvre. According to Minden, to Schmidt the human being is not capable of taking in the world as it is; biologically we are granted only a limited perspective:

When talking about the actual stuff of consciousness, Schmidt stresses its role in constituting ›reality‹. If human beings are in no position to see nature as it is in itself, then what they do see must clearly be a reality which is partially subjective in makeup. The human consciousness becomes a point of reference from which perceptual data take their bearings. This process, although in Schmidt's very oft-repeated phrase ›biologisch ausreichend‹, is contingent compared to the real nature of things (whose existence, on the other hand, is not disputed).[111]

Identity is an experience of fragmentation rather than continuity, something which Schmidt expresses with excellent precision in *Aus dem Leben eines Fauns* (1953):

Mein Leben?!: ist kein Kontinuum! (nicht bloß durch Tag und Nacht in weiß und schwarze Stücke zerbrochen! Denn auch am Tage ist bei mir der ein Anderer, der zur Bahn geht; im Amt sitzt; büchert; durch Haine stelzt; begattet; schwatzt; schreibt; Tausendsdenker; auseinanderfallender Fächer; der rennt; raucht; kotet; radiohört; »Herr Landrat« sagt: that's me!): ein Tablett voll glitzernder snapshots. […]
Aber als majestätisch fließendes Band kann ich mein Leben nicht fühlen; nicht ich! (Begründung).[112]

The model of consciousness set out in *ZT* seems to rely on a similar understanding of human perception and experience, but coupled with a conception inspired by Freud consisting of the subconscious, the ego, the superego and a »4te Instanz«. This last entity helps the individual to gain control and restrain the freedom of language.

For Schmidt, understanding consciousness and writing prose are two closely related occupations. Minden sees in the preoccupation with consciousness in Schmidt's writings a progression from an experimental representation of consciousness to a »kind of potentially limitless surrogate of Schmidt's own consciousness on paper«.[113] In his early writings Schmidt's aim is to develop a form of prose which corresponds to the fragmented experience of the world. In the essays »Berechnungen I & II«, published in 1959 in *Rosen & Poree*, he introduces four mental processes (»Bewußtseinsvorgänge«) which he aims to use as models for developing new forms of prose. The first one is »Sich-Erinnern«, which describes memory as being made up of instant flashes and the less spontaneous material which

---

111 Minden, p. 22.
112 Schmidt, Aus dem Leben eines Fauns, pp. 9-10.
113 Minden, pp. 116-17.

these flashes inspire.[114] The second is »Löchrige Gegenwart«, which refers to our experience of the world as made up of disconnected events, a »Tagesmosaik« without an »epischen Flusses«.[115] Reality is regarded as fragmentary and this influences the rendering of the literary text. The third and fourth mental processes are what he terms »Längeres Gedankenspiel« and the »Traum«. The thought-games are of an escapist nature in so far as they imply a privileging of that which consciousness can conjure up as opposed to reality. Both the thought-game and the dream become increasingly important in Schmidt's later oeuvre, inspired by his encounter with the writings of Lewis Carroll, James Joyce and not least Freud's theory of the interpretation of dreams, and it is thus highly prevalent in *ZT*. However, the notion of human consciousness and perception revealed in the first two forms provides an important background for understanding the workings of the thought-games and the dream, and how the link is established between Schmidt's conception of the workings of consciousness and his prose writings. This is where we see his theory of consciousness turn into a discussion of narrativity and representation.

In »Berechnungen I & II« Schmidt stresses the need to develop forms of prose that correspond to the four types of consciousness patterns outlined above, all of which replace an epic flow with fragmentary collections of disparate material:

Um der ›Wahrheit‹ willen – d.h. um einer konformen Abbildung unserer Welt durch Worte näher zu kommen – ersetzte ich die unberechtigte Fiktion des ›epischen Flusses‹ durch die bessere Nährungsformel vom ›epischen Wassersturz‹.[116]

What he aims for is an »objektive Mittelbarkeit«[117]; i.e. that the subjective forms of consciousness become objective by being turned into prose forms. However, the project is essentially a subjective one, especially the process of »Längeres Gedankenspiel« which allows for some people (so-called »Gedankenspieler«, amongst whom he seems to count himself) to create texts of general validity.[118] In »Berechnungen II« Schmidt explains »Längeres Gedankenspiel« as being made up of »Erlebnisebene I« and »Erlebnisebene II«. EI designates empirical reality »die objective Realität« and EII subjective reality, i.e. the imagined events of the thought-games. The same

---

114 Schmidt, Rosen & Porree, p. 293.
115 Ibid. p. 290.
116 Ibid. p. 293.
117 Ibid. p. 302.
118 As Minden has pointed out, the Romantic notion of the genius artist who is a particularly gifted spokesman is thus reinstated, although this traditional conception of art is what Schmidt aims to transgress in his essays (Minden, pp. 90-91). See also Schmidt, ZT, p. 915 for a discussion of the »4. Instanz« at work in the writings of Sterne, Smollet, Carroll, Freud, and Joyce.

distinction between EI and EII can be found in dreams, but those are experienced much more passively than the thought-games, because they bestow far less control on the individual.[119] Minden has shown how the separation and intermingling of these two levels become problematic and inconsistent for Schmidt due to the close affinity between the writer and his work[120] – in *ZT* we hear that: »›Bücher‹ sind halt auch nur zerfusseltes Autoren-Lebm. – ?«.[121] The artist deposits part of himself in his work and they become inseparable. What Schmidt therefore aims to describe is essentially his own consciousness, because this is the only reality available to him. Nonetheless, the concept of »Längeres Gedankenspiel« is also the very concept that opens the text up towards the reader and allows for his or her »Gedankenspiel« to become part of the text.

For our present purpose Schmidt's conception of consciousness is illuminating in so far as, in especially the first two concepts (»Sich-Erinnern« and »Löchrige Gegenwart«), we see a discussion which links up with Strawson's argument for a non-narrative way of experiencing and representing the world. Arno Schmidt's conception of the world seems to be informed by an episodic rather than a diachronic view of consciousness and human experience; the formal structures he develops consequently incline towards a non-narrative mode of representation. In this chapter we have seen that the formal structure which best embodies the structure Schmidt finds in *ZT* is that of the game; this comes most clearly to the fore in the importance ascribed to »Längeres Gedankenspiel« in *ZT*. Going back to Schiller's notion of a »Spieltrieb« as mediating between a sense-drive and a form-drive we see that the game may be regarded as something which allows for representation of what our senses experience; allowing for life to be represented in a certain form. Likewise the »Längeres Gedankenspiel« in *ZT* is what allows Schmidt to approach a representation of the working of consciousness – bringing what he calls EI and EII together.

The game emerges as an adequate figure for describing the workings of consciousness as Schmidt views it and consequently for the text *ZT*. *ZT* embodies the duality of chaos and chance in the play of the etyms and the intertextual references, on the one hand, and the need for restraint, the imposition of mathematical rules and formal principles which allows for the free play of consciousness to be approached and portrayed at all, on the other. Approaching the fictional world of *ZT* in terms of the imaginary

---

119 Schmidt, Rosen & Porree, p. 294. In *ZT* the distinction between objective and subjective reality is captured in the following sentence: »/Das sogenannte Wirkliche Lebm. (Und das viel=wirklichere in unserem Gehirn.-:-« (Schmidt, ZT, p. 1020).

120 Minden, p. 93ff.

121 Schmidt, ZT, p. 433.

worlds built up by games helps explain the open character of the work, its web of cross-references, intertextual pointers, and pieces of information whose affinity with the rest of the text is often opaque. The text is a glimpse into a working consciousness, an ongoing process, not a well-rounded narrative. It shows us the mind of an episodic consciousness trying to understand the world but failing to turn it into a consistent representation that can be narrated. Consciousness and the text alike thus present themselves as aggregations of discrete entities in a force field between the writing and the reading mind.

To understand the negotiation of narrativity which is thereby created, let us have a closer look at the fictional world and the notion of time and space which are established in the text. Rather than being a vehicle for telling a story, the fictional world seems to be present in order to allow for an exploration of the workings of consciousness. The narrative is a frail layer surrounding the extensive conversations which aim to explore human experience and consciousness. The notion of time as a progression thus also becomes problematic, as is evident from the very first page by virtue of the existence of the three columns, which means that it becomes practically impossible to identify exactly where the text begins. Wolfgang Hink relates the concept of time in *ZT,* and Schmidt's work in general, to the analogy between memory and photos which Schmidt establishes in the essay »Berechnungen I«. He describes time in Schmidt's writings as having a »statisch-zeitlosen Charakter« and goes on to argue that:

Simultaneität – nach [Walter] Jens ein Merkmal des modernen Romans – ist überhaupt ein zentraler Begriff für die Prosa Schmidts, denn sie läßt sich in vielen Varianten bei ihm finden, sei es in der Übereinanderschichtung verschiedener Lesemodelle, in der vertikalen (typographischen) Aufgliederung des Textes (Mehrspaltigkeit) und vor allem in der ›Verschreibkunst‹.[122]

The replacement of causality and progression of time by simultaneity and fragmentation comes to the fore, particularly in the way quotations are cited in *ZT*. The multiplicity of citation and the thought-games they result in emphasise a conception of time and history as a layering of aggregated material which can constantly be modelled in new configurations. Rather than being held together by a plot with a beginning, middle, and end, *ZT* seems to be made up of the conglomeration of everyday details and fragments of information:

Ich bin ein weit indolenterer Verehrer des ›non liquet‹, als Ihr (anschein'd) meint. Die ›Bestimmung des Menschn‹, (falls er überhaupt eine habm sollte), besteht, Meines

---

122 Hink, p. 209.

Glaubms, da=rin: große=Massn von Details zu sammln; und durch den Druck zur Aufbewahrung zu gebm.[123]

Schmidt attempts the impossible task of letting consciousness narrate itself and his method is to narrate the trivial in incidental details of everyday experience, while leaving out the larger narrative framework. The narrative progression of the novel thus arises despite itself and the multiplicity of details of which the text is made up. Time, as well as history, appear as a field of simultaneity – a conglomeration of aggregated material drawn from English pop songs, Freud, Edgar Allan Poe, landscaping, mathematics, astronomy, and painting.

Also, the idiosyncratic writing style plays a role in the rendering of this fictional world and its challenging of linear narrativity. Langbehn comments on Schmidt's use of apostrophes, semi-colons and other punctuation:

The variety of functions assigned to non-phonetic signs suggests that their function in *Zettel's Traum* is to resist narrative, since the sign depends on the contextual circumstances under which it appears.[124]

The coherence of the narrative is shattered right down to the grammatical level. The sentences become a collection of words, letters, and signs which disregard grammatical structures. Multiple meanings are created for every word in a way that opens up the text as an immense field of potential meaning. As Langbehn comments:

For the ›ideal reader‹ of *Zettel's Traum*, the text unfolds in the play of its incompletion and its deliberate practice of disturbing prior existing narrative experiences that claim to define and represent reality.[125]

Employing the game both as a figure of interpretation of the fictional world and as a means of negotiating narrativity in *ZT* have thus revealed the ways in which this figure is relevant to describing the wordplay and language games going on in the text. But is it also possible to trace the game in its more concrete sense as an actual physical event? Initially the answer seems to be negative, in so far as we have seen the extreme degree to which *ZT* deals with consciousness and language, thus creating a fictional world which seems to be highly figurative and even abstract. However, as we saw in the excursus on the conceptualisations of the figure of the game, the figurative and the concrete aspects of the game are, in practice, almost impossible to separate, as is also the case of *ZT*. This is where we find a possible explanation for Schmidt writing *ZT* not as a theoretical work, but as a work

---

123 Schmidt, ZT, p. 1201.
124 Langbehn, p. 76.
125 Ibid. p. 19.

of fiction with fictitious characters and a loosely narrative framework. At the same time as ZT is one long peek into the internal workings of consciousness, it is also staged as a word-game between the four players, Franziska, Paul, Wilma, and Dan, and as the wall against which they bounce their balls, namely Edgar Allan Poe and his writings. The suspension of time as progression means that, rather than performing as characters who carry the narrative forward, their dialogue adds to the sense of the »statischzeitlosen Charakter« of the text as a field of simultaneity. The dialogue between the characters thus becomes a macro-reflection of the way in which the etym-analysis shows every sentence in Poe's work to be laden with subconscious meaning and all the inserted quotations reveal the diverse material from which every representation is drawn. To interpret the four characters as representing the subconscious, the ego, the super-ego, and the »4te Instanz« respectively would probably be taking the parallel too far and making the characters more one-dimensional than the text allows for, but the interaction between the characters definitely adds an extra dimension to the depiction of the workings of consciousness going on throughout the text, which would not have been accomplished without the presence of the fictional world. Narrative is therefore – although problematized to the most extreme degree that we have seen so far – not abandoned.

2.3.4 Shuffling Text

Michael Minden quotes the following criticism of Schmidt raised by the avant-garde artist Oswald Wiener:

Statt einer einzigen neuen beobachtung, statt einer neuen formulierung gibt uns SCHMIDT rauhe mengen von naturwundern aus dem bildungsschatz des lexikonlesers, statt eines einzigen details, welches revision des rahmens erforderte, in welchem es detail ist, häuft er uns den schutt ewig wiederholter und bestens bekannter einzelheiten aus den zyklen einer sozialen maschine.[126]

This disapproval of providing the reader with encyclopaedic amounts of material is something which will echo through the criticism of the more recent novels to which we shall now turn. Significant for our purpose is the fact that ZT seems to reflect the rapid increase in the amount of information encountered by the individual, something which was accentuated by the spread of television sets to most people's homes during the post-war period, when Schmidt was writing his books. The television is also frequently referred to in ZT, creating starting points for discussions between the characters. In the article »Das Werk auf den Schultern vergänglicher Riesen. Arno

---

126 Minden, p. 2.

Schmidt an den Grenzen der Speicherbarkeit kulturellen Wissens Ulrich« Blumenbach argues that Schmidt is pointing out how the immateriality of news communication in post-war Germany indicates the dissolution of closed narratives.[127] There seems consequently to be scope for arguing that the technological development of communication and media promotes, as well as articulates, the feeling that a well-rounded narrative is an inadequate form of representation, or at least that it is something which should be challenged and questioned the more our everyday lives are bombarded with information. In our aim to trace this uneasiness with narrativity, *ZT* challenges a narrative mode of representation in a very radical form. In the following chapters we shall look more closely at how three concrete material signs of information technology as a symbolic form (the database, the hyperlink, and the computer game) provide figures for reformulating, in a manner adequate for the present time and culture, the negotiation of narrativity that we have seen in the preceding three chapters.

---

127 Blumenbach, p. 212. See also Voigt, pp. 306-8 and Langbehn, pp. 1165-173.

3. Digital Information Structures in Literary Fiction

3.1 Database Structures: Combinatorics and Complexity Management

Ich sitze mehrere Stunden da und mache Querchecks im Datenchaos, überprüfe Ausdrucke und Mappen, verfolge Möglichkeiten, die aufgrund der Random-Funk-tionen aufgetaucht sind. Der Kaffee bleibt unberührt, wird kalt. Ich baue, ich forsche, ich schraube. Die Geschwindigkeit der Finger imponiert mir beinah. Manchmal lassen sie den Gedanken hinter sich. Ich webe, ich hebe, ich spiele. Dann, während die Maschine mit einem Suchwort sucht – die Gedanken sind vielleicht auch anderswo –, drängt sich plötzlich die Frage vor: Wenn nun die *ganze* Datenbank die Lösung ist, nicht mehr und nicht weniger, so daß es unmöglich ist, es zu reduzieren? Oder: Wenn nun ein so mächtiges Design dahinterliegt, so grandios, daß das menschliche Denken es nicht erfassen kann?[1]

In this quotation from Jan Kjærstad's novel *Rand* (1990) the database is described almost as an artistic instrument and the handling of the data as an inspired occupation that stands in opposition to rationality. The language is out of breath; the short sentences become a rhythm which fluctuates and increases the pace, thus evoking the experience of searching a database. The revelation that the protagonist has in this passage comes as an inspired touch of insight that in a moment of distraction allows him to see what he describes a couple of pages later as: »eine Öffnung, eine Spalte, ein Durchgang zu etwas ganz anderem. Eine ganze Zone im Dasein, die keine Sprache hat«.[2] The rational, mathematical-logical form of the database is thus used as a metaphysical motif which generates imagination and creativity.

---

1 Kjærstad, Rand, pp. 389-90. »Jeg sitter i flere timer og kryssjekker i datakaoset, konfererer med utskrifter og mapper, forfølger muligheter som er dukket opp på grunn av random-funksjonene. Kaffen står urørt, blir kald. Jeg bygger, jeg forsker, jeg skrur. Jeg nesten imponeres over fingrenes hurtighet. Noen ganger ligger de foran tanken. Jeg vever, jeg løfter, jeg spiller. Så, mens maskinen søker på et stikkord – tankene er kanskje også andre steder – springer spørsmålet fram: Hva om hele databasen er løsningen, verken mer eller mindre, at det er umulig å redusere det? Eller: Hva om det ligger en så mektig design bak, så grandios, at den menneskelige tanke ikke kan fange den?« (Kjærstad, Rand, pp. 248-49). The original Norwegian quotations will appear in the footnotes, while the German translation by Angelika Gundlach is quoted in the main body of the text.

2 Kjærstad, Rand, p. 393. »en åpning, en sprekk, en gjennomgang til noe helt annet. En hel sone i tilværelsen som ikke har noe språk« (Kjærstad, Rand, p. 251).

The database is central both thematically and structurally in *Rand*. The protagonist, who is a computer specialist, murders a number of people whom he meets randomly and neither he, the reader, nor any of the other characters in the novel ever find a motive which can give the murders a rational explanation or place them within a larger causal framework. Each murder gives the protagonist new trivial knowledge, and the amount of data possessed continuously increases both for him and for us as readers. This is where the database appears as a concrete motif in the fictional world. In his capacity as computer specialist the protagonist is hired by the police to co-ordinate the data on the murders. To the protagonist the database is a concrete tool for finding a system, or perhaps even a higher meaning, behind the murders he has himself committed. It becomes a tool to explore the vast amount of data gathered, hunting for connections not determined by causality. To the reader of the novel *Rand*, the database motif presents itself (as we shall see later in this chapter) as a reference point which provides a way of thinking about how the fictional world of this novel works.

The aim of the present chapter is to uncover the ways in which the database as a concrete material sign of information technology as a symbolic form feeds back on to the novel genre's ongoing problematisation of narrativity. In *Rand* we see an example of such feedback; the database occurs as an explicit motif and thematic pivotal point, as illustrated by the quotation above. However, as we shall see, it is also integrated into the narrative structure of the novel, thereby underscoring the argument that information technology should be regarded as more than a metaphoric vocabulary and can indeed be regarded as a symbolic form. So far in this study we have looked at a number of novels from the nineteenth century onwards which display different forms of uneasiness with narrativity as a mode of representation. Goethe's *Wanderjahre* (1829), Musil's *MoE* (1930-42), and Schmidt's *ZT* (1970) all simultaneously address the issue of narration, resist it, and yet also make it possible. These works thus explore the relationship between narrativity and the perception and representation of human existence. The aim of the following three chapters is to pursue this discussion into the present and look at the way in which figures and forms deriving from information technology contribute to this debate and continue problematizing narrativity in contemporary fiction. What we have seen in *Wanderjahre*, *MoE*, and *ZT* are examples of the ways in which the archive, the network, and the game, respectively, operate as figures that suggest a transgression of the narrative representation of the novel. In its encounter with information technology, the genre of the novel acquires figures for articulating this ongoing negotiation of narrativity through the database, the hyperlink, and the computer game. Furthermore, the implications of a late twentieth-century / early twentyfirst-century information society, characterised by information overload, both facilitates and necessitates an accentuation of this negotiation. The subsequent analyses thus all aim to substantiate the argument that information technology can be regarded as a symbolic form. We shall explore three examples of concrete material signs of information technology as a symbolic form in recent novels. The database is the first we shall consider.

3.1.1 Database Structures

One of the distinctive characteristics of digital databases is their ability to store, handle, and access large and complex amounts of data more quickly than previous archival systems. However, the art of storing and managing data has its antecedents and kindred forms in the archive, the encyclopaedia, the library, and the museum – the possibilities and challenges of which have increased with the advent of digital databases. One historical antecedent of the database, which we have already encountered in chapter 2.1, is the archive. However, owing to the distinct capabilities and characteristics of print and digital media, there are significant differences between an archive and a database. Whereas the materiality of the files in an archive means they are only ever situated in one place and can only be found if one looks precisely in that location, the virtuality of a database makes it possible to access the same information in multiple contexts, thereby detaching it from its original order and source. The relationship between content and structure in a database is thus less strong than in an archive organised according to the principle of provenance, because the latter implies that the situation of data is restricted to the original order and the origin of the material. This results in the provenance archive abiding more to causal and temporal parameters than a digital database.

The concept of databases originated in the 1960s. A database can be defined as a collection of data stored in a computer in a systematic way allowing a computer program to consult the data and retrieve information. The structural description of the objects held in the database and the relationship between them are called a *schema*. The schema can be organised in various ways, known as *database models*. Examples of these are a flat model, a hierarchical model, a network model, a relational model, an object-oriented model, or a deductive model, all of which describe different ways in which the database's structure is modelled.[3] However, in this chapter we shall not

---

3 An argument can be made for regarding hyperlinking as a specific type of database. However, hypertext will be treated separately in this study, since it brings out issues of navigable space which are not necessarily inherent in a database. Database and hyperlink should, however, not be

focus on the technicalities of the individual database models, but look at the database in more general terms as a cultural phenomenon.

In our daily lives our encounters with databases are numerous, be they through using our social security number, searching Google, or getting the shop assistant to check the stock on green armchairs in IKEA. It is thus no surprise that the implications of the database are not fully grasped through its technical definition, but must also be dealt with as phenomena increasingly present in contemporary culture, art, and theory. Hayles quotes James Martin's analysis in *Computer Data-Base Organization* from as early as 1977:

> In all walks of life and in all areas of industry, data banks will change the realms of what it is possible for man to do. In centuries hence, historians will look back to the coming of computer data banks and their associated facilities as a step which changed the nature of the evolution of society, perhaps eventually having a greater effect on the human condition than even the invention of the printing press.[4]

The hopes were high, but they would soon be accompanied by fears of surveillance and identity theft, thus echoing the oscillation between utopian hopes and dystopian prophesies we know from the conceptualisation of the computer more generally.[5] Looking closer at the cultural and aesthetic implications of the database in more recent years, we see that the database as a cultural phenomenon has gained increasing influence on contemporary culture, especially over the last decade, not only as a way of describing the conditions of contemporary culture, but also as a metaphorical tool for artists. In the almost manifesto-like introduction to the volume of the journal *AI and Society* on »Database Aesthetic« (2000) Victoria Vesna states:

> It is in the code of search engines and the aesthetics of navigation that the new conceptual field work lies for the artist. These are the places not only to make commentaries and interventions, but also to start conceptualising alternative ways for artistic practice and even for commerce. [...] In an age in which we are increasingly aware of ourselves as databases, identified by social security numbers and genetic structures, it

---

regarded as completely different types of logic, but they highlight different aspects of information technology as a symbolic form, when regarded as cultural phenomena in the present context.

4 Martin, p. 2.

5 In the article »Fathoming the Archive: German Poetry and the Culture of Memory« (2003) Erk Grimm explores how, in the 1960s, the archive – due to its role in reconstructing the fascist past through written documents – had uncanny connotations as a bureaucratic apparatus. In contrast, the archive trope of the 1990s is influenced by poststructuralism and computer technology. Grimm's highlighting of the archive and its shifting connotations in German poetry and memory culture points to the fact that the archive has undergone significant changes in Western culture since the ancient Greek public archives. The last decades have witnessed an increased interest in the archive as a theoretical principle and art metaphor, not least due to the challenges and increased possibilities that archiving faces with the advent of digital databases.

is imperative that artists actively participate in how data is shaped, organised, and disseminated.[6]

In this quotation a link is established between the physical presence of the databases and the conception of the human subject as mediated and displayed by the artist. The database works simultaneously as a symptom and a tool; a symptom of the conditions of contemporary life and a tool for an ample representation of these conditions. The present aim is not to focus on new media artworks (which are what Vesna refers to) but rather to uncover the ways in which the logic of new media feeds back on the printed novel's ongoing negotiation of narrativity. In order to do this, it is, however, necessary to understand more fully what is meant when the database is referred to as a cultural object, and why it may count as a concrete material sign of information technology as a symbolic form. Lev Manovich's conceptualisation of the database, reference to which has become almost mandatory in any discussion of the cultural implications of database aesthetics, is a good starting point for this. It serves as an example of a more general cultural definition of the concept of the database that also includes phenomena which, in a strictly technical sense, are not databases:

New media objects may or may not employ these highly structured database models; however, from the point of view of the user's experience, a large proportion of them are databases in a more basic sense. They appear as collections of items on which the user can perform various operations – view, navigate, search. The user's experience of such computerized collections is, therefore, quite distinct from reading a narrative or watching a film or navigating an architectural site.[7]

Manovich thus adopts a more general definition of the database as a cultural form, and continues defining the database and the way in which it organises information in opposition to how information is structured in narrative, arguing that: »After the novel, and subsequently cinema, privileged narrative as the key form of cultural expression of the modern age, the computer age introduces its correlate – the database«.[8] The database's non-causal characteristics are what make it conflict especially with narrative:

The database represents the world as a list of items, and it refuses to order this list. In contrast, a narrative creates a cause-and-effect trajectory of seemingly unordered items (events).[9]

Hayles has criticised Manovich's definition for being too general in scope and delineating rather loosely what a database logic entails, which accord-

6 Vesna, p. 155.
7 Manovich, The Language of New Media, p. 219.
8 Ibid. p. 218.
9 Ibid. p. 225.

ing to Hayles results in a conflation of data with databases. A database is not just randomly collected and unordered data. The way in which the data entries stand in relation to one another in a database is meticulously programmed. By not distinguishing clearly between data and databases Manovich glosses over the fact that databases do indeed represent a specifically structured order which makes each database useful for retrieving some information and unsatisfactory for obtaining other information: »The database, in short, represents only a small slice of actual and potential data«.[10] It is just as much a representation as a narrative is, only of another sort.

This fact – that the database represents an organisation of information to the same degree as a narrative – is crucial when thinking about database logic in opposition to narrative. In Galen Strawson's article »Against Narrativity« it is argued that form-finding can exist in the absence of narrativity, i.e. that »episodics« may also have an inclination towards »form-finding«.[11] The fact that we are not dealing with a narrative does not mean that there is no order. It is just a different order. However, Hayles' aim is not to identify oppositions to narrative, but rather to establish narrative's »co-evolution partners«. Referring to psychologist Jerome Bruner and cognitive scientist Mark Tuner, among others, Hayles (unlike Strawson) subscribes to a conception of narrative which regards the ability to construct stories as an intrinsic human capability. She labels the database a modern phenomenon that, at its earliest, dates back to the birth of statistics in the eighteenth century. Hayles therefore replaces the term »database« with that of »possibility space«, which allows her to explore the unarticulated-but-possible outcomes of a narrative as well as the neither-articulated-nor-anticipated-but-possible outcomes of a narrative. We shall return to the implications of this »possibility space« in chapter 3.3, which deals with reader interaction and multiple narrative strands in more depth. In this chapter we are concerned with what we shall continue to call the »database«, because this term highlights issues that challenge causal and temporal modes of organisation through combinatorics and complexity management which are in dialogue with the negotiations of narrativity we have seen in *Wanderjahre*, *MoE*, and *ZT*. However, Hayles' objections to Manovich's definition show that the term as generally culturally interpretated should be used with caution and needs qualification in order to be useful.

To understand the type of configuration with which we are dealing when looking at a database logic, Whitney curator Christiane Paul's description of database aesthetics as a cultural practice is useful:

---

10 Hayles, Narrating Bits, p. 168.
11 Strawson, p. 442.

Database aesthetics itself has become an important cultural narrative of our time, constituting a shift towards a relational, networked approach to gathering and creating knowledge about cultural specifics.[12]

What she describes here as characteristic of the database is the way in which it generates knowledge as a process of »gathering and creating«. This points to two central characteristics of the database. Firstly, the database embodies a conception of a huge amount of data from which the data that we want needs to be filtered or »gathered«. The database is the entity providing this filter, and as we have seen, it does not have to obey causal or temporal links when filtering the relevant from the irrelevant information, because content and structure are separate to a much larger degree than in an archive organised by a principle of provenance. Secondly, it alludes to the »creation« of knowledge arising from the combination and recombination of data. This is facilitated by the database's ability to handle high levels of complexity. What we constantly return to when trying to understand the logic of the database and its listing of information in columns and tables is this resistance towards temporality and causality as modes of organising information. This different approach to temporality is developed by Mark Hansen in *New Philosophy for New Media*. He distinguishes between »human time« and »machine time«, pointing out the difference between:

the lived affective temporality of human experience and the ›intensive‹ time of machine processing. If the former temporality centers around the fusion interval of the ›now‹, which, neuroscience has recently informed us, lasts approximately 0.3 seconds, the latter is, literally speaking, ›beyond experience‹, that is, beneath the 0.3-second threshold. This latter, intensive time is, consequently, the time of digital information flow: ›the time of e-mail and surfing, the time which eliminates space: arrival and departure occur in the same moment in real-time.[13]

Machine time corresponds to the more abstract concept of time we find in time-measuring devices such as the watch and the calendar, but also in more ancient ways of keeping track of the cycles of the sun, moon, and seasons. These ways of organising time are non-narrative in the sense that they create a systematic structure, rather than making the events create the order of time.[14] In digital environments, such as the ones described by Hansen, and in the database we find that a narrative conception of time as a sequence of causally connected events is replaced by a notion that everything is potentially present at the same time – linearity is replaced by simultaneity.

---

12 Paul, p. 108.
13 Hansen, p. 235.
14 Abbott, p. 3.

This notion of time and causality means that, as a cultural category, database structures do not follow the narrative way of stringing together information, because narrative relies on at the very least either a temporal or a causal sequence. The fact that the content of a database is organised in the form of variables that can be calculated and combined enables the manipulation of large amounts of material. This vastly increases the number of permutations in which the data can be organised, as well as the general levels of complexity with which the data can be analysed. From a cultural perspective, a database enables a user to manage a far greater amount of material. Compared to a narrative, in which the information must consist of causally or temporally connected links, the database gives the user, at least in theory, access to much more material that can potentially be activated – provided of course that the user searches the database in such a way that the specific piece of data that is of interest is identified. However, it also increases the risk that the user could become »lost«, because the parameters by which the database links certain data to other data, and thus allows the user to retrieve specific information, is less transparent for a non-specialist user than it is in a narrative. This reveals the ways in which characteristics of the database are connected to issues of complexity management and information overload in contemporary culture, once again highlighting ways in which the database is both a symptom and a tool for representing this condition.

The question to which we shall now turn is: what happens in the feedback from the database to the novel genre? Earlier in this study we saw how *Wanderjahre* incorporates the archive organised through a principle of provenance. In *Realismens metode* [The Method of Realism], Frits Andersen has pointed to ways in which the ambition of the great encyclopaedic projects of the Enlightenment and the archive as motif has left its mark on literature and can be traced in the works of writers such as Balzac, Flaubert, Verne, Zola, Proust, Musil, and Joyce:

[It is] the ambition of both wanting to tell it *all*, the totality of a certain world, and maintaining all the *details* in this world which creates the tensions and paradoxes in the texts. You follow the extremely carefully ornate and labyrinthine road from the solitary and fragmentary towards the general and consecutive which is never reached but remains a twinkling mirage over the desert.[15]

In *Mediensimulation als Schreibstrategie* (1999), Philip Löser refers to novels by Andreas Okopenko, Milorad Pavic, Gerold Späth, Julio Cortázar, and George Perec as »Lexikonromane«, i.e. novels which make use of alternative ways of connecting the material such as tables of contents, foot-

---

15 Andersen, p. 195. My translation.

notes, indexes, and cross-references. A movement like *Oulipo* (ouvroir de littérature potentielle), which was founded in 1961 and had Raymond Queneau, Georges Perec, and Italo Calvino as its main figures, experimented with subjecting literature to strict, arbitrary rules. As we saw in the last chapter, an argument can be made for grouping *ZT* with these works. All of the abovementioned ways of integrating other forms of organization into the novel can be recognised in literature that integrates the database form. It is thus often the shambles of precise detail, the density of information, and the wish to motivate the link between data through other means than causality and temporality, which characterise the logic of the database in contemporary novels. However, the three novels we shall consider – Jan Kjærstad's *Rand*, Thomas Hettche's *Nox*, and Botho Strauß's *Beginnlosigkeit* – all in different ways seem to emphasise that the present increase in the amount of information with which we are bombarded daily makes it more necessary than ever to think about how to handle large amounts of information. The figure of the database lends itself willingly as both a symptom of and solution to this condition, thus underscoring the impact of information technology as a symbolic form.

3.1.2 »Wenn nun die ganze Datenbank die Lösung ist?«
Jan Kjærstad's *Rand*

As we saw in the opening quotation of this chapter, *Rand* explicitly thematizes the way in which the database manages complex data material and, through its alternative way of combining information, opens avenues for new insights which investigators searching for causes and effects cannot capture. By representing this other logic it creates a hope for the main character in *Rand* that the abstraction will reveal another sort of connectivity in the world, one which only becomes visible through the database and which normal language has trouble representing:

Noch habe ich ihm nicht vom Wichtigsten erzählt, vom... Umriß, den ich selber hinter diesen vorläufigen Verbindungen sehe, in der enormen, in der gedankensprengenden Möglichkeit, die in der unbegrenzten Kombination von Daten liegt. Denn ich habe... Am Rande eines... Für ein Zehntel einer Sekunde habe ich Schatten eines...[16]

---

16 Kjærstad, Rand, p. 378. »ennå har jeg ikke fortalt ham om det viktigste, om det... skimmeret jeg selv ser bak disse foreløpige sammenkoplingene, i den enorme, i den tankesprengende muligheten som ligger i en ubegrenset kombinasjon av data. For jeg har... På randen av... I et tiendedels sekund har jeg sett skyggen av en –« (Kjærstad, Rand, pp. 240-41).

The database logic is in *Rand* connected to one of the main themes of the novel, the question:»what is a human being and how can we represent it?« This question is pivotal to Kjærstad as author, and it is one which he has also reflected on in essay form. In the essay »Litteraturens mulighet. Romanen og nettet« [The possibility of literature. The novel and the web], Kjærstad suggests that a new way of characterising the human subject is called for, and his suggestions for an adequate mode of representation seem to subscribe to the logic of the database:

I am nonetheless more interested in the tendencies we see towards a new way of characterizing the human being. On a superficial level I could claim that whereas the nineteenth-century novel (and a number of contemporary novels) depict human beings through long descriptions of looks etc. today's novelists characterize their characters through lists. In *Microserfs*, for instance, Douglas Coupland presents his characters by listing their seven dream categories as if their lives were a game of Jeopardy. I do not have any troubles creating an – indeed very ›lifelike‹ – image of the people in the novel from this information. […] Information, listed, replaces conventional characterization.[17]

Let us see how that is carried out in *Rand*. The victims in *Rand* are all characterised by the short conversation they have with the killer before they are murdered. Their identity is thus deduced from brief, meaningless exchanges which mostly resemble small-talk, but which are later ascribed enormous meaning when they are extracted from their original context and turned into key words in the murderer's hunt for an understanding of why exactly these people should have died. The characterisation of the victims is thus reduced to a number of random keywords and snatches of information that the murderer later discovers, but which nonetheless come to constitute their identity in the novel. As Bjarne Markussen has pointed out, the murderer's victims represent different aspects of human experience: the practical, the social, the communicative, the artistic and so forth. Furthermore, each victim is connected to a part of the human body, together forming an image of a complete human being.[18] The protagonist provides a reflection of this relationship between part and whole when he searches the criminal records of the police. On the one hand he registers that the human being is reduced to ornaments within the logic of the database:

Name auf Name läuft vorbei, Namen, die lebendige Menschen sind (einige im Gefängnis, einige frei), Namen, die Schicksale sind, Lebensgeschichten, Gesichter. Und

---

17 Kjærstad, Litteraturens mulighet, p. 246. My translation.
18 Markussen, p. 84.

dennoch: seltsam entpersönlicht, verdichtet, abstrahiert. Schrift auf grünem Schirm. Menschenleben, reduziert auf Ornamente.[19]

On the other hand the database contains a key to understanding the whole of the human being:

Ich weiß, es mag überspannt klingen, aber während der Text durchläuft, muß ich an die Schriftrollen in der Synagoge denken, daran, daß auch dies – was ich auf dem Schirm sehe – eine Art Heilige Schrift ist, die ebenso das Rätsel der menschlichen Existenz berührt wie die Worte der Bibel.[20]

The database is here used both to symbolise the de-personified human being and to facilitate the understanding of human existence on a mystical level. The database points to another way of conceiving identity, because temporal and causal sequences have been eliminated and replaced by momentous single words in a bombardment of information. The database's representation of the human being thus presents itself as separated points in which temporal and causal sequences are suspended, almost becoming a metaphorical force-field resembling poetry, or what Galen Strawson would describe as an episodic outlook upon the world.

Nonetheless, narrativity is not so easily disposed of. Even naked facts can become narratives, which is what happens for the protagonist when he searches the criminal records of the police:

Ich fange an, oder die Finger fangen an, die Geschichten hinter diesem Namen zu verfolgen, und was ich sehe, erstaunt mich derart, daß ich eine Stunde lang dasitze und tippe und lese (und phantasiere, muß ich wohl hinzufügen). Stichworte, nackte Fakten werden zu Geschichten, einem blutigen Epos. Der Mann ist in eine Reihe von Fällen verwickelt, die sich, wenn ich so will, in alle Richtungen verzweigen. Ich reise durch ganz Norwegen, in einer Periode von zehn Jahren. Und viele der Zeitpunkte und der geographischen Namen wecken Erinnerungen.[21]

---

19 Kjærstad, Rand, p. 309. »Navn på navn ruller forbi, navn som er levende mennesker (noen i fengsel, noen fri), navn som er skjebner, livshistorier, ansikter. Og allikevel: merkelig avpersonifisert, fortettet, gjort abstrakt. Skrift på grønn skjerm. Menneskeliv redusert til ornamenter.« (Kjærstad, Rand, p. 199).

20 Kjærstad, Rand, p. 310. »Jeg vet det kan lyde overspent, men idet teksten ruller forbi, kommer jeg til å tenke på skriftrullene i synagogen, at også dette – det jeg ser på skjermen – er en slags hellig skrift, at den rører like mye ved den menneskelige eksistensens gåte, som Bibelens ord.« (Kjærstad, Rand, p. 200).

21 Kjærstad, Rand, p. 308. »Jeg begynner, eller fingrene begynner, å forfølge historiene bak dette navnet, og hva jeg ser, forundrer meg i den grad at jeg sitter i én time og taster og leser (og fantaserer, må jeg vel legge til). Stikkord, nakne fakta, blir til historier, et blodig epos. Mannen er involvert i en rekke saker som, hvis jeg vil, forgrener seg i alle retninger. Jeg reiser i hele Norge, over en periode på ti år. Og mange av tidspunktene og de geografiske navnene vekker minner.« (Kjærstad, Rand, pp. 198-99).

The name on the screen brings back memories which generate stories in the mind of the murderer. This reminds us of the way in which *Wanderjahre* displayed the process of reading an archive by providing both the disparate material of the aphorisms and the narration of the novellas. In *Rand* the isolated word that the protagonist encounters becomes a charged constellation and, even if it is not a story taking place as a temporal sequence, the constellation of the stripped facts creates a narrative which he is able to refer to as a gory epic. The elements which we concluded were suspended in the database, such as temporal and causal connections, are thereby re-established in the shape of geography and memory in the meeting with a receptive reader/user.

Narrative and database are thus on the thematic level inseparable companions in *Rand*. The aim seems not to be to do away with narrative, but rather to challenge it by confronting it with the database logic and testing the abilities of the reader to create narratives from dispersed information. In this way *Rand* explores the possibilities and the risks of an apparently never-ending number of possible combinations of data, and its consequences for the representation of the human being.

The database is, however, not only a strong motif in the novel, but seems also to function as inspiration for the structure of the novel. *Rand* consists of a repetition of the same event (the murder) in different permutations. The chart[22] below lists the victims and the information we are given about them in the novel:

Victim's name	Job	Hobby	Language	Organ
Georg Becker	Architect	Studying whales	Plastic	Sexual organs
Tor Gross	Social anthropologist	Theatre	Scientific	Brain
Eva Weiner	Typographer	Popular culture	Digital	Fingers
Dan Bergmann	Waiter	Weaving	Visual	Palate
Magnus Davidsen	Vet	Bonsai trees, acting	Bodily	Muscles
Ruth Isaksen	Musician (horn)	Travelling by train	Musical	Ear

---

22 The chart is taken from Markussen, p. 84 and translated into English.

Two of the elements which we identified as characteristic of the database are thus continuously at play in the novel`s configuration: firstly, the repeated structure which makes the events of the novel more resemble a row of equal permutating entries than actual motivated events with a cause and an effect; and secondly the repeated combination of the data material that engages the protagonist (and the reader in her attempt to understand the novel) and increases the complexity and makes the novel opaque. The novel in its entirety thus resembles a database search for the right keyword, which can ascribe meaning to the events and explain why the murders are committed, but none of the causal explanations suggested provide this. Each new murder just adds to the amount of possible explanations, while none of these become an overall framework through which everything else can be explained. The novel consequently comes to resemble a series of lists stacked upon lists, until it is not possible to see through the complexity and the unfinished is realised as being ideal. The narrative expectations of the crime novel constantly attempts to find a cause and to reach a solution, but these expectations are repeatedly overwhelmed by the many possible ways of combining the material and the inability to separate relevant from irrelevant material. The reader is denied the satisfaction inherent in traditional crime novels connected to the detection of the crime and the return to normality when the riddle is solved. The database form is consequently not only present on a thematic level, but can also be traced directly in the form of the novel, which makes *Rand* appear to oscillate between two contradictory forces: the narrative moving towards the closure inherent in the crime novel genre, and the resistance towards that type of closure inherent in the database permutations.

As a consequence, the novel and the human being stand in a similar position: placed between the narrative wish for motives and causality and the database's embodiment of insolvable contradictions which are never deciphered, but can be combined in continuously new ways. The quotation below can be read as a reflection of the novel's representation of the possibilities of a characterization of the human being in the force-field between narration and database; a reflection which comments on the way in which the novel itself tackles the description of the human subject. It paraphrases an article which one of the victims has written:

Der Artikel handelte von all diesen Hamlets, von Hamlets aus den letzten fünfundsiebzig Jahren (Frauen inklusive), von verschiedenen Sprech- und Spielstilen, von den unterschiedlichen Lösungen, was Kostüme, Bühnenbild und Beleuchtung betrifft. […] Was blieb, war der Eindruck, daß man Hamlet als Stinkstiefel und als Engel spielen kann, als… ja, Teufel und Gott. Gross selbst vermied es, zu einer der angegebenen Deutungsmöglichkeiten Stellung zu nehmen, er schätzte statt dessen die Abwechslung. Gross – ich sah ihn die ganze Zeit vor mir: das weiße Haar, die Brille, das

Tweedjackett – behauptete, Hamlet sei ein Mensch voller unlösbarer Gegensätze. Ich engagierte mich so stark, daß ich folgenden Satz unterstrich: ›Hamlet ist der Mensch par excellence; das Leben jedes Menschen ist ein unsicherer Balanceakt, gelenkt und beeinflußt von tausend unsichtbaren Kräften.‹[23]

According to *Rand*, Hamlet in his manifold versions represents a condensation of what it means to be human. By containing so many diverging personalities, Hamlet is himself a database of possible combinations who avoids an absolute unity in the same way as the novel avoids explaining the murders. The essence of man is said to consist of incompatible contradiction; there is not one solution to the character Hamlet. As the protagonist formulates it in the quotation cited at the beginning of this chapter: »Wenn nun die *ganze* Datenbank die Lösung ist, nicht mehr und nicht weniger, so daß es unmöglich ist, es zu reduzieren?«[24] In the same way as the multiplicity of personalities presents itself as the solution to the question »what is a human being?«, the form on which the novel settles arises from the bombardment of the reader with pieces of information and their possible connections. Reading *Rand* is experienced as an onrush of a large amount of irrelevant and relevant information with no corresponding means of deciphering which is which. Since none of the data provided can be connected in a meaningful sequence, the result is the dissolution of the chain of events into loosely connected fragments strung together in a manner lacking temporal or causal parameters. In this way the reader at the end of *Rand* reaches the same stage as the protagonist: a confrontation with a database consisting of incoherent fragments and cross-references which leads nowhere. Only from here can a coherent narration faintly take shape in the mind of the reader. The possibility of narration thus arises through the destruction of what is usually its primary condition – causality and temporality – by information overload. For the main character the database appears as something positive, as something that makes us aware of the many possible connections in the world, and thereby expands our vision. The risk is that we lose sight of the obvious: i.e. that the narrator is the murderer. For the novel the database

---

23 Kjærstad, Rand, pp. 84-85. »Artikkelen handlet om alle disse Hamlet'ene, om Hamlet'er fra ti til syttifem år (kvinner inkludert), om stemmebruk og ulik spillestil, om de forskjellige løsningene når det gjaldt kostymer, scenografi og lyssetting. […] Jeg satt igjen med inntrykket at du kunne spille Hamlet som en drittsekk og en engel, både som… ja, Djevel og Gud. Gross selv unnlot å ta stilling for noen av de angitte tolkningsmulighetene, han hyllet isteden variasjonen. Gross – jeg så ham hele tiden for meg: det hvite håret, brillene, tweedjakken – påsto at Hamlet var et menneske som rommet uløselige motsetninger. Jeg ble såpass engasjert at jeg streket under følgende setning: ›Hamlet er mennesket par exellence; ethvert menneskes liv er en usikker balansegang, styrt og påvirket av tusen usynlige krefter.‹« (Kjærstad, Rand, pp. 55-56).

24 Kjærstad, Rand, p. 388.

becomes a way of articulating the world of an information society in which we constantly have to separate relevant from irrelevant information. As a novel it performs a balancing act between narrating a detective story on the one hand, and, on the other hand, through the form of the database, articulating that the purpose of the murders – or life – cannot be situated in one explanation, but should be found in the combination of all of the possibilities.

The next novel at which we shall look also centres on a murder, but here the allusions to the traditional crime novel with its causal expectations are not as strong as they are in *Rand*. In fact the transgression of the narrative is even more persistent and presents itself as the very condition for the novel's existence.

3.1.3 »Kein Satz fiel mir mehr ein. F7, WP beenden?«
Thomas Hettche's *Nox*

Nox (1995) takes place in Berlin on November 9, 1989 – the night of the fall of the Wall. This is the night referred to in the title, and this is the night that witnesses not only the historical circumstances surrounding the opening of the Wall and the merging of two separated parts of a city and a country, but also a young woman who murders a man – our narrator, who is a writer.

The novel begins dramatically with the slitting of the narrator's throat. However, this act does not prevent him from narrating the story, but instead elevates him to an omniscient position from which he can follow the murderess, who proceeds on a nocturnal sexual stroll through the agitated city searching for her own name, which she has forgotten. The tale of her nightly encounters consists of a number of symbolically laden tableaux, which perform the act of merging what is split through the use of motifs like scars, wounds, and sexual encounters. It is a symbolism which is further emphasized at the end of the novel when the border guard-dog, who follows her, retells the myth from Plato's *Symposium* of how the human race were originally round creatures who were then split into two halves by the gods and subsequently spend the rest of their lives trying to find someone with whom they can unite.

The novel takes the form of small shards of text – usually not more than a couple of pages long – separated by typographical squares. There is the story of Professor Matern in his pathological museum, a mysterious man with matches, Lara and David, Heike and Heiko, a border guard-dog, and descriptions of the historical night of November 9, 1989. All these diverging strains of narration weave in and out of one another in a way that gives the impression that the narrator is drawing his material from a larger archive, shuffling the different strains of narration, and extracting moments to linger upon.

The role of the computer in *Nox* was initially illuminated by Aminia Brueggemann in the article »Identity Construction and Computers in Thomas Hettche's novel *Nox*« (1999). Brueggemann uses *Nox* as her reference point for a more general discussion of how narration and identity construction are being influenced by the computer in society today. However, the function of the computer has not been at the centre of *Nox*'s reception. When it first came out, the critics focussed mainly on its many intertextual references and the way in which the mythology of reunification is portrayed in images that verge on sadomasochistic kitsch. However, the re-publication of the novel in 2001 initiated a renewed interest leading to an appreciation of the precision and sensibility of its language and its portrayal of the city of Berlin, and effort was made to understand it as a part of the general literary currents of the 1980s and 1990s. In the article »Mythos als Kritik. Zu Thomas Hettches Wenderoman *Nox*« (1999) Franziska Schößler describes the process which the narrator of *Nox* goes through with the highly illuminating phrase: »eine Initiation zum Dichter«[25]. This initiation as a writer is set in motion to overcome the writing crisis that the murderess imposes on him at their first encounter at a literature reading the night before the murder. After the reading she comes up to him and asks: »Können Sie selbst das auch? […] Jemandem so weh tun, meine ich, wie Sie es beschreiben«[26]. His inconsistent answers lead her to reveal her desire for him and for being hurt. Her reaction to his rejection of her desire has a threatening undertone: »Jetzt erzähl nur, du habest mich so gesehen. Wenn du noch erzählen kannst«[27]. What is being threatened is his ability to narrate – in other words the potency of his existence as a writer, and indeed, it is the same woman that later slits his throat.[28] This conception of what happens to the narrator in *Nox* paves the way for an interpretation of the novel as being about its own making, about the overcoming of a writing crisis which enables the

---

25 Schößler, p. 178.
26 Hettche, Nox, p. 15.
27 Ibid. p. 20.
28 What is at stake here is an intertextual reference to Greek mythology. As Franziska Schößler has shown, *Nox* plays on the myth of Diana and Actaeon: In Greek mythology Diana is bathing nude in the woods when the hunter Actaeon stumbles in on her. He stops and stares, amazed at her beauty. However, when she sees him watching her, she enforces the same threat on his ability to tell the tale as the nameless woman enforces upon the narrator in *Nox*: »Now you are free to tell that you have seen me all unrobed – if you can tell« (Ovid [Book 3. 192]). Diana subsequently changes Actaeon into a stag and sets his own hounds to kill him. However, the hounds are so upset with their master's death that the centaur Chiron creates an image so lifelike that the hounds think it is Actaeon. In *Nox* no picture is made of the narrator. What remains is the novel; a portrait of the conditions for the writing subject in the aftermath of the reunification of Germany.

narrator to become a writer in a changed historical context – a newly reuni-
fied Germany. Significantly, *Nox* is not a novel about computers; it is about
the reunification of Germany and the writer's situation during this historical
process. However, the computer comes to play a significant part in making
the representation of this process possible, and it thus obtains a noteworthy
position in the novel – both as a literary motif and as a principle of composition.

In order to understand the significance of the computer as a motif in the
novel, we can begin by examining an indication given by the narrator of his
own writing process. The passage on which we shall focus occurs as a
flashback 43 pages into the novel. It takes place on the night after the encounter with the woman and features the writer as he starts up his computer
in an attempt to begin writing. The description of the computer's starting-up
process is quite technically detailed, which seems to emphasize the difference between the efficient computer that promises words of perfection and
the passive writer trying to launch his imagination. What he conjures up is
the image of a woman on a bed and himself naked on a chair observing her.
The image develops as he writes, and he registers the changes in her appearance as an effect of his writing process, almost as if he were program-
ming her: »Sähe sie an, dort auf dem weißen Laken, und das, was ich sähe,
wären meine Spuren.«[29] However, he suddenly stops short and cannot write
anymore. He finds himself unable to describe the expression he saw on her
face that evening: »Ich kenne diese Frau nicht, dachte ich, und meine ei-
gene Sprache verriet mich. Kein Satz fiel mir mehr ein. F7, WP beenden?«[30]
This crisis in the imaginative process makes him liken his own situation to
that of a computer that reconfigures itself:

Wie ein Computer, den man, lange bevor er nicht mehr funktioniert, einfach vergisst.
Er wartet und saugt die Zeit auf, bis einer den On-Schalter drückt. Nur jenen Moment
des Zögerns, so, wie jemand Ruhe erbittet, um sich zu konzentrieren, braucht es, bis
wieder alle Daten konfiguriert sind und der Cursor blinkt.[31]

The analogy between human time and computer time initiates an almost
mythical experience in which the narrator »enters« the computer after having submitted passwords. It is this transcendence ritual that prepares him for
his own death:

Ich ging in jener Nacht zurück in das bernsteinfarbene Licht und beantwortete noch
einmal die drei Fragen. Träumte mich in die matte, augenschonende Dämmerung der
elektronischen Speicherräume hinein, hin zu den hellen Feuern, an denen man vorbei-

---

29 Hettche, Nox, p. 44.
30 Ibid. p. 44.
31 Ibid. p. 45.

steigt in der Tiefe und immer weiter ins Flimmern der Halbleiter hinab und in jene einfachen Zustände stummer Ladungsübertragung.
Die Gedanken, die Maschine sind, haben keine Zeit. Und ihr Nichtvergessen verändert die Dinge. Nichts mehr kann nicht angesehen werden. Nichts an den Dingen vergeht mehr. Erinnerung entsteht auf neue Weise. Es gibt keine Spur mehr jenseits der Speicher. Spät erst, als bereits der erste Dämmer des Tages, an dem ich sterben würde, über den See kroch, kam ich zögernd wieder an die Oberfläche zurück. [32]

Thus the writer who in this mythical experience merges with the mechanical memory recomposes himself through the machine:

Ächzend begann der Laserkopf, die Daten des Programms von der Festplatte in den Arbeitsspeicher zu laden. Dann baute sich, Zeile für Zeile, das Bild auf und darüber der rote Schriftzug SIMCUNT.[33]

The mythic experience with the computer in the night is an important key to understanding what the novel says about the writing process and the role of the author in post-reunification Germany. In this sense the novel is all about how we structure imagination; the computer being a tool and a model for the shape that imagination takes, since it enables the writer to undertake the necessary descent into the land of the dead and emerge as reborn. We shall return to the relationship between the form of narration and the computer again, but before that we shall briefly linger on the chronology of the novel in order to make the significance of the computer passage clear.

A curious feature of the computer passage is the problems it raises relating to the chronology of events. However, this gives us a central key for interpreting the novel. Due to the mythological atmosphere in which the novel takes place it may seem futile to try to establish a chronology. However, as we are dealing with an actual historical event occurring on November 9, 1989, a sense of historical time is not completely erased, which makes the inconsistencies in the temporality of the text interesting. We are given three flashbacks to the life of the narrator before he is murdered. The first two flashbacks tell of the evening preceding the murder, when the narrator meets his murderess at the literature reading. She invites him to her place the following evening. After this first encounter the narrator returns to his room: »als ich hinaufstieg in mein Zimmer unter dem Dach.«[34] The third flashback (which contains the passage with the computer) follows about 20 pages later and begins: »Als ich in der Nacht von ihr kam, stand ich lange am Fenster.«[35] The phrase »von ihr kam« seems to imply that we are now in

---

32 Ibid. p. 45.
33 Ibid. p. 46.
34 Ibid. p. 21.
35 Ibid. p. 43.

the night following the reading, and that he has already met with her again, otherwise he would have been more likely to say that he came from the reading. More strikingly, the sequence: »immer wieder dachte ich an das, was ich nicht hatte sehen dürfen. Deshalb war ich noch da. Und mußte nun zusehen bei dem, was in mir geschah und ihr«[36] seems to imply that this passage takes place after the murder. The phrase »what happened in me« situates the time of narration to after the murder, also suggested by the interest he takes in the decaying process of his own body. However, the passage concludes with: »Spät erst, als bereits der erste Dämmer des Tages, an dem ich sterben würde, über den See kroch, kam ich zögernd wieder an die Oberfläche zurück«,[37] and we are subsequently back to the night before he is murdered. These inconsistencies in the chronology seem to point to the significance of this passage. Somehow the first and the second night of their encounter and the exact time of the murder become indecipherable. The ending makes the passage with the computer even harder to situate chronologically. In the very last passage we are back in the murderess' apartment, two wine glasses are on the table, and as she bids him to leave she reveals her name.

A possible solution to these inconsistencies would be to consider the murder and all of the following events as the product of the narrator's activity in front of the computer which suspends temporal sequence. His death and merging with the computer become one and the same operation whose product is his resurrection as the author of the novel *Nox*. The narration consequently comes to consist of layers of narrative: firstly, the narration about the writer writing the story, and secondly, the experiences of the people in Berlin on November 9, 1989 which the narrator envisions while merged with the computer.

These observations demand a closer look at the position of the narrator. The narrator obtains his omniscience by dying and thus becoming simultaneously elevated to a godlike position and merged bodily with the surroundings:

Und über Nacht würde in den Wechselstuben der Kurs der Ostmark weiter steigen, und die Unruhe, die in meinem Kopf echote, würde unsichtbar als elektrische Entladung aus der Stadt hinauszittern und durch die atlantischen Kabel dorthin, wo Tag war, zu den überseeischen Käufern und ins grelle Licht des Dow Jones.[38]

This combination of being at the same time paralysed and immersed, like an immobilised player of a computer game, makes the narrator the unwilling

---

36 Ibid. p. 45.
37 Ibid. p. 45.
38 Ibid. p. 28.

yet implicated witness of the sadomasochistic spectacle that his murderess displays before him during her walk through Berlin. However, as the analysis above indicates, we are in fact dealing with a layer of narrators and our omniscient narrator is controlled by another narrator sitting behind his computer. The computer passage functions to make us aware of this intricate set of narrators and allow us a glimpse of this other narrator behind the narrator we thought to be omniscient.

In the article »Identity Construction and Computers in Thomas Hettche's novel *Nox*«, Brueggemann argues that the voice of the narrator that emerges when he is murdered is dehumanised and disembodied – in other words a computer voice. Brueggemann explores the novel's depiction of identity construction as a reflection on how our experience of identity has changed with the advent of the computer and can be regarded as merging the porous boundaries between human and machine:

> According to Hettche, narration goes on and on with or without a living narrator. In a subtle way, the human being and the computer are regarded as being interchangeable. For Hettche does not portray the voice or consciousness of a corpse, but the voice or consciousness of a human in interaction with a computer, or one could call it a downloaded person.[39]

Our analysis of the computer passage above underscores this argument. However, the computer also becomes a tool that helps the narrator regain his ability to narrate and thus acquire a sense of his own identity. In many ways *Nox* is the story of a search for identity. The main character next to the narrator – the nameless woman – is on a constant search for her identity which is somehow tied up with her name. This identity is only revealed in the end by the border guard-dog, which enables her, on the very last page of the novel, to give her name to the narrator who can then begin his narration. But the person who is really finding his identity through this process is the narrator, who is initiated into his identity as a writer. Identity is thus closely linked to the ability to narrate. As the border guard-dog explains to the narrator:

> Wir alle drei, sagte er, du und ich und sie, gehören zu einer Geschichte. Zu einer alten Geschichte, die sich wieder ereignet. Warum? Wer weiß? Nichts von dem, was du kennst, wird nach dieser Nacht bleiben, wie es ist. Und nur die Geschichten, die man sich davon erzählt, bestimmen, was wird.[40]

---

39 Brueggemann, p. 342.
40 Hettche, Nox, p. 134.

Identity and the way in which we understand the historic night of November 9, 1989 are thus said to be made up of narrations. The question that remains is what form this narration takes.

Let us now turn to the composition of the novel and have a closer look at the significance of the merging with the computer for the mode of narration. In an interview Thomas Hettche described how he composes his books from detached fragments that he subsequently models into a coherent whole:

Vor der Geschichte, vor dem Plot hat mich eigentlich immer das Bild interessiert: Beschreibungen von Szenerien, Natur, Licht oder Musik. Der Arbeitsablauf ist immer noch derselbe: Ich sammle Fragmente, die ich dann, manchmal erst nach Jahren, innerhalb eines Buchzusammenhangs montiere.[41]

In *Nox*, this compositional style becomes a powerful way of representing the woman's personal memory: »Wieder schloß sie die Augen. Wußte, dieser Moment würde wiederkehren, immer von neuem, bis sie ihren Namen fände.«[42] However, it also points back to the computer passage in so far as we are reminded of how a database shuffles between data drawn from a larger archive:

Ächzend begann der Laserkopf, die Daten des Programms von der Festplatte in den Arbeitsspeicher zu laden. Dann baute sich, Zeile für Zeile, das Bild auf und darüber der rote Schriftzug SIMCUNT.[43]

It has already been noted that the novel consists entirely of loosely assembled tableaux that seem to flick between each other as if drawn at random from a constantly shuffling database. We encounter Professor Matern in his pathological museum, the mysterious man with the matches, Lara and David, Heike and Heiko, the border guard-dog, and descriptions of the night of November 9, 1989. Strains of narration, each of which seems to stem from a larger whole, are taken out of their temporal and spatial order and brought together and interwoven as if they represent the results of a search performed on a database: they become images rather than plot. It thus seems reasonable to claim that, apart from appearing as a motif, the database in this instance also serves as inspiration for the representation of imagination and memory and consequently for the form and construction of the narrative. It provides us as readers with a framework for interpreting the novel and a way of understanding how the novel itself conceives of imagination and memory.

---

41 Hettche, Es gibt keine Kriterien für Texte, p. 207.
42 Hettche, Nox, p. 100.
43 Ibid. p. 46.

Sie sah, daß sich Kirchberger mit Schween unterhielt. Neben den beiden standen schweigend die Blonde und der Vollbärtige, Heike und Heiko, und etwas abseits entdeckte sie auch den Senatsrat. Sah im selben Moment, daß Kirchberger zu ihnen herüberkam.

Haben Sie gehört, was geschehen ist? fragte er und wandte sich, ohne ihre Antwort abzuwarten, dem Geräuschemacher zu. Ob er die Synchronisation noch machen wolle. Der andere nickte. Gut. Wir erledigen den Transport heute nacht noch. Sie holen die Filme dann morgen bei Schween ab. Geht es in einer Woche?

Ja, sagte er und drückte seine Zigarette aus.

Kirchberger legte seine Hand auf ihren Unterarm und führte sie durch die Menge der Betrunkenen und Feiernden hinaus in den schmalen Gang. Dort, wo die Stiege an Deck führte, stand Wibke und wartete auf sie. Kalt wehte die Nacht von oben herab.

■

So bewegungslos und still, wie es ein Zuschauer nur sein kann, folgte ich jeder ihrer Bewegungen, und es hörte in mir noch immer nicht auf, hinzusehen. Und ich hörte nicht auf, mich bei Namen zu nennen. Leicht war das gewesen im Schmerz. Nun, da von Minute zu Minute alles, was ich gewesen war, fremder wurde, war sie es, die mich hielt. Als wäre, was mir geschah, nur eine seltsame Metamorphose, die jenen Blick, den sie mir nicht verzeihen konnte, nach außen stülpte.

62

Und ich sah, wie auf dem Schwarz des Nachthimmels jenseits des Parks tiefe Wolken schwammen. Grau und niedrig standen sie über den Häusern, bäuchlings orange von den Lichtern der Straßen. Manchmal schwenkte ein Scheinwerfer vom Flughafen durch sie hindurch. Kein Stern. Wenn die Wolken für Momente aufrissen, konnte ich den Mond in der linken oberen Ecke des Fensters sehen. Eine Windböe, die durch das offene Fenster hereinfuhr, warf Sprühregen auf meine Haut.

Spät noch hatte ich Geräusche aus der Wohnung über mir gehört und Schritte im Treppenhaus. Einmal, draußen im Park, die Rufe nach einem Kind. Jetzt war es still. Das Parkett knackte in der Kälte. Die Vorhänge hingen schwer und starr neben dem Fenster. Die Wasserlache war blind. Auf dem Boden das Messer.

■

Ein enger, mit Kisten und Möbeln, Regalen und Metallspinden vollgestellter Raum. Ein Waschbecken, ein Spiegel und, unterhalb der Höhe der Ufermauer, ein Bullauge. Wibke verschloß die Tür. Man hörte ganz nah das Lachen und Schreien der Feiernden.

Kirchberger zog Jackett und Hemd aus, drehte das Wasser auf, begann sich zu waschen und sah sie dabei im Spiegel an. Sie wollte hinaus, doch das Mädchen hielt sie und strich ihr mit der Hand langsam über das Gesicht. Sie mochte die Berührung. Er wird dir nicht weh tun, sagte es.

63

Thomas Hettche, *Nox*

As we have seen, the database involves a different logic than that of narration. Whereas in a narrative the acts and events are ordered in a sequence, in the database these acts and events are represented as isolated moments. The important difference is that narration establishes connections between the events and thereby ascribes meaning through an overall plot, whereas the database lets the moments flicker in sequenceless simultaneity. In *Nox*, the narrator regains his ability to narrate and his identity as the writer of the novel precisely by appropriating this narrative-challenging form, i.e. the database form taken by the novel as a whole. The narrator's recovery of his ability to write in *Nox* seems to stem from the liberation from temporal and spatial restraints that the database logic provides and which he presumably encounters while merged with the computer. This is significant, because it shows how the database form can be integrated into a narrative genre such as the novel and given a vitalising function, rather than representing a threatening »other«. The database, as it occurs in *Nox*, comes to represent a virtual space one can step into, a room where creativity runs free and overcomes writing blocks. The database facilitates this experience because it represents a different logic than that of the narrative form which has become problematic for the writer due to the changed political and cultural circumstances following the fall of the Wall.[44]

The function of the computer has not been at the centre of the critical reception of *Nox*, and rightly so, because *Nox* is not first and foremost a novel about computers. It is about the reunification of Germany and the role of the writer in the new Germany. But, in describing this, it uses information technology as a motif and as a symbolic form. What the foregoing close reading has revealed is that in *Nox* the computer works as »a medium« (so to speak) between the imagination of the writing subject and the form that the novel has to find. It is this medium, along with the murderess, his muse, which paves the way for the writer. The muse sends his imagination on a wild tour through Berlin by threatening his ability to narrate; the computer and the database form – by transgressing the narrative logic – provide ways of structuring this imagination, thus enabling him to perform his own death and rebirth and thereby become capable of writing in a new historical context characterized by transgressions and unifications.

As in *Rand*, the database is granted creative potential because it represents an order other than the narrative, turning the rules of causality and temporality upside down. In *Rand* this was a necessary result of the overload of information. Within the logic of *Nox* it is a necessary step when the order of the surrounding world is overturned by the fall of the Berlin Wall. However, narrativity is not abandoned completely, but rather recomposes itself through its meeting with the database logic. The last example we shall look at in connection with the database is Botho Strauß's *Beginnlosigkeit. Reflexionen über Fleck und Linie* (1992), which takes the challenge a step further and declares narrativity obsolete. *Beginnlosigkeit* is (as it says on the cover) »keine Fabel, keine Erzählung«. In this text narrative has become but a melancholy memory. However, it nonetheless thematizes the wish for being able to tell a story and explicitly grants information technology a role in this quest. It is thus a useful preliminary endpoint for our investigation of ways in which the database can be employed to negotiate narrativity, illustrating the very limits of how far it is possible to go in incorporating the database logic into a narrative.

---

44 Hereby the characteristics of the computer medium are also linked to the rest of the novel's imagery with its transgression of conventional boundaries in a variety of senses that are linked to the fall of the Wall.

3.1.4 »Wer mag schon einen Chip zum Gleichnis nehmen? Und doch gehörte es sich.« Botho Strauß's *Beginnlosigkeit*

In the interview »Der abwesende Herr Strauß. Ein Treffen mit dem unbekanntesten Schriftsteller der deutschen Literatur« in the Sunday edition of *Frankfurter Allgemeine* (March 2004), Botho Strauß says: »Wenn es den Computer nicht gäbe, wäre aus mir vielleicht ein richtiger Romanautor geworden«.[45] He thereby creates a dichotomy between the computer and the novel: the computer belongs to the world as it actually is, whereas the novel, along with the possibility of Strauß's ability to become an author of novels, is an imaginary construct. Whatever it entails to be »a real novelist« and whether this is at all desirable remain unsaid, though we are left with the impression that the *form* in which Strauß writes is linked to the computer and that this medium somehow stands in the way of the novel's epic impetus. We are reminded of Friedrich Nietzsche's famous remark in a letter written at the end of February 1882 to his secretary Henrich Köselitz, shortly after Nietzsche had started writing with his newly acquired typewriter: »Sie haben recht – unser Schreibzeug arbeitet mit an unseren Gedanken. Wann werde ich es über meine Finger bringen, einen langen Satz zu drucken!«[46]

Strauß is known for being interested in new technological developments, and he started using the computer more than twenty years ago. The indication that the medium has had an effect on the stature of his oeuvre is therefore interesting. Strauß is a well-known playwright and polemical debater in essays and aphorisms, but he is also a novelist and far from unfamiliar with the formalities and challenges of the genre. *Beginnlosigkeit. Reflexionen über Fleck und Linie* (1992) takes the merging of aphorisms and the novel to its limit. It is neither merely a collection of approximately 250 aphorisms nor a »real« novel. However, there is a thin layer of narration that occasionally reaches the reader like small bubbles of oxygen at the bottom of the ocean, providing the reader with vague points of reference. We are thus able to identify a male protagonist and see blurred markers that point to the world that surrounds him. Fred Hoyle's Steady-State theory of a universe without beginning or end is the theoretical pivotal point of the text. This is the universe in which the protagonist has to find his place and come to terms with his existence. *Beginnlosigkeit* is thus a confrontation with the idea of an utterly anti-narrative world. There is no beginning, no end – only the vast desert-like middle. In such a world there seems to be no other option than to be what Strawson calls »an episodic« (that is to have no clear

---

45 Weidermann.
46 Günzel, p. 419.

sense that the self that one is was there in the past and will be there in the future). People with a narrative approach to life will feel in thoroughly foreign territory. The question which the protagonist grapples with is thus:

Wie kann der Mensch mit der Erkenntnis der absoluten Beginnlosigkeit, die eine Beginnlosigkeit nicht nur der Schöpfung, sondern, davon ausgestreut metastatisch ins Geäder des Bewußtseins, eine Beginnlosigkeit *von allem und jedem* sein muß – wie kann er in einem solchen Erkenntnisstand sich und die Welt erleben und welche Folgen hat dies unweigerlich für alles und jedes?[47]

By obliterating the concept of a beginning the text aims to rethink the notion of causality, referring to the Greek dramas, the crime novel, and psychoanalysis as points of reference for an obsolete search for causes and origins. The notion of a beginning and an end is replaced by a conception of the world in which any beginning is in fact the effect of a long process, which cannot be ascribed to any one reason, but rather presents itself as an emergent structure with no predetermined aim: »Wenn eine Geschichte ein Ziel hat, wird sie schon unglaubwürdig. Folge und Ziel sind schlimme Gesellen.«[48] The image of the world that we acquire from *Beginnlosigkeit* is thus in, many ways, that of an autopoeitic system[49] as we find it in system theory. It is a world of simultaneity rather than sequence.

The concept of a beginning, or one sole principle on which the world relies, consequently presents itself as, myths and metaphors which humans reach for in order to make meaning out of the world. The form of the novel is thus also an inadequate mode of representation: »Was tut man nicht alles, um das Einstweh zu stillen! Kein Erzählen, kein Erinnern, nicht der tiefste Roman füllt diesen Zeitenschlund.«[50] The way in which a story is told – a novel narrated – necessarily has to be rethought:

Als er einem Freund der Fortschrittsmelancholie anläßlich einer Aitmatow-Novelle leise einwand, daß ihm zwar die poetischen Zeremonien des Abschieds teuer seien,

---

47 Strauß, Beginnlosigkeit, p. 6.
48 Strauß, Beginnlosigkeit, p. 94.
49 »Autopoiesis« literally means »self-creation« and was originally coined by the two Chilean biologists Humberto R. Maturana and Francisco J. Varela in the 1970s with regard to the biological cell. An autopoietic system is characterized by being an autonomous and self-maintaining unity which reproduces itself. It stands in opposition to an allopoietic system which produces something other than itself. According to Maturana and Varela the nervous system is such an autopoietic system. Through the theory of the autopoietic system Maturana and Varela aimed to answer the questions what is life and what is cognition. The answer they arrived at was that life is not a property of a system's parts, but emerges as a result of the interaction of its parts, and cognition is the process of this interaction (Maturana and Varela). Although unfortunately beyond the scope of this study, regarding cognition as a process of interaction between the parts of a self-generating system seems an interesting analogy to the implications of the database form which forsakes sequence in favour of simultaneity (see my essay »Once upon a time there was a Database« for further elaboration).
50 Strauß, Beginnlosigkeit, p. 54.

daß gleichwohl das Erinnern selbst ungerührt nicht das alte bleiben könne und es wenig wahrhaftig erscheine, wenn einer noch schildere, wie Technik die Heimat, die Lebenswelt zerstöre, da man längst in eine Phase übergewechselt sei, in der gerade die neuere Technik ein Rücksichern erst ermögliche und inspiriere, so daß es dem Roman nicht weiterhin darum gehen könne, die Spinngewebe des Vergehens über Mensch und Landschaft zu breiten, ja, daß Vergänglichkeit in einem größeren Kristall- oder Glasfibergedächtnis ihren Raum erst neu zu finden hätte, inmitten der empfindlichsten Spiegelungen und Retrospekte, die an die Stelle der zerbrochenen Überlieferung getreten seien und dem Lebensgefühl der ›epischen Wehmut‹ den geschichtlichen Grund entzögen – ach, während er es aussprach, torkelte er in seinen Eröffnungen schon, denn er erschrak darüber, wie sehr von Wunsch und Illusion verseucht diese ganz und gar zutreffenden Feststellungen waren.[51]

The novel is encouraged to give up on epic melancholy – the longing for explanations and a world before technology – and find a new space for itself within the computer database (»Kristall- oder Glasfibergedächtnis«). The wish for another kind of novel that is able to deal with a world without a beginning is thus linked to the world of modern technology. As in the quotation by Strauß in *Frankfurter Allgemeine*, there is a fundamental conflict at play between the condition of modern life and the genre of the novel. When there is no beginning, the soothing qualities of the novel, which Ulrich in *MoE* described as »sun on your tummy«, are also rendered apparently useless: »Es schmerzte ihn das Lesen im Roman, jede Zeile wurde ein Streckbett, weil die Vorstellungswelt leer blieb.«[52]

Significant, for our purpose here, is the implication that digital media and information technology contribute an adequate metaphor for describing a world without beginning:

Viele gängige Metaphern, die bildkräftig sind – der Prägestock, Kette und Schuß, Hammer und Amboß –, stammen aus einer technisch längst vergangenen Welt, ja, sie sind insgeheim wohl sogar Metaphern, Übertragungen, Bezüglichkeiten von einst zu heute. Wer mag schon einen Chip zum Gleichnis nehmen? Und doch gehörte es sich.[53]

And information technology becomes a key tool for understanding such a world:

Was für eine Welt, da sich der Dichter noch der Anschauung hingeben durfte, um die Natur der Dinge zu ergründen! Ein Sommerwald, ein Mineral, ein pockennarbiges Gesicht – und nun in die konturlose Schwingung der Materie verstoßen, da alles Wesentliche im Unsichtbaren geschieht. Seit langem sind Einsichten in die Natur nicht

---

51 Ibid. pp. 25-26.
52 Ibid. p. 77.
53 Ibid. pp. 94-95.

mehr eidetisch, sondern technisch inspiriert. Der Computer ist das Mikroskop der heutigen Naturforscher.[54]

In the world of *Beginnlosigkeit* the computer is thus both a descriptive image and a tool for exploration of this world, not least because the notion of time and space in a digital environment bears resemblance to the world-without-beginning described by Strauss in *Beginnlosigkeit*. In *Mediensimulation als Schreibstrategie* Philip Löser argues with regard to the function of the computer references in *Beginnlosigkeit* that:

> Der Verweis auf Computertechnologie fungiert dabei sehr präzise als doppelte Argumentationshilfe. Zum einen wird der Computer als Intensivierer einer Entwicklung gedeutet, bei der dem Menschen das Interesse an klar umrissenen Bedeutungen oder fest gefügten bildlichen Vorstellungen abhanden kommt. [...] Der zweite Gesichtspunkt, unter dem der Computer einen Bewußtseinswandel vorantreibt, ist die Möglichkeit, dank seiner Hilfe bisher ungeahnte Komplexitätsgrade von Wechselwirkungen in der Natur handhabbar zu machen.[55]

However, the computer also serves a third purpose in *Beginnlosigkeit* in so far as its logic (as seen in the database) embodies the search for a form that responds to a world without beginning – a space without temporal constraints. The digital database can thus be viewed as a structural model for the composition of *Beginnlosigkeit*. In many ways *Beginnlosigkeit* presents itself as if Goethe had chosen only to publish the archive sections of *Wanderjahre* and shredded the epic plot altogether. However, there is no archival organising principle of either pertinence or provenance to be identified. Original order and origin are both rendered obsolete. Content and structure seem completely separate and the text therefore has more of the characteristics of a database than a print archive.[56]

Through its structure *Beginnlosigkeit* thus thematizes the conditions for telling a story in a world in which beginnings and causality are rendered obsolete. In order to fulfil this task the database is evoked as an image that embodies the new conditions of representation in which narration is not an adequate mode:

---

54 Ibid. p. 68.

55 Löser, p. 248.

56 Interestingly, the archive is a recurring metaphor in Strauß's œuvre. In *Paare, Passanten* (1981) he writes: »Indem wir die Maschinen der integrierten Schaltkreise erfanden und bauten, die Computer, Datenbänke, Superspeicher – wurden wir nicht insgeheim von der Idee geleitet, daß die entscheidende kulturelle Leistung unseres Zeitalters darin bestehen müsse, Summe zu ziehen, eine unermeßliche Sammlung, ein Meta-Archiv, ein Riesengedächtnis des menschlichen Wissens zu schaffen, um uns selbst gleichzeitig von diesem zu verabschieden, unsere subjektive Teilhabe daran zu verlieren? Im Grunde ist die Idee des Computers eine der Lagerung, des Horts und der Zusammenfassung und als solche scheint sie eher die Ablösung vom bisherigen Fortschritts- und Expansionsdenken zu begleiten.« (Strauß, Paare, Passanten, pp. 193-94).

Die Unmittelbarkeit der technisch inspirierten Entrückung erfährt man allerdings um den Preis ihrer epischen Mittelbarkeit. Sie zu *erzählen* wäre ebenso unangemessen, als wollte man den ›Handlungsstrang‹ einer Epiphanie knüpfen. Man entfällt in einer zufälligen Minute an einen zufälligen Ort der Vergangenheit. Dieser Vorgang kommt der Ohnmacht näher als der bewußten Erinnerung.[57]

The condition of Beginnlosigkeit is consequently not only present as a motif and recurring theme – it is also explicitly manifested in the structure of the text, which consists of approximately 250 aphorisms (few of which are over one page long) that make the text as a whole appear as a vibrating field of simultaneity rather than a coherent narrative. This brings us to one of the central features of the text: the search for form, which we have seen figure so prominently in *Wanderjahre, MoE*, and *ZT*. In a certain sense, *Beginnlosigkeit* is essentially about perception and about finding form between order and chaos. And as we saw in the discussion of the database, form-finding does not have to be linear, continuous, or even narrative: »Form ist nicht nur Marmorlinie. Nicht nur Versprofil. Form ist auch: unabsehbare Form.«[58]

The idea of exploring this in a literary genre whose subject matter is published in print is a bold one, because this medium appears to favour linearity and temporality.[59] Considering the text's aim of finding a form that is adequate for a world without beginning, which we see on both a thematic and a structural level, it is interesting that the text nonetheless offers small drops of narrative in which we encounter a male protagonist and see the blurred contours of his world. Narrative should, per definition, stand in opposition to a world of Beginnlosigkeit in so far as a narrative plot enforces a notion of sequence (beginning, middle, and end), because even in its most basic form it involves a character coming into a world and doing something in it. Despite this, the text cannot rid itself of this »epic melancholy«. But it transforms narrative into something very different from that which is traditionally implied by the novel genre; challenging it to the very limit and ensuring that the justification for describing the text as a novel becomes doubtful.

---

57 Strauß, Beginnlosigkeit, p. 81.

58 Ibid. p. 61.

59 However, Barbara Maria Stafford argues in *Echo Objects* that even printed books embody the notion of fragmentation within them: »Printed book formats, for example, embody a foliated order that perceptibly intermingles scattered information. But the ritualized act of turning a leaf also breaks up the assembly of the text. The practise of thread binding, both in the West and in China, created an interruptive ›economy of reversal‹. The mere fact of tying loose papers together enabled accidental manifestations of the unexpected and the unknown to show themselves. Discontinuity and fragmentation was thus lodged at the heart of serial structure.« (Stafford, p. 53).

The inclination towards form-finding in what has no form finds its outlet in the subtitle of *Beginnlosigkeit* »Reflexionen über Fleck und Linie«, which refers to a central dichotomy in the text between the blurred spot and the wilful line, an opposition which becomes a leitmotif:

Der Fleck und die Linie.
Er ist alles seelisch Gemeinte, nicht konturierbar, in mehrdeutiger Gestalt verlaufend.
Sie ist die gebündelte Helle, und ihr Mysterium ist ihr offenes Ende, ihre Unabsehbarkeit. Liebe ist Fleck, Schrift ist Linie. Gesicht ist Fleck, Schritte sind Linie.[60]

In this quotation the relation between the spot and the line is beautifully summarised in almost poetic terms. We encounter the spot and the line as opposites – representing contrasting logics resembling *MoE*'s characterisation of the oscillation between emotion as condition and process – but also as personified and gendered species in a symbiotic love affair. In its short form this passage thus condenses the dilemma of the text in choosing between narration and non-narration. The issue here is highly theoretical – it is not a topic that lends itself to narration – yet the abstract concepts »Fleck« and »Linie« are transformed into persons and a story arises in spite of itself. The spot is vibrating standstill and simultaneity; the line is ephemeral movement and sequence. In the description of this relationship between the spot and the line we obtain an insight into why narrative is not abandoned even in a world without a beginning where causality and temporality have been rendered obsolete. The movement that a narrative lends to a text is one half of a complementary pair. The other half, the non-narrative challenge of linear temporality and continuous space, is articulated by the concrete material sign of the database. Reading this text we are not in doubt that, had it not been for the computer, Strauß would have written a very different book.

3.1.5 Combinatorics and complexity management

In the article »Narrating Bits. Encounters between Humans and Intelligent Machines« N. Katherine Hayles writes:

The larger goal is to open new possibilities for understanding the changing roles of narrative in a digital age, when the age-old ability of narrative to shape and express human subjectivity is coming into intimate contact with the capacity of intelligent machines to store, process, and generate massive amounts of data. [...] I cannot imagine a human world without narrative, but I can imagine narratives transformed and

---

60 Strauß, Beginnlosigkeit, p. 71.

enriched by their interactions with the possibility space in the complex ecologies of contemporary media and culture.[61]

Rand, Nox, and *Beginnlosigkeit* each illustrate in different ways the implications that the database may have had for printed novels in the early 1990s in their approach to narration and human identity. These novels show us the challenges and possibilities that face the contemporary novel in its mediation between the narrative and the database's subversion of causal and temporal sequences. Furthermore, they provide us more generally with an example of the ways in which information technology can act as a symbolic form for conditions of contemporary culture, offering modes of description and tools for handling information overload and its resulting complexitiy. The narrative negotiations going on in these novels are in dialogue with those that have been present in the novel genre since its emergence, and should not be regarded as a »machine-logic« only coming into being with the pervasive impact of information technology on our world. However, the conditions of living in an information society have accentuated the need for narrative negotiation, and the rendition of this negotiation in the three examples at which we have been looking in this chapter, gives us an insight into how the impact of information technology is reflected in our cultural imagination. In *Wanderjahre* we saw how the figure of the archive, organised according to a principle of provenance, was incorporated into the narrative expectations of the novel. The disparate form of *Wanderjahre* as an »Archivroman« thus reflects the novel's representation of the condition of human existence played out between a fixed role in life and a continuous process of becoming in the early nineteenth century. By focussing on the database we gain an insight into the nature of the relationship between human beings and technology in the late twentieth century. In the negotiation between narrative and database logic in the three novels dealt with in this chapter we have seen the combinatorics and complexity management that the database embodies reflected in the novels' representation of human existence as a multitude of possible combinations which, while avoiding an absolute unity, do not abandon all hope of achieving the closure inherent in narrative representation.

The three works discussed in this chapter are all from the early 1990s, This is not to imply that the database characteristics we have identified are not equally prevalent today. It merely suggests that imagery based on information technology evoked in a European context in the early 1990s was often linked to that of databases, because that was the dominant association

61 Hayles, Narrating Bits, p. 185.

of digital technology in this period. When we turn to the hyperlink as a mode of navigation, which in common perception is closely linked to the internet, other connotations ascribed to information technology are emphasised. This is reflected in the way information technology is used, not only as a metaphor and motif, but also in the construction of narrative structures in the course of the 1990s during which the internet became known in circles outside the limited academic and technical ones in which it had developed. As we shall see, in comparison with the database, the hyperlink emphasises navigation between data rather than the data's configuration. This highlights other characteristics of information technology as a symbolic form and it is to these that we shall now turn.

3.2 Hyperlink Constructions: Navigating the Connections

Of all the concepts used in this study, that of the hypertext is probably the one that has been the most used and misused since it was first coined in the mid-1960s. We shall therefore consider it cautiously. Before attempting to get to grips with its manifold theoretical connotations we shall observe how the principles on which it relies are discussed and enacted in the novel *Finder sted* [Taking place] (1998) by the Danish author Svend Åge Madsen. By first observing the principle of the hyperlink as it is discussed and incorporated as part of a fictional narrative, it becomes easier to recognise the characteristics that make it so foreign to linear narrative exposition, while it remains engaging for narrative experiments.

3.2.1 »I have the modest plan of leaving behind my brain« Svend Åge Madsen's *Finder sted*

During lunch Luis carefully explained how he occupied himself after he had retired. […]
›I started writing my memoirs. I have met many famous people. Created their style, or just worked for them occasionally or met them in another connection.‹
He mentioned a long list of people, some of whom were famous in different areas, others Kaare recognized without being able to place them.
›But I quickly discovered that it was not my genre. It became an empty, clumsy listing of events. Or rather: It was not what I wanted. I did not dream of creating an easily read, superficial story of my many different experiences, one after the other. What I wanted was to capture the events and situations of my life in their totality, in their complexity.‹

While he was talking he arranged three different kinds of cheese on the plate. He separated tomatoes, lettuce leaves, bread, grapes.

›Separately they are nothing special, but already two of them together make an exciting combination for the taste buds.‹

He stuck the fork in a cube of pepper and an exquisite piece of cheese. Tasted it with pleasure. Carefully finished chewing before he allowed a mouthful of red wine to follow.

›Therefore I started to collect my memories. All sorts of memories, large and small, as they entered my mind. I transferred them to the computer. The sequence was, so to speak, unimportant. What was important for me were the connections between them. I try to store them the way we must imagine that they are stored in our brain. With countless available couplings between them.‹[62]

The novel *Finder sted* (1998) tells the story of Kaare, who, after a failed suicide attempt and subsequent hospital admission, tries to find his way back to life. He is hired by a mysterious woman who aims to give attempted suicides new zest for life by giving them an assignment: either be shadowed by or shadow others. This provides them with a purpose in life and attempts to re-establish a stable sense of causality. However, Kaare tires of the project and flees to Madeira, where he meets and falls in love with a local woman, Catarina, whose actions he discovers he can control with his thoughts, just as she can control his. Cause and effect are thus turned upside down. On Madeira he also meets the retired fashion designer Luis, who claims to have created Catarina and who is in the process of transferring his memory into a gigantic computer. However, Kaare's shadowers catch up

---

62 The novel has not been translated into English. The translation is my own. The original text will be quoted in footnotes: »Under frokosten forklarede Luis omhyggeligt hvad han fik tiden til at gå med efter at have trukket sig tilbage. […]

›Jeg begyndte at nedskrive mine erindringer. Jeg har truffet mange berømte mennesker. Skabt deres stil, eller bare arbejdet for dem lejlighedsvis, eller truffet dem i anden sammenhæng.‹

Han nævnte en lang række navne, hvoraf nogle berømte fra forskellige områder, andre genkendte Kaare uden at kunne placere dem.

›Men jeg fandt hurtigt ud af at det ikke var min genre. Det blev til tom, klodset opremsning. Eller rettere: Det var ikke det jeg havde lyst til. Jeg drømte ikke om at lave en letlæst, overfladisk fortælling ud af mine mange forskellige oplevelser, den ene efter den anden. Det jeg ønskede var at fange mine livshændelser og situationer i deres totalitet, i deres kompleksitet.‹

Mens han fortalte arrangerede han tre forskellige stykker ost på tallerkenen. Han adskilte tomat, salatblad, brød, vindrue.

›Hver for sig er de ikke noget særligt. Men allerede to af dem sammen udgør en spændende kombination for smagsløgene.‹

Han stak gaflen i en terning peberfrugt og et udsøgt stykke ost. Smagte nydende på den. Tyggede omhyggeligt af munden før han lod en mundfuld rødvin følge efter.

›Derfor begyndte jeg at samle mine erindringer. Alle mulige, store og små som de faldt mig ind. Jeg kørte dem ind på computeren. Rækkefølgen var så at sige ligegyldig. Det der var vigtigt var forbindelserne mellem dem. Jeg prøver at lagre dem sådan som vi må forestille os de er opbevarede i vores hjerne. Med utallige frie koblinger mellem dem.‹« (Madsen, pp. 93-94).

with him, and when one of them falls off a cliff close to where Kaare has settled, he stands accused of murder. He now has to search through his own memory to find out how he has become who he is and what kind of man he would like to be in order to clear his name and restore his connection with Catarina after the supernatural correspondence which allowed them to read each other's minds wears off.

On the thematic level of *Finder sted* we see a desire for the simplicity of linear narrativity. The story of how Kaare and Catarina come to understand one another by telling each other stories seems to advocate storytelling as the best way for human beings to understand themselves and each other. However, on the level of the novel's structure we can identify a radical hesitation towards telling the story in a straightforward manner which goes beyond mere postponement of the dénouement of the plot. The way in which the novel is narrated displays a preference for presenting a huge amount of data with a countless number of non-linear couplings. The principle of Luis' pompous, computer-generated copy of his own brain is thus echoed in the form in which this novel is told.

In the above quotation, Luis outlines his considerations on how to write his memoirs. He continues with the words:

This comprehensive database constitutes *Luis Mendes Viera's Memoirs*. Not just the pitiful extract other self-centred people publish. Three hundred pages of small talk about how this happened and then that happened. The database can, of course, be read in that way. I have the modest plan of leaving behind my brain. Or at least the content of my memoirs, unedited and yet easy to orient oneself in.[63]

What Luis creates is essentially a gigantic database containing all his memories. Rather than writing a straightforward narration, he aims to maintain the complexity of his mind's associations of, thus replacing the importance of sequence with a focus on connections. In his conversation with Kaare, Luis elaborates on the vast system of connections between his memories and how this sytem can be read. This shows the particular sense of spatial arrangement and the importance of navigation in what he is attempting to do:

The quality of the work does not depend on me, but solely on the reader: how good you are at choosing material and combining it.‹
    While Luis spoke Kaare looked at the dizzying view before his eyes. Luis noticed.

---

63 »Hele den omfattende database udgør Luis Mendes Vieiras Erindringer. Ikke bare det sørgelige udkog som andre selvoptagne mennesker udsender. Tre hundrede siders småsnak om så skete der dét, så skete der dét. Sådan kan basen selvfølgelig også læses. Jeg har, i al beskedenhed, planer om at efterlade mig min hjerne. Eller i hvert fald indholdet af mine erindringer, uredigerede og alligevel lette at finde omkring i.« (Madsen, p. 99).

›In the same way as you can approach the landscape before us. You can focus randomly, here and there. You can form an overview; you can follow a road or what moves. Or carefully observe what takes place at a certain spot. Therefore you can enjoy the view for a long time every day and still have a new experience. You can say that *My memories* constitutes a mental landscape.[64]

Bringing to mind the way in which the network formation of *MoE* encouraged a reading similar to that of de Certeau's distinction between the viewer and the walker, which we saw in chapter 2.2, memory is in this quotation described as a spatial field in which one can linger. It is a space where you are obliged to make your own choices rather than having a story presented to you, one in which the decisive choices have already been made for you. This points back to the novel's title *Finder sted*, »Taking place«. The word »finder« in Danish has the connotation of »finding« – the novel is not only *taking* place, it is also constantly *finding* its place. The title is derived from a quotation by the Portuguese poet Luis de Camões (1524-1580) cited at the beginning of the novel. During his stay on Madeira Kaare embarks on translating his most famous work, Portugal's national epos, *Os Lucíadas*. *Os Lucíadas* is an epic poem focusing on the expedition of Vasco da Gama, but written in the tradition of Homer's *Odyssey* and Virgil's *Aeneid*. It portrays the Portuguese as descendants of Lusus, a companion of Dionysus who, according to myth, founded Lusitania, a Roman province which approximates to present-day Portugal. Through the shared first name of Luis de Camões, our retired designer (Luis), and Dionysus' companion (Lusus), a parallel is established between the epic – depicting grand geographical discoveries – and Luis' project of presenting his memories as a giant landscape that can be explored. Whereas the movement of *Os Lucíadas* is extrovert, going out into the world to conquer new land, the movement of Luis' computer is introvert, penetrating the hidden recesses of the mind. Both projects are, however, driven by the aim of »finding« something, of finding or creating a place or a space. This occupation with the spatial is also reflected in the structure of the novel itself. It consists of twelve chapters, but instead of being called chapters, which would indicate a temporal sequence, they are

---

64 »Kvaliteten af værket afhænger ikke af mig, men udelukkende af aflæseren: hvor god man er til at udvælge stof og kombinere det.‹

Mens den anden talte gled Kaares blik over den svimlende udsigt der udbredte sig foran hans øjne. Luis havde åbenbart bemærket det.

›På samme måde som man kan gå til landskabet foran os. Man kan slå ned tilfældigt, hist og her. Man kan danne sig overblik, man kan følge en vej, eller hvad der bevæger sig. Eller nøje iagttage hvad der udspiler sig på et bestemt punkt. Derfor kan man nyde synet lang tid hver dag, og stadig få en ny oplevelse. Man kan sige at Mine erindringer udgør et mentalt landskab.‹« (Madsen, p. 100).

called »first place«, »second place«, and so on, which fuses the chronological sequence with the spatial sensation of moving through a landscape.[65]

In the disruption of causal and temporal sequences that occurs in this novel we encounter many of the traits of a database logic that we identified in the previous chapter. However, the novel also introduces us to another theme that is similarly related to information technology, but not accounted for by the aesthetics of the figure of the database: the linking of the computer to issues of memory and the functions of the human mind as an associational network. At play are issues of connections, navigation, and networks, which are accentuated in a way that resembles what Manovich calls »navigable space«.[66] By navigable space Manovich means the computer's preference for representing abstract information as spatial experiences. This means that all kinds of data is rendered in three dimensions through computer visualisation. This is not only something we find in the interactive 3-D spaces of computer games and virtual reality, but in most interfaces; and hyperlinking is one of the principles that have been at the heart of envisaging text in spatial terms. Having encountered Luis and his desire to turn his memory into a navigable landscape, we are now in a position to approach the hyperlink as a technological and cultural phenomenon, before returning to look more closely at how the hyperlink principle can be employed in the structure of a printed novel and thereby point to the way in which the hyperlink can be regarded as a concrete material sign of information technology as a symbolic form.

3.2.2 Hyperlink configurations

A hyperlink may be defined as the connection through which one moves from one text or image to another in a computer environment. It resembles a citation or cross-reference in so far as it refers the reader of a given text to another text or image. Usually these links are represented by highlighted words or images which, when clicked, lead to another location. Hyperlinks provide a way of linking large bodies of information – and they do so by

---

65 This focus on the spatial qualities of text brings to mind Mikhail Bakthin's notion of the chronotope which emphasises the interdependency of time and space. According to Bakthin different types of chronotopes (i.e. relationships between time and space) manifest themselves differently in different types of writing. In *Finder sted* the inherent linearity of time is constantly contrasted and challenged by space as a way of breaking open and reassembling the chronological events: »It was as if he lived contrary to time« (Madsen, p. 21).

66 Navigable space is one of the two cultural forms which Manovich focuses on in *The Language of New Media* (the other is the database). We shall return to this notion in chapter 3.3 on computer games, but I want to evoke it here in connection with what we see in *Finder sted* and as a transition to looking at what the concept of hyperlinking entails.

presenting specific information in a spatial rather than a linear fashion. Like a database, a hyperlink can be regarded as an attempt to counter information overload. A hugely successful implementation of the hypertext principle is, of course, the World Wide Web, invented and implemented by Tim Berners-Lee in the 1990s.

Hypertext was one of the first principles derived from the computer medium to spark off considerable conceptual interest within the humanities. First coined by the American sociologist and philosopher Theodor Nelson in the mid-1960s, its development coincided with the dissemination of poststructuralist ideas on the death of the author, multi-linearity, and an endless postponement of the signifier – all of which hypertext seemed to embody. In 1994, George P. Landow, one of the first literary theorists to occupy himself with hypertext, remarked:

Hypertext, an information technology consisting of individual blocks of text, or lexias, and the electronic links that join them, has much in common with recent literary and critical theory. For example, like much recent work by poststructuralists, such as Roland Barthes and Jacques Derrida, hypertext reconceives conventional, long-held assumptions about authors and readers and the texts they write and read. Electronic linking, which provides one of the defining features of hypertext, also embodies Julia Kristeva's notions of intertextuality, Mikhail Bakhtin's emphasis upon multivocality, Michel Foucault's conceptions of networks of power, and Gilles Deleuze and Felix Guattari's ideas of rhizomatic, ›nomad thought‹.[67]

This statement can be regarded as emblematic of the first generation of studies bridging information technology and literary studies. Poststructuralist theory has had an enormous influence on the understanding of hypertext. As Rasmus Blok has noted, this convergence between critical theory and information technology meant that the reception of hypertext was infused from the beginning with a utopian potential, and for this reason hypertext was primarily regarded as a laboratory for the principles voiced by poststructuralist theories.[68] This can likewise be seen in the early literary experiments with hypertext published on CD-ROM and online in the 1990s.[69] This convergence between information technology and contemporary critical theory has been extensively discussed, for instance by George P. Landow, Jay David Bolter, J. Yellowlees Douglas, and Stuart Moulthrop. However, as early as 1997, Espen Aarseth warned against relating hypertext directly to poststructuralist theories:

---

67 Landow, Hyper/Text/Theory, p. 1.
68 Blok, p. 407f.
69 In the 1990s two software programs especially designed for electronic fiction became available: *Storyspace* and *Intermedia*. Michael Joyce's *Afternoon. A story* is probably the most discussed work of electronic fiction created in this period.

Some of these writers used words such as *network* and *link* to illustrate that texts are not isolated islands of meaning but ongoing dialogues of repetition, mutation, and re-combination of signs. However, to read these theorists' claims as a call for a new type of text (hypertext) is to mistake their descriptive, epistemological investigation of signification (and their critique of certain previous paradigms) for a normative attack on the limits of a specific communication technology (printing).[70]

This statement highlights the caution with which this convergence should be approached. We shall not go into detail here on the way in which the in-dividual theories of Barthes, Derrida, Foucault, Kristeva or Deleuze resem-ble the hypertext principle, as they are issues which have been dealt with extensively elsewhere.[71] We shall limit ourselves to observing that such a convergence can be identified and may be taken as an indication that infor-mation technology is indeed in dialogue with current epistemological and philosophical trends, whether or not poststructuralist theorists intended to go beyond printed text. However, we want to avoid the utopian belief in hypertext often found in this first generation of enquiries into its potential for literary and cultural studies. What is important for this study of the hy-perlink as a concrete material sign of information technology as a symbolic form is not so much those theories that it potentially illustrates, but what kind of representation it facilitates on a much more basic level. Only then can we proceed to look at the way in which the hyperlink as a concrete ma-terial sign is in dialogue with contemporary literary undertakings.

Theodor Nelson coined the term hypertext in the mid-1960s in connec-tion with the development of Project Xanadu (software aiming to go beyond the simulation of paper by the technique of hypertext). However, the cue had been given almost twenty years earlier by the American engineer Van-nevar Bush. The first description of the principle behind hypertext is gener-ally ascribed to Bush's article »As We May Think« from 1945 which sug-gests a new cataloguing technique – a device by the name of »Memex« which works through associational selection (like the way in which the hu-man brain was believed to work) rather than alphabetical selection:

When data of any sort are placed in storage, they are filed alphabetically or numeri-cally, and information is found (when it is) by tracing it down from subclass to sub-class. It can be in only one place, unless duplicates are used; one has to have rules as to which path will locate it, and the rules are cumbersome. Having found one item, moreover, one has to emerge from the system and re-enter on a new path. The human mind does not work that way. It operates by association. With one item in its grasp, it snaps instantly to the next that is suggested by the association of thoughts, in accor-

---

70 Aarseth, Cybertext, pp. 83-84.
71 See, for instance, Landow, Hypertext; or Landow, Hypertext 2.0.

dance with some intricate web of trails carried by the cells of the brain. It has other characteristics, of course; trails that are not frequently followed are prone to fade, items are not fully permanent, memory is transitory. Yet the speed of action, the intricacy of trails, the detail of mental pictures, is awe-inspiring beyond all else in nature. Man cannot hope fully to duplicate this mental process artificially, but he certainly ought to be able to learn from it. In minor ways, he may even improve, for his records have relative permanency. The first idea, however, to be drawn from the analogy concerns selection. Selection by association, rather than by indexing, may yet be mechanised.[72]

Here we see the motivation for the development of the hypertext principle and its affinity with research into cybernetics and artificial intelligence which also got under way in the 1940s: the wish to come up with a way of linking information which was as effective as the brain's memory and allowed for efficient retrieval from, and navigation in, large data material.

When we talk about hyperlinks we are essentially talking about how information is linked and therefore about how information is navigated. It is precisely this idea of navigating information through association and seeking to imitate the brain's way of working which separates the hypertext principle from other ways of cataloguing material. This parallel between the associational abilities of human memory and the development of hypertext has been explored by, among others, Janine Wong and Peter Storkerson, and Peter Matussek, who in different ways argue that antiquity's »ars memoriae« can be seen as a predecessor of hypertext. In *The Art of Memory* (1966), the English historian Frances A. Yates outlined how the rhetoricians of antiquity learned their speeches by heart by placing the pieces of text they had to remember in an imaginary physical setting – for instance the rooms in a house. Thus memory could be regarded as a stroll through this imaginary environment. Hypertext is in the same way a spatial arrangement which takes the form of a movement between sets of information that are already situated and internally connected. As we have seen, at the heart of hypertext is a conception of the text in which each link leads to another text in a movement that resembles the mind's ability to associate. However, the difference[73] is first and foremost that, whereas for the rhetoricians of antiquity the material was situated in their own mind, the hypertext navigation takes place in a virtual space which exists separately from the individual human mind. Hypertext can thus be regarded as a form which communicates an experience and a representation of the world in which the mind's

---

72 Bush, p. 106.

73 For a more detailed problematization of the analogy between mind and computer see, for instance, Tabbi, p. 120f.

associational patterns have become external and thereby less subjective. Lev Manovich indicates something along these lines when he describes hypermedia and interactivity:

Before, we would read a sentence of a story or a line of a poem and think of other lines, images, memories. Now interactive media asks us to click on a highlighted sentence to go to another sentence.[74]

If we regard the hyperlink as a concrete material sign of information technology as a symbolic form in Cassirer's sense, we are looking at a form which primarily accentuates the transitions between the textual fragments and the spatial qualities of the text, rather than the establishment of a coherent temporal sequence with a beginning, a middle, and an end. As was the case with the database, it can thus be argued that the principle of hyperlinking carries characteristics which challenge a traditional narrative sequence. It does so in a way that resembles the characteristics of the network which we looked at in chapter 2.2 in relation to Robert Musil's *MoE*. Here we saw the network as a figure with an inherent resistance towards causal linearity, which in *MoE* is employed to discuss the conditions of modern existence and how it can be represented. *MoE* is historically situated precisely in this period of semantic transition of the word »network« in which it becomes more and more common to use the figure as part of a social analysis. If we look at how the significance of the network figure developed between Musil's time and our own, we see that, in the second half of the twentieth century, the network figure became more and more dominant in mathematical, philosophical, and sociological discourses as a cultural and social metaphor for the complexity of modern life. Most radical is probably system theory, which relies on a conception of the world as having a network structure. General system theory was proposed by the Austrian biologist Ludwig von Bertalanffy in the late 1940s; developing through cybernetics and chaos theory through to complex adaptive theory, it is an interdisciplinary field which deals with any complex system ranging from ant hills to the nervous system. A complex system is defined by having a network topology, and issues such as nonlinearity, feedback loops, autopoiesis and nesting are especially addressed under this rubric. In particular, the German sociologist Niklas Luhmann has worked to develop system theory as a way also of approaching social and cultural aspects of society.

Apart from system theory, the contemporary understanding of networks is to a great degree informed by Gilles Deleuze and Felix Guattari's famous

---

74 Manovich, The Language of New Media, p. 61.

notion of the *rhizome*.[75] The rhizome can best be described as a non-hierarchical network:

The rhizome is an acentered, nonhierarchical, nonsignifying system without a General and without an organizing memory or central automaton, defined solely by a circulation of states.[76]

To Deleuze and Guattari the introduction of the rhizome is part of a deconstructive project that aims to do away with the hierarchical root-tree model which they regard as enforcing organized systems of power and domination.[77] We thus see how the interest in the network figure hinges on the manner in which the nodes are connected, which carries significant connotations for the comprehension of the network structure at hand. In the early twentieth century the image of the network (as we saw in *MoE*) carried labyrinthine connotations, highlighting as it did the alienation and confusion felt by man in a modern world filled with railways, telephones, and telegraphs. However, it also embodied the vague beginnings of a social interpretation of the network and the possibilities it holds (conceptualised as Möglichkeitssinn in *MoE*) which we see accentuated in the connotations ascribed to the network figure in the conception of the network informed by system theory and the rhizome in the later half of the twentieth century.

The connections made in a hypertext are – although programmed by the programmer – largely dependent on the reader. In *Writing Space. The Computer in the History of Literacy*, Jay David Bolter remarks that:

A hypertext has no canonical order. Every path defines an equally convincing and appropriate reading, and in that simple fact the reader's relationship to the text changes radically. A text as a network has no univocal sense; it is a multiplicity without the imposition of a principle of domination.[78]

---

75 Interestingly, Carl Jung had already described life as a rhizome in the prologue to his autobiography *Memories, Dreams, Reflections*.

76 Deleuze and Guattari, p. 21.

77 Deleuze and Guattari set up a number of principles to define the concept of the rhizome. Firstly and secondly, the rhizome is governed by the principles of connection and heterogenity. This means that any point of a rhizome system can be connected to any other point. It is non-hierarchical in its structure in so far as no point comes before another when all points are connected. Thirdly, thinking rhizomatically means that it is the lines between the nodes that are important, not the point of contact. What influences a certain node comes from a multiplicity of angles; not one force of influence in particular. Fourthly, we find the »principle of asignifying rupture«; this means that the rhizome may be »shattered at a given spot, but will start up again on one of its old lines, or on new lines«. Finally, there are the principles of »cartography« and »decalcomania«. These principles state that the rhizome is not a tracing mechanism, but is a map with multiple entry points (Deleuze and Guattari, p. 7f.).

78 Bolter, p. 25. See also David S. Miall's writings for a discussion of these aspects of hypertext.

The network form of the hypertext means that navigation and reading become non-linear and with no predetermined order. This gives, on the one hand, an enormous amount of options for the reader, but on the other hand, it also means that navigation can easily become incalculable, incomprehensible and, in its extreme form, pointless. Like a database, a hyperlink can be described as a model for organising information, but it is more difficult to study without implicating a user than a database is. As Luis says in *Finder sted*: »the quality of the work does not depend on me, but solely on the reader: how good you are at choosing material and combining it.«[79] What characterises the hyperlink is thus the *navigation* from one fragment to the other, which transforms the sequence into an associational network that allows for several different options at each crossroad. The less hierarchical manner of organisation is a central part of the reason why the hyperlink facilitates experiments that challenge linear narrativity.

The genre of hypertext fiction published online or on CD-ROM distinguishes itself by often exploring non-linearity and reader interaction. Besides referring to electronic literature, the term hypertext fiction is also used to describe printed novels such as Vladimir Nabokov's *Pale Fire* (1963) and Julio Cortazar's *Rayuela* (1963), both written around the time the term hypertext was coined by Theodor Nelson. However, the associational, fragmentary way of narrating which the hyperlink represents can be found from Laurence Sterne to Salman Rushdie. Musil's *MoE*, which we looked at in chapter 2.2, is but one particularly illuminating example that explicitly contemplates narrativity and its implications for the understanding and representation of human existence. The invention of hypertext might thus be said to radicalise already existing artistic tendencies, which is a recurring point in most writings on the literary implications of hypertext from Espen Aarseth to Janet Murray. Jay David Bolter in particular has worked on placing hypertext fiction in the same literary tradition as the avant-garde movements and modernism, comparing their attempt to destabilise the literary text:

In disrupting the stability of the text, interactive fiction belongs in a tradition of experimental literature [...] that has marked the 20th century – the era of modernism, futurism, Dada, surrealism, letterism, the nouveau roman, concrete poetry, and other movements of greater or lesser influence.[80]

Although such comparisons are useful for understanding the impact of information technology in a larger historical framework, they should be addressed with caution. The danger of such a view is that the literary tradition

---

79 Madsen, p. 100.
80 Bolter, p. 131.

comes to be seen as moving towards the redeeming computer screen, which can finally do what printed text has not been able to. By regarding the hyperlink as a concrete material sign of information technology as a symbolic form, it becomes possible to look upon it as a phenomenon which stands in a reciprocal relationship to the issues dealt with in the printed novel, rather than being its successor. Also, it is worth keeping in mind that, whereas fragmentation seems to be a key word for many of the literary movements which Bolter points out above, the hyperlink in fact seems rather to emphasise connection.[81] This will also become apparent from our reading of the fiction by Jan Kjærstad (1993-1999) and Reinhard Jirgl (2005). By approaching hypertext in a way that maintains an awareness of its historical heritage at the same time as acknowledging the accentuation of this form brought about by the daily exposure to hypertext-constructions in our everyday life and environment and the conceptual development of the figure of the network in the twentieth century, we can begin to scrutinize the exchange between the novel as a narrative genre and hypertext as a vocabulary for negotiating narrativity.

We shall now look at two particularly illuminating examples of printed novels which explicitly allude to hypertext principles in their way of representing contemporary society and the conditions of the human subject in a time which Reinhard Jirgl describes as »die nervöse Zeit«. For Jan Kjærstad, the hyperlink works as a generator for making a large, uneven, and even internally contradictory narrative material work together. For Reinhard Jirgl it becomes a much more performative, almost physical undertaking drawing the reader into the experience of the world that the novel opens up.

3.2.3 »Als ich das erste Mal von einem Computernetzwerk hörte, dachte ich sofort an Großmutters Kristallkandelaber.« Jan Kjærstad's *Forføreren, Erobreren, Oppdageren*

Rather than posting a novel on the web as a hypertext, I wish to bring the experiences from the web and the hypertexts (with their new possibilities of experience and recognition) into the novel. From one point of view *The Seducer* (1993) and *The Conqueror* (1996) are attempts in this direction. It is possible to incorporate the fan-

---

81 Stafford describes contemporary remix art as narrative taken to the extreme: »Unlike twentieth-century cut-and-paste collage techniques – juxtaposing recognizable snippets of the world – or earlier divisionist intarsia from mosaics to caricature, the new electronic recombinant media are seamless and endless. Such aggressive repurposings are not about creating physical and spatial adjacency among incongruent fragments. Rather, their intent is to produce morphed synchronization across complex multidimensional data.« (Stafford, p. 161).

shaped, multi-tracked forms that you see in an electronic text – the jumps from level to level – into a novel.[82]

That Kjærstad's Wergeland trilogy was inspired by the non-linear mode of writing of hypertext has frequently been remarked upon in the critical reception of the three novels,[83] and as illustrated by the quotation above Kjærstad himself has been quite explicit in his essays on the fact. It is thus hard to avoid mentioning this series of texts that became remarkably popular among the wider public in Scandinavia in the 1990s, although they did not avoid criticism for bombarding the reader with encyclopaedic amounts of information. Despite the experimental nature of the texts and Kjærstad's reputation for being a difficult read, the novels evidently hit a nerve which made them feel relevant for a large audience. The trilogy thus provides an intriguing point of comparison with Reinhard Jirgl's *Abtrünnig* to which we shall subsequently turn.

The Wergeland trilogy consists of *Forføreren* (1993), *Erobreren* (1996), and *Oppdageren* (1999).[84] It tells the story of the celebrated TV personality Jonas Wergeland, who returns from a business trip to Barcelona and finds his wife, Margrete, dead on the floor in their home. That is the starting point for the three volumes, in which four different narrators[85] give their version of Jonas Wergeland's life and the reason for Margrete's death. All circle around the question: »what is a human being?«

The story of Jonas Wergeland is in many senses a traditional narration of the »Bildung« of a man and his journey towards recognizing his own potential, which draws on intertextual references to Goethe's *Faust* and Henrik Ibsen's *Peer Gynt*. This thematic heritage clearly distinguishes it from other (especially online) experiments with the adaptation of hypertext conducted in 1990s, in which the story often became less important than the experiments with the new form and medium. Precisely because the Wergeland trilogy does not compromise its wish to tell a story about the conditions of existence for the modern human being in order to explore form, but manages to fuse these two, it is particularly interesting to examine how the form of the hypertext is put to work in these texts.

---

82 Kjærstad, Litteraturens mulighet, p. 259. My translation.

83 See, for instance, Mogensen.

84 In the following I shall refer to the German translations by Angelika Gundlach and Hinrich Schmidt-Henckel: *Der Verführer*, *Der Eroberer*, and *Der Entdecker*. The original Norwegian quotations will occur in the footnotes. The translations of Kjærstad's essays are my own.

85 Respectively Kamala Varma (Jonas' voluntary visitor from the prison) in *Forføreren*, Rakel (Jonas' sister) who dictates her story to an ageing professor in *Erobreren*, and finally Kristin (Jonas' daughter) supplemented by Jonas himself narrates in *Oppdageren*. This gives us three different versions of his life.

From the level of sentences to the level of chapters the story of Jonas Wergeland is told in small associative jumps which cause one story to be constantly interrupted by other stories which weave in and out of each other. The first two volumes consist of a number of smaller chapters which link to each other, while the third volume allows the stories to change within the same chapter. For instance, the chapter on how Margrete broke up with Jonas in sixth grade in *Forføreren* ends with a desperate Jonas lying in the ice rink with his heart broken. The following chapter takes place in 1972 when Jonas goes to Timbuktu in order to avoid the commotion around the Norwegian referendum on whether to be a part of the EU. The connection is emotional rather than causally or temporally motivated, since the story that leaves Jonas devastated on the ice is followed by a story about the wish to go as far away as possible. At the same time both chapters link to other chapters by the use of recurring words and images. Connection rather than fragmentation is thus emphasised in the trilogy. Words and images occur repeatedly and are connected to other stories through association, so that a network of connections is created within the text.[86] It is the navigation (the transition from one story to another), which on the one hand marks a selection, but on the other hand directs attention to the immense network of stories from which the stories that we are in fact told are chosen. This is the central approach to narrating employed in the Wergeland trilogy. As a comment on this way of telling a story, the professor who writes down the narration in *Erobreren* remarks:

Es passiert in den Zwischenräumen. Ab und zu habe ich Lust, bei diesen schwarzen Löchern, die an den Schnittpunkten zwischen Geschichten entstehen, innezuhalten, zu verweilen. Bei allem Ehrgeiz, das Wesentliche aus Jonas Wergelands Leben zu erzählen, kann ich mich von dem Verdacht nicht befreien, daß die größten Geschichten oder die Schlüssel hier verborgen liegen.[87]

The meaning that the narrator wants to capture escapes the stories, and this lost meaning is located in the movement from one story to the next. The se-

---

86 In comparison with *MoE* it is interesting to note that Kjærstad in the essay »Menneskets Nett« from 2004 reflects on *MoE* by using the figure of the web. Though writing in two significantly different historical contexts, Musil and Kjærstad seem to be struggling with parallel projects that deal with a wish to overcome a crisis in the genre of the novel which they both sense and link with the likewise problematic role of the human subject. Musil was informed by the discoveries and discussions in physics and psychology in the early twentieth century. Kjærstad is overwhelmed with information and information technology in the early twenty-first century.

87 Kjærstad, Der Eroberer, p. 376. »Det er i mellomrommene det skjer. Noen ganger får jeg lyst til å stoppe opp, dvele, ved disse svarte hullene som skapes i skjæringspunktet mellom to historier. Tross ambisjonen om å fortelle alt vesentlig i Jonas Wergelands liv, kan jeg ikke fri meg fra mistanken om at de største historiene, eller nøklene, ligger skjult her.« (Kjærstad, Erobreren, p. 320).

quence of the overall narration is thus made into a series of associative jumps. The same applies to time. Frederik Tygstrup worded this very well in a comment in 1994:»In *Forføreren* the sequence of time has been dissolved and frozen in a non-chronological row of time flakes whose mutual relations are more important than the sequence of time«.[88] As a principle of navigation the hypertext allows each fragment to contain a story. The challenge to the temporal sequence of the narrative and its preference for causal connections lies rather in the construction of the connections between all of the narrations.

In *Oppdageren* we see an example in miniature of the associative jumps in Kjærstad's way of narrating. It is also an example of how small narrations are woven in and out of each other even at the sentence level. In the following passage Jonas Wergeland tells a story from his childhood about the way in which you experience the world when you are standing with your head in the middle of a cut-glass chandelier and are putting the individual crystals back in their place:

Der Umgang mit diesen handgeschliffenen Glaskristallen hat mein Leben geprägt. Nichts kam diesem Erlebnis gleich, der festlichen Stimmung, die mich unter diesem Reifrock aus Kristallen erfüllte, in dem Licht, das er zugleich verteilte und sammelte. Als ich das erste Mal von einem Computernetzwerk hörte, dachte ich sofort an Großmutters Kristallkandelaber. Ich besaß eigentlich schon ein Prisma, seit ich ganz klein war, und spielte oft damit, fand es etwas Hübsches und in sich Vollkommenes. Erst als Großmutter ihren Kronleuchter hervorholte, begriff ich, dass mein Prisma zu einem größeren Ganzen gehörte. Es würde mich nicht wundern, wenn diese Erkenntnis für mein Projekt X bestimmend gewesen sein sollte, die Idee, die mir beinahe den Hals gebrochen hätte.[89]

Each sentence in this passage forms an independent unit that points to a certain place in Jonas Wergeland's life, but together they form a story that allows us to see – if not all of Jonas Wergeland's life – then, at least in glimpses, a considerable amount of it. Or – to remain within Kjærstad's use of metaphors – you could say that each sentence consists of a crystal that is a unit in itself, but whose function and full potential is not unleashed until it is placed in connection with the others. In the first 12 lines at least four sto-

88 Tygstrup, p. 26. My translation.
89 Kjærstad, Der Entdecker, pp. 157-8.»Omgangen med disse håndslipte glasstykkene har forfulgt meg hele livet. Ingenting kunne danke ut de opplevelsene jeg hadde, den feststemningen som grep meg, under denne kjolen av krystallbiter, i dette lyset som både ble spredt og samlet. Første gang jeg fikk høre om et nettverk skapt av datamaskiner, tenkte jeg straks på mormors lysekrone. Jeg hadde faktisk eid et prisme fra jeg var helt liten. Jeg lekte ofte med det, oppfattet det som noe fint og fullstendig i seg selv. Først da mormor fant fram kronen sin, skjønte jeg at mitt eget prisme hørte til i en større helhet. Det skulle ikke forundre meg om den erkjennelsen var bestemmende for mitt Prosjekt X, ideen som nær knekte nakken på meg.« (Kjærstad, Oppdageren, p. 135).

ries are at work. There is the main story about the grandmother's chandelier, which is the axis that the narration continuously returns to. From this story three smaller narrations, which are also reciprocally connected to each other, branch out: the structure of the internet, Jonas' memory of when he had a single crystal as a child, and finally the memory of the so-called Project X of his youth. As a reader you can easily imagine these movements as hyperlinks in which the marked word links to a new subject and back to the main axis – at least until what you thought was the main axis is replaced by another trail, and so on, forming the structure of a network.

None of these smaller stories are fully developed in this passage, but they linger as loaded words whose significance simultaneously reaches back to episodes of which we have already been told and points forward to so far untold stories. Here we see an example of the novel's mediation between the bubbling pleasure of narrating and the principle of the hypertext that constantly intervenes in the linear sequence and reconfigures the narration. For instance the reference to Project X points to a story from when Jonas was a student which we do not encounter in the novel for another 200 pages. Only then do we discover that Project X is the title of Jonas' attempt to construct a new classification system for knowledge which challenges the American librarian Melvil Dewey's system. A project of linking information – of putting the individual parts in new places in relation to the whole – and thus creating a constellation resembling that of a network. The reference to Project X in the quotation above is consequently not arbitrary, although the connection is neither causal nor temporal, but follows the logic of thought, even if the reader does not have the freedom of the hyperlink to jump 200 pages forward in the novel and instantaneously discover what Project X refers to.

The reason why Kjærstad writes printed novels and does not put his novels on the web or CD-ROM is, he tells us, that he does not want to give up the privilege of the author to create a hierarchy within the text. In the essay »Litteraturens mulighet. Romanen og nettet« he writes:

When the sequence of the text [in a hyperfiction] is controlled to that degree by the reader (and by chance) and not by the author – even if the author decides which words and paragraphs should be linked – we lose what to me is the goal of fiction: to create knowledge, recognition. A bit solemnly you could say that you lose the possibility of the moment of catharsis.[90]

Kjærstad is thus not willing to pass on his position as an author to random readers, and since he has not developed the »4te Instanz« which Arno Schmidt introduces to restrain the freeplay of language, this means that

---

90 Kjærstad, Litteraturens mulighet, p. 257. My translation.

there is an outer limit to how far he wants to go in undermining the narrative when it comes to the possibility of user interaction.

Espen Aarseth describes the involvement of the reader in cybertexts in the following way: »the reader has to become a meta-reader, mapping the network and reading the map of her own reading carefully.«[91] This is what Aarseth calls an *ergodic* process. »Ergodic« derives from the Greek words *ergon* and *hodos*, which mean »work« and »road« respectively. The term describes the reading of open dynamic texts (such as hyperfictions), which demands that the reader takes an active part in creating a narrative sequence by choosing the roads by which the narration should go. However, a printed novel – such as the Wergeland trilogy – does not demand the same amount of activity from its reader as digital hyperfiction does; neither does it give the reader the same amount of influence. Aarseth's terminology can nonetheless be used to understand how the principle of hypertext influences the Wergeland trilogy. This is the case because the trilogy uses the tension that arises between a controlled and carefully prepared hierarchical structured sequence on the one hand and, on the other, the number of stories which weave themselves in and out of each other without giving the reader the opportunity of identifying a larger paradigm in which it all fits. The associative nature of the form demands that the reader grabs the links (e.g. Project X or the crystal) that he has been given, and holds on to them for the next 200 pages when an elaboration is finally given. However, this does not mean that the reader is capable of breaking the code and finding an overall structuring principle for the trilogy. Using hypertext as a paradigm thus results in a radicalised version of the German literary theorist Wolfgang Iser's theory of so-called *Leerstellen* or »gaps of meaning« which the reader fills out during his reading.[92] The reader is constantly reminded that none of the four narrators is capable of giving a definitive representation: »Is this the most important story in Jonas Wergeland's life?« the narrators ask themselves over and over again, while the best friends, the love affairs, and the relative importance of other events in Jonas' life change from volume to volume. This means that the reader's experience comes to resemble a search on Google in which you have to navigate through more or less rele-

---

91 Aarseth, Cybertext, p. 93.

92 Wolfgang Iser is together with Hans Robert Jauß one of the main figures of the so-called »Rezeptionsästhetik«. A literary theory which developed in the 1970s and which focuses on the way in which a text acquires its significance in the encounter with a reader: »Der Leser wird die Leerstellen dauernd auffüllen beziehungsweise beseitigen. Indem er sie beseitigt, nutzt er den Auslegungsspielraum und stellt selbst die nicht formulierten Beziehungen zwischen den einzelnen Ansichten her. Daß dies so ist, läßt sich an der einfachen Erfahrungstatsache ablesen, daß die Zweitlektüre eines literarischen Textes oftmals einen von der Erstlektüre abweichenden Eindruck produziert.« (Iser, Die Appellstruktur der Texte, p. 235).

vant links in a hunt for trustworthy information, and every time you choose one path, other potential results are simultaneously excluded. Kjærstad does not give the reader the option of choosing; rather he tells multiple incompatible versions of the same life without making them exclude one another. The trustworthiness and the desired understanding of the whole is placed in the simultaneity of all the versions – all the fragments – as when the daughter, Kristin, simultaneously plays all the 23 episodes in the TV series which made her father famous:

Ich drehte mich langsam auf dem Bürostuhl, das Licht der gut zwanzig Bildschirme traf mich wie heilende Strahlen. Ich begriff oder ahnte, welche geistige Planung, welche Arbeit – und nicht zuletzt: welche Grundidee – hinter diesem komplizierten Zusammenspiel stehen musste, diesen Tausenden winziger Querverweise, die sämtliche Sendungen zu einem sich wechselseitig kommentierenden Netzwerk verschmelzen ließen.[93]

What we see here is a reflection on how Kjærstad challenges narrative by using the hypertext form as a structuring skeleton for the novel – the unity of the text thus emerges from a pulsating network of connections. However, we also see how Kjærstad reaches the limits of the merging of the novel and the hypertext when he wants to maintain the privileges of his authoritative role as an author – even if it is in a problematized version.

In the Wergeland trilogy the temporal sequence is suspended and transformed into associative jumps. Time becomes a multiplicity of moments connected in a network. Consequently, the life and identity of the human being is also understood and described differently. As we shall see, it can be argued that the implications of the hypertext form do, in fact, constitute an answer to the question posed by the trilogy of »what is a human being?« The American theorist Mark C. Taylor presented the concept of *nodal subjectivity* in *The Moment of Complexity. Emerging Network Culture* (2001). This is a conception of the subject that breaks with traditional binary oppositions such as nature/culture, subject/object, consciousness/body, organism/machine, inner/outer, life/non-life and conceives of the human being almost as an incarnation of the World Wide Web and complex global networks:

As the webs in which I find myself become ever more complex, I eventually realize that the currents rushing through me are tributaries in a vast river of information.

---

93 Kjærstad, Der Entdecker, p. 602. »Jeg dreide langsomt rundt i kontorstolen mens jeg merket hvordan lyset fra noenogtjue TV-apparater traff meg som stråler. Som legende stråler. Jeg skjønte, eller jeg ante, hvilken mental planlegging, hvilket arbeid – og ikke minst: hvilken idé – som måtte ligge bak dette innviklede samspillet, disse tusentalls av ørsmå koblinger som fikk alle programmene til å gli sammen til et gjensidig kommenterende nettverk.« (Kjærstad, Oppdageren, pp. 514-15).

Tossed and turned by the turbulence this river perpetually generates, the I unravels but I do not completely dissolve. [...] The self – if, indeed, this term any longer makes sense – is a node in a complex network of relations. In emerging network culture, *subjectivity is nodular*.[94]

Taylor's theory is that the so-called network society, which he argues lies at the root of our economic, political, social, and cultural existence, affects the individual to such a degree that the subject should likewise be considered a network in which earlier well-defined boundaries are broken down. This idea of the human being as consisting of a series of nodes bound together in a network, and that of the boundaries between the subject and the forms of the outer world as porous, represent an illuminating theoretical viewpoint from which one can consider the trilogy's depiction of the human subject. However, whereas Taylor emphasises the nodal points, we see – with the trilogy as well as *MoE* in mind – how the emphasis should perhaps be rather on the associative jumps, the spaces in between consisting of cross-references and connections.

The recognition that a human being has a multiplicity of potential personalities is a theme which runs through the entire trilogy and above all reveals itself in the composition of the three volumes, which portray Jonas as divine, demonic and resurrected respectively.[95] As Jonas comments when he stands with his head inside the chandelier and sees Margrete: »Sieben Menschen, einer in der Mitte und sechs ringsherum. Ich erkannte, wer es war. Es war Margrete.«[96] The unity of the human being thus flickers in the network of all the connected possibilities – there is not only one correct definition or identity.

Rather than regarding human life as a continuous sequence that assembles the discordant concordance of life in a plot (as a narrative understanding of human life would have been), existence presents itself as an associative jumping between nodal points which are all connected in a huge network. It thus continues a tradition of narrative negotiations which we have traced from *Wanderjahre* through to *MoE* and *ZT*. In *Erobreren* it is explicitly said that narration is that which is capable of ascribing meaning and thus saving a life from »Sinnlosigkeit«.[97] Narration is crucial to the understanding of the human being, not least the human being's understanding of its own life in the trilogy. But, rather than make the internal oppositions of

---

94 Taylor, p. 231.

95 In the book *Så hvad er et Menneske?* Thomas Thurah outlines the explicit resemblance of the three narrators to God, the devil, and Christ. These characteristics are likewise represented in the image they give of Jonas (Thurah, p. 210ff).

96 Kjærstad, Der Entdecker, p. 187. »Sju mennesker, én i midten og seks i en ring rundt. Jeg så hvem det var. Det var Margrete« (Kjærstad, Oppdageren, p. 159).

97 Kjærstad, Der Eroberer, p. 311. »meningsløsheten« (Kjærstad, Erobreren, p. 265).

life and identity fit into a neat and tidy narration, Kjærstad turns the construction inside out and, by using the hypertext form, creates a network of associatively connected stories that suspends time and causality as organising principles. He thereby recognises the qualities of identity construction that narrative has, at the same time as he exposes its shortcomings.

Kjærstad's concern with the description of the human subject is thus closely connected to the form that he chooses. The construction of the trilogy finds its inspiration in the associative jumps of the hypertext, and the character sketches arise from a number of individual stories that are linked associatively. This means that the human subject is represented as a complementary spatial category for whom meaning arises in the network of relations. The human subject is situated in the same place as the novel: in the leap from one narration to another. However, what we see in the trilogy is not a fragmentation in the terms of the avant-garde or modernism, but rather an accentuation of the connections and the significance of the whole as they are created by the reader.

This use of the hyperlink to facilitate a narrative construction that binds together hugely diversified and internally contradictory material, such as that of the Wergeland trilogy, will be worth keeping in mind when we turn to Reinhard Jirgl's *Abtrünnig* (2005), which addresses the materiality of the hyperlink and turns reading into a physical, almost performative act.

3.2.4 »?Was heißt Eigenresonanz der-Internet«
Reinhard Jirgl's *Abtrünnig. Roman aus der nervösen Zeit*

Jirgls Buch ist eine Flaschenpost. Sie enthält keine Erzählung, weil der Faden von Chronologie und Folgerichtigkeit gerissen ist. Sie hat keinen Anfang und auch kein Ende, sie trotzt dem Leben und ist dem Leben abgetrotzt. Sie lebt von dem verzweifelten Versuch, schwarze Lettern zu verketten zu einem roten Faden, der das verlorene Ich für die Zeit einer Lektüre zusammenfügt.[98]

Thus Martina Meister describes Reinhard Jirgl's *Abtrünnig. Roman aus der nervösen Zeit* (2005) in her review in *Frankfurter Rundschau*. *Abtrünnig* takes place between 2000 and 2004. Apparently we are dealing with two first-person narrators. One is a border guard from Frankfurt an der Oder whose wife dies from cancer. He tries to create a new life for himself in Berlin while searching for a young Ukrainian woman he helped enter Germany illegally with her brother. The other is a journalist from Hamburg who finds himself in a mid-life crisis, divorced from his wife and in love

---

98 Meister.

with his therapist. When the therapist moves to Berlin with her husband he decides to follow her, and the tale of the two men's lives in the metropolis, which toss them around emotionally and physically, commences. The story is framed by an introduction and an exit by an unnamed narrator reflecting on the creation of what we assume is the present novel.[99] But this is just the apparent story, as Meister points out. This story provides a concrete point of reference for the reader to hold on to in a novel which is best described as a massive overload of information – articles, dreams, manifestos, German history, all in a giant pool of information beneath which lies the *possibility* of a consistent story – a narration with a beginning, a middle, and an end. Maybe. Or maybe just the hope of one, as indicated by the three sections of the novel: »Geburtstage«, »Arbeitstage«, »Todestage«.

Essentially, *Abtrünnig. Roman aus der nervösen Zeit* is a novel about the possibility of writing a novel in »nervous« times. Living and writing are presented as identical projects. As in Musil's *MoE*, one of the main challenges is finding a form for life and writing alike. In *MoE* we saw that the form of the network created an underlying structure for the novel at the same time as the network semantically gained weight as a way of describing social interactions. The form for which we are on the lookout in *Abtrünnig* shares many similarities with that of the network form we discovered as essential to the narrative structure of *MoE*. However, there are significant differences in the rendering of this network structure which prompt an awareness of how the connotations of the network figure have developed between Musil's day and Jirgl's. As the subtitle »Roman aus der nervösen Zeit« indicates and many reviewers[100] have observed, the novel presents itself as characterising the conditions of life in contemporary times. This also gives a possible clue to understanding the insertion of essayistic sections of a sociological and political nature, something which has disturbed reviewers. Telling a story is not the sole objective here.

The picture painted does not have a rosy hue. Berlin, epitomizing contemporary society, is merciless, and the fates of our two protagonists are ferocious. The border guard from the GDR is murdered shortly after he is finally reunited with the young woman he helped escape to Germany, and our journalist is driven to the edge of insanity, lost in the city and his own mind,

---

99 We may assume that this narrator is the journalist-narrator in so far as we learn of his literary aspirations in the novel, but no decisive proof of that is given. For a consideration of to whom this introduction should be ascribed see Dieter Stolz's article »»Das Aufbrechen der verpanzerten Wahrnehmung‹: Reinhard Jirgls Roman *Abtrünnig* - ein (un)vermeidbarer Amoklauf«: »Eine Art ›Über-ich‹, eine noch immer namenlose, nicht genau zu fixierende Stimme zwischen reflektierendem Autor und Schreibendem Amokläufer oder demjenigen, der beide erfand.« (Stolz, p. 248).

100 See, for instance, Funck, Wutschnaubend und düster; Funck, Die Rache des freien Mitarbeiters; JP; Langner; Meister; Mohr; Müller; Nord; Radisch; Schoeller; Sdun; and Vogler.

on a journey which ends in a tumour operation. *Abtrünnig* thus shows the traces of a classic modernist novel grappling with modern life in the city – in dialogue with Alfred Döblin's *Berlin Alexanderplatz* (1929) and Knut Hamsun's depiction of the starving artist in *Hunger* (1890). So what makes it feel so contemporary? The answer to this question might be found by taking a closer look at what separates the modernist metropolis from the contemporary cybercity. To answer this question let us first look at Jirgl's unique writing style.

A distinctive characteristic of Jirgl's novels is the way in which he uses abbreviations of the conjunctions »und« and »oder« (»u«, »u:«, »od«), numbers written as figures rather than spelled out (also as indefinite articles: »1 Leben«), and an unusual positioning of question marks, exclamation marks, and punctuation. As a result of this his writings are often compared to those of James Joyce and Arno Schmidt. In the essay »Das poetische Vermögen des alphanumerischen Codes in der Prosa« (2003), Jirgl explains the thinking behind his characteristic way of using not only the content, but also the textual appearance, as a means of conveying meaning and creating a textual image.[101]

Jirgl's aim is to create a bodily sensation of the text – to force the reader into an abrupt reading rhythm where the text-body exists in its own right not merely as a vehicle for conveying a message. Taking his cue from Vilém Flusser, Jirgl argues that the linearity of the alphabet has fundamentally influenced Western culture. Jirgl wishes to bring back some of the image material to the letters of the alphabet and lend them a bodily quality. To Jirgl numbers are connected to the ideogram and thus stand in opposition to the letters, which makes them helpful for breaking open the linearity of the letters. He speaks of »die Wirklichkeit des Alphabets und die Wirklichkeit der Ziffern«, referring to the alphabetic reality as linear and the reality of the numbers as »insular«.[102] It is this opposition which Jirgl uses as a poetic strategy in his novels.

The textual iconography that Jirgl creates is not intended merely to substantiate the content of the text, but also to convey a statement in its own right:

Der differenzierte Umgang mit Zeichen und Ziffern stellt indes keine Illustration des übrigen Textes dar, vielmehr hat er den Rang einer zusätzlichen Dimension als Ausdruck für all jene sich verändernden, erweiterten Diskurse im gesellschaftlichen wie im Leben des Individuums selbst.[103]

---

101 See also De Winde and the introduction in Jirgl's *Das obszöne Gebet*.
102 Jirgl, Das poetische Vermögen des alphanumerischen Codes in der Prosa, p. 57.
103 Ibid. pp. 51-52.

The visual impression of the text while being read thus adds another layer of comprehension to the world Jirgl aims to describe. Jirgl explains that, when he uses »1« rather than »ein«, he wishes to indicate some sort of shortness of breath: »kurz, eilig, rasch vorübereilend«[104] as opposed to the graphically broad »ein« which describes »langsame Vorgänge, zäh fließende, eher dauerhafte mit geringen Veränderlichkeiten«.[105]

In the essay Jirgl explicitly mentions the computer as a factor in the interaction between letters and numbers and the quality of text in the contemporary world:

Augenfällig, daß in den letzten dreißig Jahren auch im Gelände der Schrift Grundsätzliches sich verändert hat, und wer heute zum Schreiben sich hinsetzt, sollte wissen, daß er damit etwas schon grundsätzlich Verschiedenes beginnt gegenüber dem scheinbar gleichen Tun von vor drei Jahrzehnten. – Weder bin ich meiner Zeit so gram noch will ich durch mein Schreiben jene auffälligen Bewegungen, die in der Gegenwart die Schrift schlechthin betreffen, ignorieren. Denn spätestens seit oben erwähnter Popularisierung der Computer ist deutlich geworden, das *innerhalb* der Schrift zwei Haupttendenzen zum Driften *aus* der Schrift sich manifestieren: Zum einen die Rückkehr zum *Bild* (von den Piktogrammen bis zu den Computeranimationen der *virtual reality*); zum anderen der Vorausschritt zu den *Zahlen* (denn Computer waren und sind letztlich bloße Rechenmaschinen). Kurz gesagt, das erste bedeutet die Wiederkehr der Imagination, das zweite die Festigung der Kalkulation – hierin findet das bezeichnete Spannungsverhältnis innerhalb des alphanumerischen Codes seinen deutlichsten Ausdruck wie auch seine besten Verwendungshinweise. Denn wie oftmals, so auch hier, finden Problemlösungen im Innern des problematischen Systems bereits ihren Lösungsansatz.[106]

To Jirgl the computer thus brings out some of the fundamental characteristics of writing: the image and the number, which it is important for Jirgl to accentuate in the way he constructs his writing, because they participate in re-connecting writing with the body:

Die Schrift, zusammenfassend gesagt, ist vor viertausend Jahren aus den Körpern ausgebrochen; im gelungenen Text findet sie dorthin zurück. Somit sucht *im* Schreiben das Inszenatorische – der Körper-Text, der auf der Bühne steht – seinen Ausdruck.[107]

Although the reference to the computer in this essay is primarily used to support his argument about the characteristics of writing, it is interesting that he makes this connection to the computer medium, because it is something which becomes more prominent in *Abtrünnig*. Here the layout of the

---

104 Ibid. p. 70.
105 Ibid. p. 72.
106 Ibid. p. 63.
107 Ibid. p. 59.

text becomes even more visual – even more bodily – than in his previous books, and interestingly the inspiration for this seems to be the internet and the hypertext principle it employs. In *Abtrünnig* Jirgl introduces the use of *links* in the text. As in a hyperlink, certain words are underlined and the text refers, firstly, to a part of the text which is separated from the continuum of the rest of the text and framed by a box, and, secondly, to another page or chapter of the novel. The reader is thus prompted towards a non-linear reading. Compared to Kjærstad's trilogy, the hyperlinks are here much more unavoidable visually.

Reinhard Jirgl: *Abtrünnig. Roman aus der nervösen Zeit*

This mimicking of the logic of the webpage and the hyperlink lends a certain »three-dimensionality« to the appearance of the printed page. It becomes more visually provocative. Furthermore, it becomes a physical experience to read, because it involves action from the reader to flip to the other end of the book when encountering a reference that requires it. In this way Jirgl comes a step closer to his goal of making the text a bodily experience.

The reason that Jirgl nevertheless chooses the printed page, and not the internet, as his medium can most likely be found precisely in his quest for infusing writing with this sense of body. One can consider whether it does not in fact require more action on the part of the reader to flip to the other end of the book than to click on a link on a computer screen, and this might be a reason for Jirgl's choice. Also, as Hayles has argued in *How We Became Posthuman. Virtual Bodies in Cybernetics, Literature and Informatics* (1999), the computer was for a long time affiliated with a lack of contact with the human body. Although contemporary internet artworks and theory have in recent years become especially concerned with issues of the body and performance, the immaterial reputation of the computer might have made Jirgl hesitant about taking the leap from the physical printed page to the virtual screen.[108]

The internet is, however, not merely an inspiration for the layout of *Abtrünnig*. It also plays a significant part on the thematic level. Throughout the novel there are frequent references to information technology, which is not surprising in a novel that aims to describe life in the modern metropolis of Berlin and to characterise contemporary times. Information technology is an integrated part of any modern city, and it could be argued that it would have been more noticeable if there were no mention of information technology at all in a novel such as this. Nonetheless, precisely because it is such a characteristic element of the world in which Jirgl's characters move, and because the hyperlinks manifest themselves so conspicuously in the textual body, the thematic function of the internet becomes important.

The internet is primarily debated in the chapter »Freak Waves. Jähe Wut«, which occurs towards the end of the novel as part of the larger section termed »Todestage«. The chapter reproduces an article on the internet allegedly written by an author of whom we have previously heard, because the journalist-narrator has written about him and his book on artificial intelligence. The article is inserted at the stage where the narrator has lost just about everything and is psychologically at a point just before he runs amok. It is drawn up in 13 short clauses marked with a section mark (§) and strikes a critical note, using what appears as Marxist terminology analysing society in terms of the bourgeoisie, capitalism, religion, and technology. The internet is characterised in the following manner:

Als die künftig spektakulärste Ruine dürfte das Internet verbleiben, allerdings in weitgehender Unsichtbarkeit. Aber nicht wegen seiner hauptsächlichen Immaterialität wird diese Ruine in ferneren Zeiten nicht zum weithin sichtbaren Symbol aufragen wie Ritterburgen und Fabrikhallen; das rhizome Aderngeflecht der Internetkabel ist niemals zur Erdoberfläche vorgedrungen: Es blieb Zeit seines Lebens beerdigt; Inter-

---

108 This argument can be substantiated by the fact that Jirgl in *Abtrünnig* shows knowledge of these discourses, for instance by quoting Jean Baudrillard: »Die Gewalt des Bildes (und allgemeiner der Information und des Virtuellen) besteht darin, daß es das Reale umbringt. Alles muß gesehen werden, alles muß sichtbar sein. Das Bild ist der Ort dieser Sicherheit par excellence.« (Jirgl, Abtrünnig, p. 83).

net-Kultur ist eine Sepulkral-Kultur. Und zwar die letztmögliche, die ironische: Leben und Wünsche allzeit begraben – Menschsein zieht sich unter die Erde in elektronisch leitfähige Bunkersysteme zurück. Was oberirdisch verbleibt – biologische Gehäuse –, ist beständig absterbendes Fleisch, Zellmasse, in krieglosen Regionen inflatorisch die Welt verstopfend; zu Friedenszeiten am eigenen Daseinmüssen zuweilen verzweifelnd –.[109]

For the author of the thirteen clauses the internet is a significant reason for the condition of the contemporary world: the undermining of the boundaries between the private realm and society, the individual and the crowd, subject and object. It embodies capitalism and is envisioned as a weapon.

The journalist reacts with laughter when reading the article, but nonetheless contemplates the content of the article. Towards the end of the chapter the author of the article materialises as if emerging from the monitor as a Faustian figure to attack our narrator: »Der blanke Monitorschirm erstrahlt im kristallin weißen Licht, heller als das Tageslicht durch die zerbrochenen Scheiben, – ein Leuchten nicht aus diesem Tag u aus keinem.«[110] It can be argued that this article reflects much of the desperation felt by our first-person narrator at this stage; his feeling of being caught in a web which controls his movements and the wish to subvert this network; a feeling of being controlled by a world governed by humans striving for money, power, and success.

This is not the only instance of a critical attitude towards the internet. Throughout the novel the references to the internet that we find are charged with scepticism. For instance, in the chapter »Bittere Neige«:

?Was aber geschieht mit allen vorrangig immateriellen Gebilden, wie beispielsweise dem Internet (das-Internet zählt steuerrechtlich nicht zu den materiellen, beweglichen Gütern), sobald diese in Eigenresonanz verfallen. ?Was heißt Eigenresonanz des-Internet; ?wie stellt die zerstörerische Selbst-Schwingung sich dar -- [111]

This scepticism is interesting because it appears at odds with the fact that the textual layout of the novel seems to rest on the form of the hyperlink. However, this apparent contradiction underscores the proposition of the present study. It shows us the impact of the hyperlink as a concrete material sign of information technology as a symbolic form, even in a context where the characters of the novel regard the medium with suspicion. To regard information technology as embodying a worldview and the hyperlink as a material sign of this worldview means that the influence can be traced even when the texts dealt with are not themselves consciously propagating a

---

109 Jirgl, Abtrünnig, p. 487.
110 Ibid. p. 500.
111 Ibid. p. 212.

positive view of the impact of information technology in the way that, for instance, the Wergeland trilogy does.

A question that remains unanswered and which has been an object of discussion for reviewers is the uncomfortable question of irony. How sincere is Jirgl's attack against capitalism and the world it has created? The article on the internet is one of many angry assaults on a society governed by the drive for money, power, and success. However, at the same time there is in both our protagonists a strange attraction towards the city governed by these urges, an attraction towards the nervousness it imposes upon them. In order to understand this further, a brief excursus which compares *Abtrünnig* to Knut Hamsun's *Hunger*[112] might be fruitful and bring forth both the correspondence to the modernist »Großstadtroman« and the inherent difference that marks Jirgl's work out as a novel of the twenty-first century.

Hunger likewise takes place in a big city (at least by the standards of 1890), and it commences with the famous words: »It was in those days when I wandered about hungry in Kristiania, that strange city which no one leaves before it has set its mark upon him...«[113] Many initial readings focussed on the novel as an expression of the horrifying conditions for a struggling artist in the late nineteenth century, as an autobiography of Hamsun's own hardships. However, as Jørgen Haugan eloquently points out, *Hunger* is composed in a strict manner which deliberately focuses attention on the hunger episodes – everything in between is cut out. It is the periods when our protagonist is hungry that are described in the narrative. When he does get some money and is able to support himself for a little while, the narrative breaks off and only starts again when a new hunger period commences. The hunger is thus – although described as destroying the protagonist – at the same time the best thing that happens to him while he is wandering around Kristiania and something which he voluntarily seeks, because it is here that he finds the fuel for his aesthetic undertaking.[114] Now let us return to *Abtrünnig* to see where the comparison takes us.

The ending of the introductory scene seems to indicate that the parallel is appropriate:

Damals wußte ich noch nicht, wieviele Abschiede u Enttäuschungen, allsamt schon gehäuft zur Jahrzehnte=hohen Lebenshalde, ich noch in Unwürde=ertragen könnte, bis !Der-Moment einträfe der mich zurückschlagen ließ.

Davon blieb in=mir – so wie in Jedemmensch der gefangen ist im Spiralnebel Alltäglicher Kränkungen & dessen Da-Sein mehr-und-mehr Aufenthalt heißt in kahlen

---

112 The novel seems to invite such a comparison in so far as Hamsun is repeatedly mentioned in the novel.

113 Hamsun, p. 3.

114 Haugan, p. 73ff.

weißgetünchten Zellen – eine Zeitbombe zurück, deren Werk, 1mal=in-Gang-gesetzt, Nichts mehr zu stoppen vermag. Und jeder Herz-Leben's Schlag wird fortan von zwei von ein ander getrennten Uhrwerken geführt : Eines zählt gleichmäßig, unabhängig vom Willen, voran. Das-Andere, voll eigen-Sinn, zählt rückwärts, sowohl in langsam schleichender Gangart als auch, unvorhersehbar, in Sprüngen Hetzjagden Raserei im Countdown von Leben's Zeit. Unvermeidbar wird !Der-Moment eintreten, in dem die Eine Leuchtziffer erscheint & im-Innern rot gellend der Aus=Ruf !GE-NUG. ES !REICHT.

Weitundbreit die Menschen & ihre Geschichten, die nach=mir greifen u mich schrecken. Ich werde sie einsperren in Meinembuch. Denn der Schrecken ist das Gefängnis der Wörter. Ich gehe auf sie zu, und gehe in Fremder Landschaft hinein.[115]

Reading Jirgl's other books and tracing his story as a GDR author who did not publish the books he wrote until after the reunification, there is no doubt that he is critical of society, critical of the state and of institutions that assume power over the individual and threaten the subject with »Ichlosigkeit«[116]. His project as an author is fundamentally different from that of Hamsun, who aims to break free from the conventional pattern of the Bildungsroman and create art that seduces rather than educates. Nonetheless, reading *Abtrünnig* in correspondence with *Hunger* emphasises that, although money, power, and the internet are seen as negative phenomena when they take hold over the individual and control his faith, there is simultaneously a strong urge towards these things, and for the narrator of the introduction and exit chapters these destructive powers hold an aesthetic vitality which fuels his project as an author and facilitates the emergence of the novel. *Hunger* reminds us that negative conditions can have a positive outcome for the right artist. Viewed in this way it is no longer surprising that the internet and the hyperlink become an inspiration for the form of the novel, even though the internet is regarded with suspicion on a thematic level. Let us now turn to have a closer look at how this is conducted in order finally to reach a likely answer to the question of the contemporary »feel« of the novel.

In the essay »Das poetische Vermögen des alphanumerischen Codes in der Prosa«, Jirgl repeatedly emphasises that his characteristic way of inserting numbers and signs in unconventional places in the text establishes a level of enunciation in its own right. The printed page becomes an image, an ideogram with its own message. This enables us to recognise the significance of the hyperlink in the layout of the text and as a thematic node. The point, which remains to be clarified, is the role of the hyperlink in how the narrative is constructed and how the novel as a whole is read. How does the

---

115 Jirgl, Abtrünnig, p. 11.
116 Jirgl, Das poetische Vermögen des alphanumerischen Codes in der Prosa, p. 59.

characterisation of contemporary times given by a novel which describes itself as a »Roman aus der nervösen Zeit« arise? What is it that makes the style and construction of the plot in *Abtrünnig* different from early twentieth-century avant-garde experiments?

The two main characteristics of this novel are its intense pace and expressionistic flow on the one hand, and its overload of essayistic insertions and information on the other. The contemporary feel of the novel seems to stem from the excessiveness by which these two elements come together, and the conceptual form which makes this effect possible can be found visibly in the layout of the novel in the form of the hyperlinks. It can thus be argued that the accentuation of the characteristics we find in Musil, Döblin, and Hamsun is facilitated by the hyperlink as a concrete material sign of information technology as a contemporary symbolic form. Regarding information technology as a symbolic form means approaching it as a form which influences the perception and representation of our own time, but also permits a historical awareness of the concrete material signs that information technology contains. Viewing the hyperlink figure in *Abtrünnig* in comparison with the network figure in *MoE* allows for a fuller understanding of both the way in which the forms of information technology influence contemporary fiction and the way in which these forms are in dialogue with other previous examples of narrative negotiations. In *MoE* we saw how human existence, narrativity, and the novel genre alike were rendered problematic. When the human subject was felt to be disintegrating, as it did for Ulrich, narration appeared less fulfilling as a mode of representation, because it presumed an acting subject. The genre of the novel thus needed to be rethought, and the network figure as an ambiguous image, which has both confining and liberating connotations, occurred as a way other than the linear narrative of grasping and organizing life, story, and text. It is the same duality of network connotations which we find in the conceptualisation of the hyperlink in *Abtrünnig*. However, the pace with which this is mediated has increased dramatically; in Berlin there is no »anderer Zustand« to resort to. Instead of the impression of the network as a large conglomerate of plot nodes and reflection-spaces balancing one another in the manner of a large, slow organism, *Abtrünnig* appears as a nervously flickering billboard in which the characteristics of the network have penetrated the text to an even more explicit degree by physically showing the narrative network as links on the printed page. What is being characterised is not the noise and turmoil of the modern metropolis of the early twentieth century; what is blown open and dissected are the conditions of life in information society by which we are constantly bombarded, not only with the impressions of the street on which we move, but also by information rubble which piles up alongside us and which we do not know how to dispose. In *Abtrünnig. Roman aus der nervösen Zeit* these fragments of information turn up visibly on the printed page as hyperlink-like boxes inserted into the continuum of the text and creating new connections. They disturb us as we read – tending as they do to break open the linear flow of our reading and direct us somewhere else in the text. If we follow their invitation we lose track of what we were reading immediately before, and we do not know when to stop reading and return to where we broke off. By encouraging this nervous mode of reading, which does not disturb us when surfing the internet, but somehow appears more upsetting in the context of a printed novel, this work creates a powerful illustration of the conditions of the novel genre today. As a reader one struggles to follow the development of the narrative: what happens to our two first-person narrators? But as we read we are faced with the challenge of manoeuvring the book and the world it opens up, and we realise that to understand fully the fictional characters and the society in which they are immersed we have to follow the logic of the hyperlink, give up on a linear reading, and search out the new connections, because that is the way in which the world confronts the characters in the novel. The world of Möglichkeitssinn envisioned by Ulrich has become an actual choice for the reader of *Abtrünnig*, but rendered in a much more hectic and unsteady pace than that which Ulrich seems to have imagined. In his article on *Abtrünnig*, Dieter Stolz has shown that following the links opens the way for a more positive experience of the fate of the protagonists, because the reader who follows the links: »der landet am Ende garantiert nicht beim blindwütigen Amoklauf des oben vorgestellten Protagonisten. Die Pointe: Es führt einfach kein Link-›Befehl‹ (*sic!*) in dieses Kapitel.«[117] Following the links thus opens up alternative worlds, alternative modes of encountering the world of *Abtrünnig. Die Welt* remarks that the statement »Um sein Glück zu erfinden, muß man Eigensinn entwickeln« counts as Jirgl credo.[118] *Abtrünnig* seems to assert that that statement also applies to the mode in which his latest novel should be read.

3.2.5 Navigating the connections

By identifying the hyperlink as a concrete material sign of information technology as a symbolic form and tracing its relation to the figure of the network, as well as its function in the novels *Finder sted*, the Wergeland trilogy, and *Abtrünnig*, we become aware of the way in which information technology as a symbolic form simultaneously relates to ongoing narrative

---

117 Stolz, p. 250.
118 JP.

negotiations in the novel genre and is intricately linked to the condition of cultural imagination in our specific period of time. The network form of the hyperlink and the emphasis on the text as navigable material become principles of composition for all three novels, just as we saw the database become in *Rand, Nox,* and *Beginnlosigkeit,* discussed in the previous chapter. The result is a number of texts which allow all the possible options of combinations to flicker in sequenceless simultaneity, turning Ulrich's notion of Möglichkeitssinn into textual worlds: our encounter with Luis and his computer-generated brain in *Finder sted* gives us an image of identity as a matter of combining memories, creating connections that make sense; Jonas' experiences in the Wergeland trilogy are not made to concur in one consistent narration, but rather support one another through principles of complementarity; and the portrait of the conditions of life in Berlin in *Abtrünnig* is characterised by a massive overload of information in which the characters and the reader alike have to learn to navigate and find their own circuitous route. Consequently, these novels can more generally be regarded as providing us with examples of the ways in which information technology functions as a symbolic form for the conditions of contemporary culture, offering modes of description and tools for stringing large diversified bodies of material together. However, we also see how these novels – precisely by using the figure of the hyperlink – place themselves in a tradition of narrative negotiations which has parallels to the way in which the figure of the network is employed in *MoE.* Our reading has shown both the similarities and the differences stemming from the development of the network figure in the twentieth century, in which it becomes increasingly common as a descriptive figure of the workings of society and social interactions.

The hyperlink dominated the discourse of information technology throughout the 1990s, which the selection of the works discussed in this chapter reflects: *Finder sted* is from 1998 and the Wergeland trilogy was published between 1993 and 1999. The more recent *Abtrünnig* is included here partly to emphasise that all three of the concrete material signs treated in this study are equally prevalent in contemporary culture, even if a certain succession in their dissemination might be observed – the intention is not to set up rigid chronological boundaries. Another reason for the inclusion of *Abtrünnig* here is that the emphasis on the performative implications of the hypertext principle, a particular feature of this work, seems to provide an appropriate transition to the next material sign of information technology as a symbolic form which we shall consider: the computer game. The hyperlink anticipates part of the discussion of user interaction and navigable space which becomes central in relation to the game, but whereas the hyperlink challenges narrativity by focussing on navigation – the movement from one textual node to another – the game also raises the issues of immersion within navigable space and the effect of repetition, highlighting the difference between reading a narrative and playing a game.

3.3 Computer Game Configurations: Immersion and Emergence

The computer game belongs in a tradition of games and play that has been the subject of anthropological, psychological, and sociological examinations. However, as we saw in chapter 2.3, games have also been conceptualized throughout the history of philosophy by thinkers from Aristotle to Kant and Schiller; and in the course of the second half of the twentieth century the figure of the game has seen an immense accentuation – especially in the wake of deconstructionist and poststructuralist thinking about language and signification as games, and in response to the influence of »game theory« in economics.[119]

In the article »Über den ästetischen Begriff des Spiels als Link zwischen traditioneller Texthermeneutik, Hyperfiction und Computerspielen« (discussed in chapter 2.3), Kocher and Böhler distinguish between a figurative understanding of the game (whose occurrence they date to the eighteenth century) and a performative-communicative understanding of the game that was prevalent before the eighteenth century and which they argue is revived in the computer game. One of the aims of this chapter will be to explore whether this accentuation of a notion of the game as an actual physical event is reflected in the way in which the selected contemporary novels deal with the figure of the game. However, the advent of the computer game not only marks the rise of a renewed interest in the game as an actual physical event as opposed to an analogy for aesthetic considerations, as Kocher and Böhler argue, it also marks an interest in examining games as aesthetic objects in themselves. A likely reason for this is that the computer game, more than other games, takes the form of an object which can be examined in a way other games that primarily exist as social exchange cannot. It does not only exist when being played, but presents itself as an aesthetic phenomenon that must be addressed in its own right. Consideration of the concept of computer games thus requires mediation between the notion of the game as

---

119 In economics, »game theory« studies choices made in an environment where the costs and benefits of each choice are not fixed, but depend on the choices made by the other individuals. It became a field of its own when John von Neumann began publishing on the issue in 1928 and has especially flourished since the 1950s. Today its use has spread and it is used in biology, philosophy, psychology, and sociology.

social event, aesthetic analogy, and as aesthetic object in itself, which is what we shall attempt by looking at the computer game as a concrete material sign of information technology as a symbolic form in this chapter.

Hans-Georg Gadamer's chapter »Spiel als Leitfaden der ontologischen Explikation« is a significant example of an early treatment of the game situated in between aesthetic object, analogy, and social act. Gadamer's notion of »play« is developed as part of his characterization of the artwork and the aesthetic experience. In his description of the game he looks at the game not from the point of view of the player, but at the game in itself and argues that: »Die Seinsweise des Spieles ist also nicht von der Art, daß ein Subjekt da sein muß, das sich spielend verhält, so daß das Spiel gespielt wird.«[120] Moving from game via cultic acts and plays (as we find them on a stage) to the artwork, Gadamer reaches the position that: »Die Darstellung der Kunst ist ihrem Wesen nach so, daß sie für jemanden ist, auch wenn niemand da ist, der nur zuhört oder zuschaut.«[121] Whereas a game is played for its own sake, an artwork represents something for someone even when there is no viewer. The transition from game to art thus signifies an opening towards the viewer. For Gadamer, the concept of the game is a useful point in his inquiry into the aesthetic experience, because the consideration of the game supports his thesis that an artwork is not an independent object that encounters an independent subject. An artwork's being unfolds only when it is experienced, yet at the same time it has an independent, consistent form which is intrinsically linked to this experience. The game enables him to reach an understanding of this intricate interaction between viewer and artwork. As we shall see in this chapter, the computer game can be regarded as removing itself from Gadamer's conception of the game as an activity pursued for its own sake and moving towards his conception of the artwork which simultaneously realises itself through the encounter with the viewer, while remaining independent of the consciousness of the viewer.

The first computer games were developed in the 1950s and 1960s. Coin-operated arcade games first became widespread in the 1970s. Since then a number of different genres have emerged as new technology has been developed. Originally this mainly took the form of arcade games found in entertainment venues such as cinemas, restaurants, and video arcades. Later these games were developed for home use, especially by the Japanese companies Nintendo and Sega,[122] but more textually based fictional environ-

---

120 Gadamer, p. 99.

121 Ibid. p. 105.

122 »Video games« are another commonly used term for these games. By definition a computer game is a game controlled by a computer. A video game is a computer game where the main feedback device is a video display such as a monitor or television (Ryan, Avatars of Story).

ments were also developed between users in online communities bearing certain similarities with chatrooms. Today the net profit of the computer game industry rivals that of the Hollywood movie industry, and games are designed with a focus on three equally important factors: gameplay (the structure and sequence of the game), graphics, and sound.

Game theorist Espen Aarseth has argued that simply talking about »games« or »digital games« seems irresponsible, because there are so many different genres, gaming situations, and game technologies which determine how the individual games should be approached.[123] To illustrate this we can identify at least five main categories, the boundaries of which may arguably overlap when considering individual games, but which are here presented to give an indication of the various types of marketing categories: *adventure games*, where the player immerses herself in a fictitious universe which resembles that of role play, *strategic games*, in which civilisations must be built or war waged, *simulation games*, in which the player navigates a plane, a car or a submarine, *platform games*, in which the player fights her way from level to level and collects points, or *sport games*, which simulate various forms of sport. Aarseth distinguishes between »digitized versions of traditional games« (card games, board games etc) and »games in virtual environments«. Thereby we allude once again to what Manovich terms »navigable space«, i.e. to the computer's preference for representing abstract information spaces as spatial experiences. This means that all kinds of data are rendered in three dimensions through computer visualisation, a category which we also touched on in the chapter on hyperlinks.[124] In the following we shall, however, continue to talk about »games« in general terms, because we are not exploring specific games, but rather more general qualities of information technology that accentuate issues which we shall consider under the headings *immersion* and *emergence* and which may, on a broader scale, be grouped under the term »game«.

Computer games were initially contextualized in relation to narratological studies, read in particular through the Russian linguist Vladimir Propps' studies of fairy tale patterns. However, as scholars have struggled to separate the study of computer games from literature and film studies and to make it a discipline in its own right, a central debate has focussed on how computer games relate to narrative. In *Hamlet on the Holodeck. The Future of Narrative in Cyberspace* (1997), Janet Murray argues that the game and narration resemble each other in so far as they both provide interpretations of experiences we have in the surrounding world. In particular the fairy tale

---

123 Aarseth, Quest Games as Post-Narrative Discourse, p. 362.
124 Manovich's category »navigable space« thus suggests qualities which are divided between the hyperlink and the computer game in the terminology used in this study.

with its schematized structure seems an obvious object of comparison. Referring to the origin of the game in religious rituals and ceremonies, Murray regards games as texts which offer interpretations of our experiences and allow us to live through life on a symbolic level:

In games, therefore, we have a chance to enact our most basic relationship to the world – our desire to prevail over adversity, to survive our inevitable defeats, to shape our environment, to master complexity, and to make our lives fit together like the pieces of a jigsaw puzzle.[125]

To Murray storytelling is a core human activity that can be incorporated into any medium.[126] In opposition to this view we find Espen Aarseth, who is among those who have endeavoured to make game studies a field of its own and separate it from narrative studies. He argues that there are essential discursive differences between narratives and computer games and that, when games are analyzed as stories, their intrinsic qualities as games become obscured:

Even if we adopt the widest (and weakest) possible notion of narratives – that they could be architectural rather than sequential, enacted rather than related, experienced personally and uniquely rather than observed collectively and statically – an ontological difference would still remain. This difference is probably best described with the word *choice*. In a game there must be choice. Even in games of ›pure‹ chance there is choice: what to bet on, how much to bet, and so on. Not only that, but the choices would have to be crucial. In a game everything revolves around the player's ability to make choices.[127]

According to Aarseth, »Choose your own adventure« books are thus examples of quasi-games, because they do not give the reader any real choice; the task is more about discovering the dominant plot which has been there all along. Aarseth's argument is not that narratives cannot be part of a computer game and used as one feature among many, but that the game cannot be understood merely from a narrative perspective, because the game qualities of a game hold fundamental traits which are foreign to that of a narrative. According to Aarseth, the quality of being playable is fundamentally at odds with being a narrative, because the simulation that a game sets forward is performative, whereas a narrative is constative.[128]

---

125 Murray, Hamlet on the Holodeck, p. 143.
126 Murray, From Game-Story to Cyberdrama, p. 1.
127 Aarseth, Quest Games as Post-Narrative Discourse, p. 366. In correspondence with the emphasis put on »choice« in this quotation the computer game designer Brian Reynolds is quoted in McAllister's *Game Work. Language, Power, and Computer Game Culture* for stating that: »A game […] is a series of interesting choices« (McAllister, p. 39).
128 Aarseth, Quest Games as Post-Narrative Discourse, p. 369. Aarseth sets forward this argument with reference to a conference paper on MUD and performance by Ragnhild Tronstad. The

My aim here is not to position myself in this dispute, which I believe is essentially about competing aims and interests. The »narrativists« are interested in exploring the fictional world of computer games: »The main reason for using narrative concepts in game studies is to come to terms with the imaginative dimension of computer games – a dimension that will be overlooked if we concentrate exclusively on rules, problem-solving, and competition«.[129] By contrast the proponents of game studies are interested in studying what makes a game different from a narrative.[130] However, the very existence of such a debate shows a tendency to challenge the omnipotence of narrativity in contemporary culture, which is what makes this discussion relevant for our overall purpose. We shall therefore look closer at some of the arguments for regarding games as something different from narratives.

One of the central arguments for a difference between game and narrative is that their relationship with time is different for each. In most narratives there is a difference between the time in which the narration takes place and the time during which the narration is told.[131] In the computer game, however, Jesper Juul argues that the player experiences a sense of interacting in the »now«. As a player you experience the events as they happen and they depend on your actions; the time of that which is told and the time of the narrative are experienced as merged.[132] This difference in relation to time means that the computer game operates with other criteria of success and thereby also with other aesthetic characteristics than those of a narrative.[133] Even though reader-response theory has accentuated the role of the reader as an active participant in the interpretation of the literary work, we are dealing with a different kind of interaction and immersion. Wolfgang Iser's theory of the *Leerstellen* of a text, which the reader fills out while reading, implies that the work does not arise until it meets a reader, but Espen Aarseth and others argue that there is a significant difference be-

---

terms »performative« and »constative« derive originally from the vocabulary of the British philosopher of language J.L. Austin. In *How to do Things With Words* he describes »constative utterances« as the type of sentences which describe or constate something. They can therefore always be said to be either true or false. In contrast to these he defines »performative utterances« as statements which not merely state something which is true or false, but perform an action. It does something rather than describe what is being done. Example: »I name this ship the ›Queen Elizabeth‹« (Austin, p. 5).

129 Ryan, Avatars of Story, p. 203.

130 Juul argues that the differences are based on different interpretations of narrative, thus highlighting that the question of whether games are narratives rely on what definition of narrative is used and which aspect of the game is in focus (Juul, Half-real, p. 157).

131 See, for instance, Genette.

132 Juul, Games Telling Stories.

133 See also Eskelinen.

tween the interaction of a reader of a narration and that of the player of a computer game:

In the adventure game or determinate cybertext, far from moving toward a story by means of a plot with significant gaps, it is the plot that is narrowed down, by designifying of the gaps. From many potential stories, a single plot is extracted (if the player is successful).[134]

Even in a text which leaves a large part of the construction of meaning to the interpretation of the reader, the interaction of the reader consists rather of the construction of an interpretative discourse that requires her to step out of the fictitious world in order to be able to conduct her interpretation. As Juul argues, the player stays in this world when she interacts, because the time of the thing told, the narrative time and the time of the game merge.[135] This conclusion corresponds to the following statement by Gadamer:

Die Seinsweise des Spieles läßt nicht zu, daß sich der Spieler zu dem Spiel wie zu einem Gegenstande verhält. Der Spielende weiß wohl, was Spiel ist, und daß, was er tut, ›nur ein Spiel ist‹, aber er weiß nicht, was er da ›weiß‹.[136]

While playing the game the player does not know that it is »only a game«, although this is, of course, clear to him when not playing. This sense of existing and moving in a »now« helps create a sense of *immersion*, which describes the physical sensation of being absorbed by a different reality.[137] The experience of having to learn to navigate is an important part of the player's pleasure of playing. The goal we reach is not necessarily the solution of the game, but the immersion which in itself contains enjoyment for the player: »Exploring the game world, examining its details and enjoying its images, is as important for the success of games [...] as progressing through the narrative.«[138]

Marie-Laure Ryan counter-argues that, when reading a book or seeing a film, we likewise experience the events as taking place in the present.[139] There is no doubt that we can also immerse ourselves in a narrative. In fact this is the desired effect of many (especially realist) narratives. However, as Juul's argument about the sensation of time in games clearly shows, the ability to act and choose in the imagined world accentuates the feeling of im-

---

134 Aarseth, Cybertext, pp. 111-12.
135 Juul, Games Telling Stories.
136 Gadamer, pp. 97-98.
137 The implications and diverging uses of the concept of immersion in game studies is, for instance, discussed in Dovey and Kennedy, p. 104f.
138 Manovich, The Language of New Media, p. 247.
139 Ryan, Avatars of Story, p. 186f.

mersion. In *Narrative as Virtual Reality* (2001), Ryan argues that immersion opposes interaction, because interaction necessarily involves reflection and thus moves the experience to a discursive level which ruins the immersion in the fictional world. She sees in virtual reality the most promising potential for reconciling the two, because it involves the whole of the body of the player in the experience of the fictional world. However, Juul's argument on the perception of time in games underscores that, even in a less technologically sophisticated phenomenon such as the computer game, we find this merging of the immersive with the interactive.[140] Rather than ruining the immersion in the fictional world, the fact that the game requires choices by the player means that she is transported directly into this world. The choices made in (most) computer games do not require discursive analysis, but rather that the player understands the world in which she moves. We can thus remain in the fictional world and still interact.[141]

The player's participation in the realisation of the game and the experience of time which this interaction involves are thus both fundamental for the logic of the game, and they provide conditions for the creation of a satisfying game experience different from those that we expect of a narrative. Juul writes:

Computer games are not narrations, but phenomena whose merits lie in exploration and repeatability – in a construction which allows that the same small elements can be combined again and again in new and interesting configurations. It is the strength of the computer game that it can do something else than tell stories.[142]

He thereby points to repetition as a distinctive characteristic. Gadamer indicates something similar with regard to the game:

Das Ordnungsgefüge des Spieles läßt den Spieler gleichsam in sich aufgehen und nimmt ihm damit die Aufgabe der Initiative ab, die die eigentliche Anstrengung des Daseins ausmacht. Das zeigt sich auch in dem spontanen Drang zur Wiederholung, der im Spielenden aufkommt und an dem beständigen Sich-Erneuern des Spieles, das seine Form prägt (z.B. der Refrain).[143]

The excitement that drives the player to the next level cannot be equated with what drives the reader of a novel. To the player, a computer game is about solving problems, confronting opponents, and refining the ability to

---

140 Ryan, Narrative as Virtual Reality, p. 354.

141 Murray also distinguishes between immersion and what she calls agency, but introduces the concept of agency with the statement: »The more realized the immersive environment, the more active we want to be within it« (Murray, Hamlet on the Holodeck, p. 126). For her too the ability to act is not contrary to a sense of immersion.

142 Juul, En Kamp mellem Spil og Fortælling, p. 66. My translation.

143 Gadamer, p. 100.

navigate. This skill is learned through repeated attempts to search for the underlying algorithm on which the code of the game builds, often in a competition with oneself to get a higher score. The repetition arises in the accumulation of knowledge about the game that is built up through practice and which puts the player in an increasingly better position to complete the game. The repetition thus becomes a central element, but in a way different than in narration, not least due to the interaction of the user which means that the game takes place in the »now«. The type of repetition with which we are dealing in a computer game has been described with the disputed term *emergence*.[144] The concept of emergence comes from evolutionary theory but has become especially popular in complex system theory. It is often accused of not really defining anything, but computer game research seems to be a place in which there is, in fact, some consensus on the use of the term. Emergence in games defines the way in which games are built where a number of simple rules are combined and give variation, and where the player develops strategies to play the game from these simple rules. Jesper Juul[145] quotes the following description of an emergence structure by John Holland, an American professor in psychology and computer technology:

Emergence [...] occurs only when the activities of the parts do *not* simply sum to give activity of the whole. For emergence, the whole is indeed more than the sum of its parts. To see this, let us look again at chess. We *cannot* get a representative picture of a game in progress by simply adding the values of the pieces on the board. The pieces interact to support one another and to control various parts of the board.[146]

The number of possible outcomes and the roads to these are thus enormous in a computer game which builds on an emergence structure. This means that the game can be repeated over and over again in new configurations. In this sense the emergence characteristics of the game as an emergent structure capture much of what N. Katherine Hayles calls »possibility space«, which she sees as being intertwined with narrative – particularly in electronic fiction and in works like George Perec's *La Vie mode d'emploi* (1978) and Milorad Pavic's *Dictionary of the Khazars* (1984):

As the machinic becomes entwined with the human, narrative moves from the causal sequences typical of traditional storytelling toward the combinatoric algorithms typical of possibility space. The results are quasi-narratives that strive to capture all pos-

---

144 See, for instance, Juul, The Open and the Closed or Juul, Half-real, p. 73f.
145 Juul, Hvad spillet betyder, p. 185.
146 Holland, p. 14.

sible combinations within causal sequences, as if unwilling to abandon either causality or combinatorics.[147]

To sum up briefly before taking Hayles' cue and moving on to look at how the figure of the computer game functions in three different examples of contemporary fiction, we have seen that the computer game can be understood as a mode of representation which accentuates repetition in the form of an emergence structure, at the same time as the significance of user interaction and immersion in the »now« of the game are emphasized. In *Narrative across Media*, Ryan aims to mediate between the standpoints regarding whether or not games should be regarded as narratives by shifting the position of enquiry. For Ryan the question is not whether the logic of new media opposes that of a narrative logic; for her the challenge is for new media to develop their own forms of narrativity which succeed in reconciling narrativity with interactivity. There is no doubt that, in so far as they provide us with a fictional world of navigable space, in many respects computer games enter more easily into a dialogue with a narrative logic than both the database and the hyperlink. However, the aim in this study differs from those of Ryan and Aarseth in that we are *not* trying to determine whether or not computer games have narrative elements; instead we are looking at how the computer game as a concrete material sign of information technology as a symbolic form influences contemporary fiction. In contrast to Ryan and Aarseth, we are exploring the figure of the game in a context where narrativity is taken for granted (i.e. the novel), and our aim is to investigate how the figure of the game occurs in this environment. Significantly, we will discover that the game mostly works as a disruptive element in the progression of the narrative, thus highlighting that, even though narrative and games might be made to work together, there are fundamental differences. However, we shall also see that, in the three novels at which we shall be looking, this disruption proves fruitful for the representation of life in the twenty-first century, thus underscoring the argument that information technology may be regarded as a symbolic form.

Faced with life in an information society, as are the characters of all these three novels, the figure of the computer game provides a way of dealing with these conditions, sometimes providing an adequate way of ma-

---

147 Hayles, Narrating Bits, p. 182. The emergence structure as defined by Holland points to resemblances with Gestalt psychology's notion of the Gestalt (cf. chapter 2.2) and thus the structure of the network as well as the database's emphasis on combinatorics. Nonetheless, it is emphasised here as a characteristic of the computer game, because it provides an illuminating way of describing the relationhip between the parts of a game. However, the correspondence may be regarded as yet another example of the close relationship between the three concrete material signs of information technology as a symbolic form which we are looking at in this study.

noeuvring in the world (as in David Mitchell's *number9dream*), sometimes with fatal consequences (as in Günter Grass' *Im Krebsgang*), and sometimes providing the framework which renders representation possible at all (as in Guy Tournaye's *Le Décodeur*).

3.3.1 »You're doomed from the first coin. You pay to postpone the ending, but the video game will always win in the long run.« David Mitchell's *number9dream*

I catch a glimpse of my father being bundled into an unmarked van parked across the baseball field. I would recognize him anywhere. He hammers on the back window, but the van is already through the gates and disappearing into the smoking rubble of Tokyo. I leap onto our patrol stratobike, take off my baseball cap and rest it on the console. Zizzi flashes me a peppermint smile and off we zoom. Lavender clouds slide by. I train my gun on a chillipepper schoolboy, but for once things are exactly as they appear. The sunroof of a midnight Cadillac flips open, and out pops a lobstermob-ster*Bang!* Shell and claws everywhere. I drill the rear window and the vehicle explodes in paintbox flames.[148]

The introduction to the third chapter »Video Games« of David Mitchell's *number9dream* (2001) operates smoothly between two levels of reality which in the narrative merge into one. The first three sentences let us believe that we are in the »normal world« of Eiji Miyake, a twenty-year-old man from the provinces who has come to Tokyo in search of his father. Then, in the fourth sentence, the word »stratobike« appears, raising the reader's suspicion about the world in which the action takes place. This suspicion is increasingly confirmed the more we read and the more surreal the world described becomes. Our doubts as to whether the action takes place in the same world as the previous chapter are also encouraged by the mention of a »console«. This might of course refer to a part of this unknown vehicle, the stratobike, but by now the reader has become guarded and it seems more likely that »console« refers to the control board of the gaming machine. We are thus situated outside the game universe, in the game centre in which we later learn that Eiji plays this game. References further on in the text, where Eiji's hand gets tired, provide the same sophisticated slippage between the game world and the real world. As readers we are thus lured into the description of the game: the references to the father let us believe that this chapter follows on from what we learned in the two previous chapters of Eiji and his search for his father. Only when we are caught up in the tearing speed of the gameplay reported to us in the present

---

148 Mitchell, p. 97.

tense, as if we were experiencing the game simultaneously with Eiji, do we realise that this is in fact a virtual scenario – a game sequence embedded in the narrative.

number9dream is interesting to consider in relation to the figure of the game which we have already identified as a concrete material sign of information technology as a symbolic form. David Mitchell is British, but the novel takes place in Japan, which places us in a different part of the world altogether from the very European focus of the novels we have looked at so far. Nonetheless, *number9dream* is included precisely for the reasons which might exclude it. It provides a full-blown reflection of the edges of an investigation that has focussed on European novels from the last two decades which, while certainly relating to information technology, do not necessarily have information technology and computers as their main thematic focus. From the beginning this has meant that many of the obvious classics of Anglo-American science fiction from the 1970s and 1980s and novels by writers such as Kurt Vonnegut, Thomas Pynchon, William Gibson, and Douglas Coupland have not been included. However, the atmosphere and vocabulary of the science fiction genre is what to a great degree shapes the world and logic of many computer games and, by looking at the game as a phenomenon, we are also looking at a whole body of cultural heritage stemming from the adventure genre as well as science fiction novels and films. *number9dream* is not a science fiction novel, and the computer is neither portrayed as something to be feared nor something in which to vest special hopes, but rather as an everyday object that Eiji encounters repeatedly. Nonetheless, the novel eloquently plays with the genre and the implications of the game for the narrative progression of the text, and in places mimics films like *Blade Runner*, the novels of William Gibson, as well as Japanese cartoons. Bringing *number9dream* into our discussion highlights the way in which the novels at which we are looking belong to a fairly new generation of novels relating to information technology. For this generation information technology is neither salvation nor apocalypse, but an everyday phenomenon which nevertheless influences the way they perceive and represent the world.

Kinship with the other novels we have looked at also stems from the fact that *number9dream* was criticised by reviewers for the same reason as most of the novels dealt with in this study: for providing an overload of information. Robert MacFarlane, for instance, wrote in *The Observer* that:

number9dream is a sprawling, wanton affair. For all its attractions, the book suffers from an imaginative hyper-fecundity. What with the alternative realities, the narrative byways and cul-de-sacs, there is just too much information coming at you.[149]

In *The New York Times Book Review*, Daniel Zalewski described Mitchell's problem as a »lack of control«[150], and a narrative spinning out of control bordering on something else and more game-like is indeed what we are dealing with in *number9dream*. The reason that this study includes *number9dream*, with its bombardment of information and different genres, is perhaps best encapsulated by the *Evening Standard*'s Jerome Boyd Maunsell when he describes the novel's cacophony of quest, romance, cyberthriller, and family saga as a text filled with »the crackling rhythms of the digital age«.[151] Whereas the database and the hyperlink present themselves as ways of reacting to and representing this condition of »overload«, for instance in *Rand* and *Abtrünnig*, the game takes on this role in *number9dream*, as it did in *ZT*.

Like the notion of »Längeres Gedankenspiel« in *ZT*, the figure of the game in *number9dream* is bound up with that of the dream in its many forms (nightmares, daydreams, memories). The dream becomes the main narrative device that allows for the novel to break down the logic of reality and take in different forms of narration. As a child Eiji used to imagine that his life was actually the dream of someone else:

I imagined there lived somewhere, in an advertland house and family, the Real Eiji Miyake. He dreamed of me every night. And that was who I really was – a dream of the Real Eiji Miyake. When I went to sleep and dreamed, he woke up, and remembered my waking life as his dream. And vice versa.[152]

This blurring of the difference between reality and dream veils the whole novel in a hazy hue of the unreal. In dreams time collapses, and Eiji is able to move effortlessly between the actual past, what is yet to come, and what will never be: »Time may be what prevents everything from happening at the same time in waking reality, but the rules are different in dreams«.[153] It is these other rules by which *number9dream* operates when incorporating the dream world into its texture. From the very beginning of the novel we see how the dream and the real overlap and intermingle. The first chapter is characterized by a repeated playing through of Eiji's attempt to talk to his father's lawyer and to get her to reveal her client's identity. However, the

---

149 MacFarlane.
150 Zalewski.
151 Maunsell.
152 Mitchell, pp. 407-8.
153 Ibid. p. 400.

narrative is short-circuited every time and revealed to be just another imaginative scenario Eiji conjures up while he summons the courage to actually walk over to the office building in which the lawyer works. What signifies most of Eiji's dreams is the fast-paced tempo. Apart from the section where Eiji is caught up in a Yakuza[154] gang showdown, it is the dream sections which most resemble popular cultural genres such as action movies, cartoons, and video games. In the following reading of the text we shall focus on the way in which games and dreams intermingle in the novel and help create its special narrative space.

Games are a central figure in Eiji's life and in the novel as a whole. The three most prevalent are football, card games, and video games. Football belongs to his childhood and life on the island with his sister Anju, who drowns while he is away playing an important game. Card games are connected to his encounter with the unpredictable city of Tokyo, most crucially illustrated in chapter seven, »Cards«, when the Yakuza forces him to play a card game in which whoever turns the queen of spades has to donate his organs while the others go free. When Eiji finally stumbles over his father accidentally he describes it as: »a card trick that Tokyo has performed«,[155] and one of his co-workers at the pizza bar describes the human condition as a card game.[156] Video games feature most prominently in chapter three,[157] but they are also found in other chapters[158] and their language and logic prevail throughout the novel in so far as Eiji's dreams often take the form and vocabulary of video games.

For Eiji dreams and games are a way of playing through reality in its many bearings and coping with the reality that actually faces him. As such, the novel may be described as a modern »Bildungsroman« which has sent Eiji on a quest from his home island to the modern cybercity to find the identity of his father. However, it becomes apparent that behind the search for his father there lies a more fundamental search for »meaning« and a need to reconcile the trauma of losing his twin sister when he was eleven. After reading the diary of his great uncle, who gave his life to the emperor of Japan during the Second World War, Eiji has several conversations with Ai, the girl with whom he falls in love in Tokyo, about finding the meaning of life. Two statements stand out, both made by Ai, which point to an un-

---

154 The Japanese mafia is a common reference point in video games as well as films. The name »Yakuza« originally comes from a Japanese card game. In 2005 Sega released a video game in Japan with the name »Yakuza«.
155 Mitchell, p. 370.
156 Ibid. p. 351.
157 Ibid. pp. 95-149. See also the quotation at the beginning of this section.
158 For instance Mitchell, p. 15.

derstanding of life as a game: »Maybe the meaning of life lies in the act of looking for it«[159] which is later modified to:

›You find your own meaning by passing or failing a series of tests.‹
›Who passes or fails you in these tests?‹
Her footsteps echo and static breezes. ›You do.‹[160]

Whereas a narrative conception of identity finds its meaning through gathering the discordant material of life into a consistent narration, identity understood in terms of the figure of the game may be described as understanding life as a series of choices with several equally likely outcomes. Eiji's quest for meaning, his understanding of his own identity, and the form of the game are thus closely tied together on the thematic level. However, as we shall see, they are also tied into the discussion of how the story is composed.

Eiji's story is told as a first person narration. It is the world as it unfolds to him which we encounter, including all the dreams and fictitious worlds which surround him. The novel thus includes the journal of his great uncle, who was a suicide pilot aboard a so-called kaiten torpedo during the Second World War; the fairy tales he finds in the study of an author in whose house he takes refuge from the Yakuza gang; letters from his mother, who is trying to give up drinking and start a new life; the story of a woman abducted by the Yakuza and forced into prostitution; and the textual representation of video game sequences which Eiji plays. Eiji's story is told as an interplay between the experiences he has in Tokyo, flashbacks to his childhood with his sister on the island, and his dreams. This uneven bundle of material is strung together in eight chapters of approximately the same length and a further one – the ninth – which is untitled and unwritten apart from the number nine. The novel's own explanation for this structure is given in one of Eiji's dreams where he meets John Lennon, who explains the title of his song #9 Dream from 1975 with the statement: »The ninth dream begins after every ending.«[161] The ending of the novel number9dream has indeed the character of a beginning rather than an end: on the last pages of the novel, after Eiji has returned home to his island, he hears the news of an earthquake in Tokyo. As readers we are left in the dark as to what will now happen to Eiji and the people he met in Tokyo and, once again, as to what is dream and what is reality. As one of the characters writes at one point: »Endings are simple, but every beginning is made by the beginning be-

159 Mitchell, p. 288.
160 Ibid. p. 309.
161 Ibid. p. 398.

fore.«[162] The novel thus comes to resemble an emergence structure in so far as it arises from the combination of the diverse material at hand, creating a portrayal of the multifaceted complexity of human experience which is more than the sum of the individual parts. The fact that the combination of the material with which we are presented is only one of potentially many – one possible way of playing the given hand – is highlighted by the blank chapter nine, which is not written but represents the beginning of a new dream, a new combination of the elements available.

In *number9dream* games emerge as equal to the other imaginary worlds of the novel: daydreams, nightmares, memories, fairy tales. A game is a certain kind of dream in the same way as a novel is, but in the novel *number9dream* the dreams often involve a form of game. However, the game seems to be more of a narrative device than an actual attempt to fuse the novel genre with the possibilities of interaction given by the game. The reader is not invited into the creation of the narrative, as would be the case had *number9dream* been released as a game. We follow Eiji and navigate in the world as he does. *number9dream* is a novel not a game, but it uses the game form as a vehicle in the construction of the narrative.

The aim of featuring the game so heavily as a motif and narrative vehicle seems to be to let the logic of the computer game (and the emergence structure it entails) open up the narrative and create a space for the inclusion of the much diversified material rather than, as we have seen in some of the other novels considered in this study, perhaps most radically in *ZT,* challenge narrativity per se. In *number9dream* the game becomes a way of creating an adequate response to, as well as representing, what Jerome Boyd Maunsell in the *Evening Standard* described as »the crackling rhythms of the digital age«. *number9dream* thus stands out as a novel which aims to encompass and represent human experience not only as consisting of what takes place before our eyes, but also as involving the imaginary worlds which we carry with us, fed by the culture and media which surround us, and the narratives they generate.

In this sense the figure of the game can be seen as providing a way in which the contemporary world, with all its information, can be communicated and represented. The novel as a whole is created as an emergence structure in which the protagonist moves through new worlds in a continuous loop between reality and imaginary realms, creating an unpredictable field of possible worlds. Only in the interaction between these worlds does the story move forward. The emergence structure of the game thus seems an

---

162 Ibid. p. 333.

adequate description of the uneven collection of material of which *number9dream* is composed.

While we have focussed mainly on the emergence structure as characteristic of the figure of the game in *number9dream*, the next novel we shall look at highlights another central feature demonstrated by the figure of the game, namely immersion. Günter Grass' *Im Krebsgang* shifts us back to a German focus, given that it deals specifically with Germany's past and collective memory. It also operates in a context where popular culture is more distant as a reference point than is the case in *number9dream*. It thus functions as a point of comparison and contrast which highlights other issues of the game as a concrete material sign of information technology as a symbolic form than those that we have encountered so far.

3.3.2 »Jedenfalls begann ein streitbares Rollenspiel« Günter Grass' *Im Krebsgang*

The role of the internet in Günter Grass' *Im Krebsgang*, which was published in 2002, has already been examined, and the mode of narration of the novella compared with the structure of hypertext.[163] However, looking at *Im Krebsgang* from the point of view of the concrete material sign of information technology as a symbolic form which we have called the computer game, with a special focus on the implications of interactivity and immersion, adds another level of understanding to the relationship between the function of the chatroom within the logic of the novella and the narrative construction of the plot. The figure of the game is in fact at work on three different levels within the body of the printed novella: on a thematic level, a narrative level, and in the construction and reading of the text.

Much of the general cultural debate about computer games has centred on the impact of violent games on children and young people and the abuse children might be subjected to by chatting to strangers online.[164] *Im Krebsgang* can be read as taking part in this debate in so far as the computer is regarded as being at least partly to blame for Konny going to the extremes that he does (his grandmother's and parents' inadequate ways of dealing with the past are clearly also factors). There seems to be no doubt that the realm of debate and the way in which the virtual and the real are dealt with in the chatroom plays a significant role in the development of the plot. In the following, we shall look more closely at how the insertion of the

---

163 See Midgley, Günter Grass, *Im Krebsgang*; and Veel, Virtual Memory in Günter Grass' *Im Krebsgang*.
164 See, for instance, McAllister.

chatroom into the narrative influences the character of the fictional world created by the novella.

Im Krebsgang covers German history from 1936 to 1999 projected onto three generations of the Pokriefke family. The middle-aged journalist Paul Pokriefke is the main narrative voice. His son, Konny, commits a murder, having been spurred on by tales of German suffering at the end of World War II related to him by his grandmother Tulla, and which Konny subsequently re-tells in neo-Nazi terms on the internet. Paul is employed to tell his family's story by the mysterious world-weary author »Jemand«, who bears a close resemblance to Grass. This means that he has to mediate between his mother's nostalgic memories of the shipwreck of the cruise ship *Wilhelm Gustloff* on 30 January 1945, and his son's reproduction of these events on the internet, which has led to murder.

Let us first trace the figure of the game on a thematic level. The contemporary events which bring the past to the surface are mainly played out on the internet. Through the website Konny sets up to commemorate the sinking of the ship *Wilhelm Gustloff*, on which his grandmother was a passenger, he encounters another young man likewise obsessed by the past. They each assume a fictional identity online and commence a debate about the historical events in question. In the novella this online debate is described in terms of role play:

> Jedenfalls begann ein streitbares Rollenspiel.
> Der fortan immer wieder auflebende Disput wurde per Vornamen geführt, indem ein Wilhelm dem ermordeten Landesgruppenleiter Stimme gab und sich ein David als verhinderter Selbstmörder in Szene setzte.[165]

Konny and Wolfgang assume identities as virtual reincarnations of the historical characters Gustloff – the German Nazi official who was killed and subsequently became a martyr – and Frankfurter – the Jewish student who shot Gustloff and stated the reasons for his deed with the words: »Ich habe geschossen, weil ich Jude bin«.[166] The metaphor of table tennis is repeatedly invoked whenever the interaction between the two boys is referred to. We are thus dealing with an imaginary space which appears to come from the realm of play or game and is dominated by the rules of this space: »Beide beteuerten, für Fairplay zu sein. Und beide bewiesen sich als Bescheidwisser, die ihre jeweils neuen Erkenntnisse wechselseitig lobten.«[167] A dialogue begins consisting of antagonism on the one hand, and respect and mutual

---

165 Grass, pp. 47-48.
166 Ibid. p. 28.
167 Ibid. p. 49.

understanding on the other. In this forum the two outsider boys have each found a person with similar interests and approaches to the past.

Looking closely at what this relationship to the past entails, we observe that the otherwise conscious distinction between present and past becomes blurred for the two boys. Konny and Wolfgang's chatroom discussions are not only a debate about historical facts, they amount to a virtual *replaying* of the fatal incidents. They not only read and reflect on the past, they relive it and interact in it. Therefore their role-play transgresses the virtual boundaries and becomes real for them, something which we see already in one of their first encounters: »Wilhelms in den Chatroom gestellte Frage »Würdest du, wenn mich der Führer ins Leben zurückriefe, abermals auf mich schießen?«, beantwortete David umgehend: »Nein, nächstes Mal darfst du mich abknallen.«[168] The distinction between present and past is blurred to an extent which allows for their disagreement to escape from the virtual and enter reality. In other words they immerse themselves so much in the roles of Wilhelm Gustloff and David Frankfurter and their interaction in the chatroom that they not only become unable to separate past from present, but also reality from virtuality.

A reason for this may be found in what we saw as characteristic of the immersion obtained in games. The feeling of immersion and agency blurs the boundaries between real and virtual space and creates a sense of being in a completely other reality that takes over the perceptual apparatus. This experience of space influences the social manners and conventions of dialogue on the internet. As Sherry Turkle, among others, has shown, the boundaries of acceptable behaviour are more easily transgressed by stepping outside oneself and taking on another role in a fictitious space.[169] Rather than providing catharsis in the Aristotelian sense and domesticating disturbing feelings or threatening fantasies, the chatroom provides a forum for Konny and Wolfgang in which there are no social norms and moral boundaries to prevent abusive language and unreflective verbal violence. Combined with the blurring of the distance between the world in actual fact and its representation, the digital narration into which Konny and Wolfgang weave themselves becomes deadly, because the violent social manners of the chatroom are transferred into the real world. The identification between the virtual »character« Gustloff of the past and the real, contemporary »reader/author« Konny causes the distance which is inherent in most narration to disappear. The representation of the past which he creates on screen becomes so real that the sense of past and present, imaginative and real space, is blurred to a degree that makes him carry out the murder in reality.

---

168 Grass, p. 49.
169 Turkle, p. 82.

His identity becomes so tied up with representing this other character – his virtual alter ego – Wilhelm Gustloff that his actual self merges with Gustloff's outlook upon the world.

On the thematic level we thus witness a discussion of the immersive effects of role-playing on the internet. Although we are not dealing with a computer game in the traditional sense, but a role-play in the form of a chatroom, we plunge right into the discussion of interactivity and immersion raised by the figure of the game in the more general sense outlined at the beginning of this chapter. The question of immersion or identification also becomes central on another level, i.e. in relation to the construction of the narrative. Throughout the story, Paul repeatedly reflects on how the story should be told, and towards the end we learn that the old writer who employed Paul to write the story has forbidden him to speculate on what Konny or any of the other characters might be thinking:

> Er sagt: ›Niemand weiß, was er dachte und weiterhin denkt. Jede Stirn hält dicht, nicht nur seine. Sperrzone. Für Wortjäger Niemandsland. Zwecklos, die Hirnschale abzuheben. Außerdem spricht keiner aus, was er denkt. Und wer es versucht, lügt mit dem ersten Halbsatz.‹[170]

This prohibition on identification with the characters in the novella or of immersion in their world (and dismissal of the possibility of such immersion) seems significant in comparison with the evidence which the chatroom provides of how wrong things can go when such identification is attempted. Konny and Wolfgang try to do exactly what Paul is warned against to imagine that they are inside the head of the historical characters Wilhelm and David. In the virtual room of the chatroom they merge with these characters and Wilhelm and David become vehicles for emotions which Konny and Wolfgang cannot find an outlet for in their everyday environment. However, »Jemand« (the looming author figure who guides Paul in his construction of the novella *Im Krebsgang*) wants to obtain something else with the novella than Konny does with his website. The figure of the chatroom and the form of immersion it represents provide him with an illustrative example of an apparently inadequate way of handling the past.

However, it becomes quite clear that, for Paul, narration is not an easy way to come to terms with the past – it is an elaborate challenge to create an adequate representation of the past, a task he describes as a dissolution of his identity rather than a construction of it: »Wenn ich jetzt beginnen muß, mich selber abzuwickeln, wird alles, was mir schiefgegangen ist, dem Untergang eines Schiffes eingeschrieben sein.«[171] The story of the ship-

---

170 Grass, p. 199.
171 Ibid. p. 7.

wreck has shaped his identity to such a degree that the act of narrating the
events becomes a disintegration of the fragile core of his personality, because he realizes the difficulties of creating a truthful representation. Thus
narration does not emerge as the easy and only right way to understand oneself and one's past. The road to an appropriate representation of the past is
more circuitous than that. In this respect it is significant to consider not only
the differences between the chatroom and the way in which the narrative
runs in *Im Krebsgang*, but also the similarities, not least because the chatroom and its implications provide an important point of reference in the
construction of the narrative space unfolding in »Krebsgang«.

The way in which the story is told is first and foremost defined by the
mode in which the narration progresses – the pace of the »Krebsgang«:

Aber noch weiß ich nicht, ob, wie gelernt, erst das eine, dann das andere und danach
dieser oder jener Lebenslauf abgespult werden soll oder ob ich der Zeit eher schräg-
läufig in die Quere kommen muß, etwa nach Art der Krebse, die den Rückwärtsgang
seitlich ausscherend vortäuschen, doch ziemlich schnell vorankommen.[172]

Moving forward while simultaneously looking backwards re-enacts the
process of remembering, and the novella thus comes to reflect on the procedural character of narrating and remembering. Rather than forming a linear
progression, the story jumps between present and past and allows for multiple stories to unfold simultaneously. This can be read as enacting the mode
of reading hypertext, as argued in my article »Virtual Memory in Günter
Grass' *Im Krebsgang*« in *German Life and Letters*,[173] but if we read the
concept of the »Krebsgang« in terms of the chatroom and the figure of the
game, we add further to the interpretation of what the »Krebsgang« entails.
In *Im Krebsgang* this way of telling the story means that past and present
appear as worlds of equal importance, and the hard work of coming to
terms with the past, which is the challenge facing all the contemporary
characters of the novella, becomes a matter of mediating between the multiple worlds open to the human subject. Rather than seeing the historical period which the novella covers as a historical progression from past to present, the novella creates a space of simultaneity in which the characters, despite their historical situation, operate on equal terms; we are thus reminded
of the description of the notion of time in *ZT* as having a »statisch-zeitlosen
Charakter«. In *Im Krebsgang* history opens up as an emergent structure – a
virtual world into which we can project ourselves by replaying the past.

Consequently, what characterizes a narration told in »crablike« fashion is
that the boundaries between the different periods of time are porous. This

---

172 Ibid. pp. 8-9.
173 Veel, Virtual Memory in Günter Grass' *Im Krebsgang*.

influences the form that the novella takes. *Im Krebsgang* consists of fictional characters moving in a fictional environment; this fictional world is folded around the actual historical event of the sinking of the *Wilhelm Gustloff*. However, the historical events are also dramatized by focussing respectively on the Russian captain on the submarine who sank the *Gustloff*, the man whose name the ship carried, and the man who shot Gustloff. The figure that incarnates this porosity between past and present in the construction of the different worlds of the novella is the chatroom. The chatroom likewise represents a breaking down of the boundaries between the past and the present, but in an extreme form for which there is no room in the genre of narrative fiction. The difference between the novella's representation of time and that of the chatroom is not only that in the chatroom the boundaries between past and present are blurred, but also that a large amount of identification with the characters of the past is added, so that their concerns become our present concerns. This opens up the possibility of an interaction with the past, which on the thematic level of the novella represents a dangerous undertaking.

The chatroom thus embodies a medium which proposes a form of representation and identification which would break open the narrative and allow for an identification and interaction which threatens the distance which the novella wants to uphold. Were true immersion/identification in the form of interaction to be allowed into the novella it would mean shifting the mode of representation from constative to performative[174] and the narrative would transgress itself. However, the novella plays with this possibility and uses the connotations of this figure to create its own negotiation between past and present and show the dangers of breaking down these boundaries.

Moreover, in the construction of the narrative and the structure of the novella as the reader encounters it, there is a playfulness in the relationship between historical and fictional figures. Within the logic of the narrative, Paul, Konny, and Tulla are the »real« characters and figures like Wilhelm Gustloff and David Frankfurter remain, if not fictional, then at least accessible only in the imagination, because they belong to the past. But to the readers of *Im Krebsgang*, Gustloff and Frankfurter present themselves in a certain sense as more lifelike, because we know that they are actual historical characters, whereas Paul, Konny, and Tulla remain fictional constructs. Grass knowingly plays with these real and imaginative levels by letting the figure of »Jemand« resemble himself and even presenting him as the author of the novel *Hundejahre* (which Grass published in 1963). This is interesting, because it shows us the variety of levels on which the discussion of

---

174 Aarseth, Quest Games as Post-Narrative Discourse, p. 369.

immersion and interaction embodied by the figure of the chatroom takes place in this novella. As readers we are not invited to interact or participate in the novella in any sense apart from the »normal« engagement a novella evokes; it is not in this sense that the figure of the game is interesting as a way of reading *Im Krebsgang*. However, for the reader the intermingling of the historical facts with the fictional narrative creates the sensation that the novella reaches out into her world. The chatroom thus proposes a form of representation which the novella warns against as an adequate way of dealing with the past, but it also – and this is significant – provides a mirror for the form and the challenges the narration itself takes and faces.

In comparison with the figure of the game found in *number9dream*, in *Im Krebsgang* we have seen another example of the way in which the game as a concrete material sign may point to information technology as a symbolic form embedded into the theme and construction of the narrative. The implications of this use are different from those that we saw in *number9dream*, as are the theme and voice of the two novels, but they both display ways in which the figure of the computer game participates in the negotiation of the way in which the narratives are conducted.

3.3.3 »Pour continuer, appuyer sur la touche Play« Guy Tournaye's *Le Décodeur*

The last example we shall consider in relation to the figure of the computer game also features a chatroom, but addresses the relationship between printed text and screen representation as a matter of form in a much more »head-on« manner than any of the other examples we have dealt with so far. The author Guy Tournaye has previously worked for the French Canal Plus and the Conseil Supérieur de l'Audiovisuel (CSA).[175] The main part of his first novel *Le Décodeur* (2005) is constructed as a textual representation of the content of an audiovisual webpage, thus drawing on the connotations of TV drama and computer games.

The introductory chapter of the novel sets the stage by telling the story of how the website for the TV series *Street Hassle* was closed down by the FBI on the basis of allegations that it functioned as a communication channel for terrorist organisations. The credibility of the story is underlined by footnotes referring to real newspaper articles from the websites of www.lemonde.fr and www.usatoday.com as well as university reports on the topic of websites carrying hidden messages. The introduction and initiation of the book is ascribed to a first-person narrator who presents himself as a

---

175 Grangeray.

previous editor of the journal *Multimédia Stratégies*. He has come into possession of a DVD which contains the content of the allegedly hi-jacked website, supposedly given to him at a cryptography conference by an anonymous member of a research group at the Center for Secure Information Systems at George Mason University. The job of this editor was to transcribe and translate every single webpage in order to publish it as a novel, a choice of medium which he explains in the following manner:

> J'ai entrepris la traduction et la transcription de chacune des pages stockées sur le support optique, convaincu qu'un livre serait le meilleur moyen de les relier et d'en révéler la trame cachée. Le contenu original du site *Street Hassle* et les données camouflées s'affichant en surimpression dans la version décodée ont été retranscrits de la façon le plus littérale possible, sans fioriture de style ni artifice typographique. Cette mise à plat délibérée ne vise pas seulement à garantir la fluidité de la lecture. Elle crée un texte à double entrée – une sorte de stéréogramme –, qui laisse le lecteur libre de choisir lui-même son point de vue, en focalisant soit sur l'intrigue de la série policière, soit sur la machination qui s'y inscrit en filigrane.
>
> D'aucuns s'étonneront sans doute de voir un tel document publié sous l'appellation ›roman‹. Il ne s'agit évidemment pas de mettre en doute l'authenticité de l'enquête menée par les chercheurs de l'université George Mason. Encore moins de surestimer la part de subjectivité inhérente à tout travail de transcription. Le mot ›roman‹, ici, a d'abord valeur de manifeste.[176]

These are the guidelines provided for reading the subsequent material presented to the reader in 21 chapters which reveal the structure of the site, transcriptions from the discussion forum, descriptions of selected scenes, information on the music, scenery, costumes, and script. The transition from the introduction to the actual website is initiated by the evocative phrase: »Pour continuer, appuyer sur la touche Play«,[177] which invites the reader into the narration as if playing a computer game.

By mimicking the logic of a webpage, *Le Décodeur* draws the reader into the construction of the plot – creating immersion – in a much more direct way than we noticed in *number9dream* and *Im Krebsgang*. Also, the emergence structure is taken much more literally in a way which brings to mind the notion of »Längeres Gedankenspiel« and the quotation practice of *ZT*. At the end of the novel it is revealed that the main part is in fact extracted from the works of other authors. The last five pages consists of a list of books from which the previous text has borrowed quotations, most often without mentioning the authors cited, and sometimes in a form adjusted to the present text. The list contains works by Rousseau, Nietzsche, Baudrillard, Freud, Perec, Borges, and Deleuze, amongst others. From this perspec-

---

176 Tournaye, pp. 17-18.
177 Ibid. p. 18.

tive the novel as a whole stands out as a combination of already existing elements which, when put together, create a product which is more than the sum of its parts – in other words a structure which resembles the principle of emergence.

The figure of the game is pivotal both as an interpretational key to the intricate structure of the text and as a theme. In one of the chats on the discussion forum the mafia boss accused of murder in *Street Hassle* is likened through his name, Franck-le-Mat, to the figure of the Fool in a game of Tarot. The 22 cards that make up what is called the »major arcane« in Tarot have names like »The Magician«, »The Emperor«, and »Wheel of Fortune«. The Fool (»le Mat« in French) is the card without a number; a figure who is outside the game, a wanderer who does not fit in anywhere, related to the Joker of ordinary playing cards and the Bishop (»le Fou« in French) which in a game of chess is not restricted by distance in each move. The 22 Tarot cards are traditionally said to symbolise a story in which the Fool is the hero and the other cards are the path that he takes through life.[178] In the novel the Fool is characterised like this:

Rôle ambigu, du reste, puisque le joker se situe à la fois à l'intérieur et à l'extérieur de l'espace ludique. À l'intérieur dans la mesure où il participe au jeu comme élément actif. À l'extérieur, parce que sa fonction est de transgresser la Règle qui l'a créé. Avec lui, rien n'est jamais acquis.[179]

Playing cards also come into the story in another manner related to the discussion of the structure of the TV series' website. In the last chapter »Réalisation« we are told that Rousseau used to have a set of 27 playing cards on which were scribbled aphorisms, sketches, pieces of text. The text muses on the likely use of these cards and concludes by pointing out their inspirational function for *Street Hassle*:

Le fait est que ces cartes à jouer ont un peu servi de matrice à *Street Hassle*. Placée sous le signe du fragment, de l'énigme et de l'errance, avec le Mat pour seul et unique guide, cette série décrit un voyage imaginaire en forme de rêverie, un curriculum vitæ au sens le plus littéral du mot – [180]

When, at the completion of the novel, we are told that the textual body is in fact made up of quotations from other texts, the reader's sense of being a player rather than a reader is intensified and the novel reveals itself as a deck of playing cards similar to the ones belonging to Rousseau, but also bringing to mind the aphorism sections of *Wanderjahre* – now in a webpage version rendered possible by information technology.

---

178 Banzhaf, p. 6.
179 Tournaye, p. 32.
180 Ibid. p. 107.

In the quotation above the text reveals itself as something else relating to the figure of the tarot cards – that is a life journey – a curriculum vitae. The novel's discussion of human existence is thereby highlighted and connected to the figure of the game. This connection has already been made in chapter nine, »Détective«, which reveals the notes of the psychologist following Franck-le-Mat who suffers from bad memory loss following the death of his companion Veronica. His problems with regaining his memory and identity stand out as he has a sudden inability to connect one event with another[181]: »Sa vie n'est plus qu'une surface lisse et miroitante, un kaléidoscope d'impressions sans lien les unes avec les autres.«[182] He compensates for this condition by continuously narrating stories:

Dépouillé de son passé récent, privé de tout sentiment de continuité, il s'invente sans cesse des fictions pour remplacer ce que son esprit ne parvient plus à fixer. Sans identité, sans for intérieur, il est devenu une sorte de Schéhérazade improvisant mille et une histoires au gré des situations.[183]

This is a condition which, to a certain degree, remains even after he regains his memory. The psychologist describes his conversations with Franck-le-Mat in the following manner:

Lorsqu'il essayait de dire quelque chose de lui, d'affronter ce clown intérieur qui jonglait si bien avec son histoire, ce prestidigitateur qui savait si bien s'illusionner lui-même, il se mettait aussitôt à recommencer le même puzzle. Rêves, souvenirs d'enfance, chaînes associatives subtilement entrecroisées, jeux de miroirs où les images se renvoyaient sans fin leurs guirlandes moebiusiennes.[184]

When, in the last chapter, the claim is made that the series is an autobiography, it is an obvious conclusion to suspect Franck-le-Mat of being behind the arrangement of the series. His psychological condition would account for the cryptic content which causes the FBI to shut down the website. However, in a more abstract sense the site and thus the novel is a tale of the conditions of the human subject told through the figure of the online game and the Fool:

Autobiographique? Évidemment. Cette série n'est même que cela: une autobiographie sans je, où le sujet tisse ses relations comme autant de fils d'araignée avec certaines caractéristiques des choses et les entrelace pour construire un réseau qui porte son existence.[185]

---

181 We are reminded of the »Mangel an Verbindungskraft« in *MoE* as discussed in chapter 2.2, and Strawson's notion of an episodic outlook on the world.
182 Tournaye, p. 45.
183 Ibid. p. 44.
184 Ibid. p. 58.
185 Ibid. p. 104.

Letting *Le Décodeur* conclude this exploration of the computer game as a concrete material sign of information technology as a symbolic form in contemporary literary fiction allows us to highlight what have been the two central questions of this study: how do we go about narrating a contemporary world? And how does such a narration position the human subject? The novels we have looked at have all grappled with these questions. *Wanderjahre, MoE,* and *ZT* turned to the figures of the archive, the network, and the game – figures that have all been accentuated by information technology and are in dialogue with the forms of the database, the hyperlink, and the computer game which we have found in the contemporary novels of Kjærstad, Hettche, Strauß, Madsen, Jirgl, Mitchell, and Grass. *Le Décodeur* chooses information technology (and more specifically the game) as a resort and finds in that figure inspiration for creating a contemporary form of narration.

To a larger degree than we saw in both *number9dream* and *Im Krebsgang*, the reader is given a choice (the characteristic which Aarseth defines as distinguishing the game from the narrative). The introductory pages of *Le Décodeur*, which present the book as a novel and propose how the book should be read, emphasise precisely the openness of the text revealing an ambition to allow the readers to judge for themselves:

Le mot ›roman‹, ici, a d'abord valeur de manifeste. L'actualité récente nous a en effet montré à quel point le besoin de vérité (›ce délire juvénile dans l'amour de la vérité‹, disait Nietzsche) pouvait servir d'alibi à de pitoyables impostures. À la différence des pseudo-documents qui font la part belle au complot et à la conspiration, le présent ›roman‹ ne prétend à aucune vérité. Il s'en tient aux faits, sans chercher à les interpréter. Ce n'est qu'à ce prix, nous semble-t-il, que l'on peut aujourd'hui dire le réel; en appréhender la complexité, l'étrangeté – la poésie ? -, loin des mystificateurs qui se targuent de le ›couvrir‹ pour mieux lui faire écran.[186]

However, it *is* a printed text and not a webpage we are reading – the sequence is thus determined beforehand, leaving no room for actual choices on the part of the reader. Nonetheless, the illusion that the reader is interacting with the material is repeatedly invoked in the way in which the webpage text is worded. Chapter four, »Production«, for instance, is written in the second person plural, inviting the reader to imagine how the idea for the series *Street Hassle* was born: »Imaginez la situation. C'est votre dernier jour de vacances à Miami«,[187] and later, drawing the reader in even more: »Car c'est à vous qu'il est arrivé, et cette coïncidence vous touche, elle vous est destinée.«[188]

---

186 Ibid. p. 18.
187 Ibid. p. 21.
188 Ibid. p. 25.

The novel thus resembles a system of boxes within one another: firstly, there is the original murder riddle in the TV series; secondly, and embedded in the first, the question of hidden messages in the series' website; and finally, on a more general level, the novel as a whole including large amounts of intertextual references and quotations. The different levels are interspersed amongst each other, providing keys for interpreting the other levels. The many »behind the scenes« reflections on the form of the TV series from the people behind *Street Hassle* can thus be read as reflections on the form and content of the novel, creating a self-interpretative loop. Let us look at a few of the comments made on *Street Hassle* which can be read as a description of the form of the novel itself. The scriptwriter writes of his old idol and advisor on this script:

Expert dans l'art du montage, Charles était avant tout un ébéniste hors pair. Avec lui, la citation savait se faire marqueterie, hologramme, anamorphose. Rien à voir avec la prose en kit, 100% contreplaquée, distillée par les script DJs en vogue...[189]

Writing on Charles and his views on scriptwriting, *Street Hassle*'s scriptwriter reveals a feeling that we are lacking an adequate vocabulary for the contemporary world which surrounds us; a world characterised by chaos and fragmentation. However, the scriptwriter is hesitant about the impersonal implication of Charles' proposition of:

une écriture anonyme, fragmentée. Ni centre, ni centres, ni histoire, ni personnages, ni sens vectoriel, flux impersonnel, multitudes d'éclats, évidé, criblé, atone, suspendu, miroir prismatique ne se fermant sur rien – pas d'univers de l'auteur -, multiplicité de traces aussitôt recouvertes.[190]

The same attempt at redefining postmodern and system theory ambitions is found in the last numbered chapter »XXI. Réalisation« which tells us that the critics have praised *Street Hassle* as indicative of contemporary modes of communication, admiring the way in which it communicates information, archiving and remixing in a way which blurs the distinction between production and consumption, broadcast and reception, creation and copy: »Le metteur en scène s'affirme ainsi comme un moteur de recherche naviguant entre les signes, un sémionaute en quelque sorte.«[191] However, the director fiercely rejects this and exclaims: »je n'ai que faire des ›combinatoires réticulaires‹ et autres ›agencements rhizomatiques‹.«[192] He continues by pointing to the similarities between his work and cave paintings, Etienne-Jules Marey (French scientist and chronophotographer

---

189 Ibid. pp. 79-80.
190 Ibid. p. 80.
191 Ibid. p. 100.
192 Ibid. p. 100.

1830-1904) and Jean Painlevé (French director of science and nature films 1902-1989) rather than postmodern icons such as David Cronenberg and David Lynch, stating that:

Street Hassle n'est pas un feuilleton, c'est un site où les sons et les images créent un jeu de cheminements et d'assocations qui tourbillonnent sans fin autour de l'énigme. Objectif: contraindre le spectateur – comme le rêve contraint le rêveur – au perpétuel glissement et à l'absence de toute certitude; dessiner un monde infini de relations et de réseaux, où chaque plan entre en correspondance toujours singulière et nouvelle avec un autre, sans jamais apporter l'assurance – la clôture – d'une signification ou d'un ›c'est ceci‹. C'est pourquoi chaque scène est construite comme un lieu de passage (et non de circonscription), un lieu d'échanges, de mise en déplacement, où les signes circulent, passent et disparaissent comme le furet. Au fil des épisodes, *Street Hassle* s'affirme ainsi comme un univers en extension, un monde en processus, en archipel.[193]

Reading this discourse on the form of the fictitious TV series *Street Hassle* as a comment upon the form of the actual novel *Le Décodeur* reveals an attempt at taking the implications of information technology beyond the conceptualisations of postmodern theory, employing it to work out new ways of narrating that feel adequate for life in an information society. This seems to be what the novel *Le Décodeur* aspires to as a whole, and significantly the game, with its connotations of immersion and emergence, is an important device in reaching this goal. In fact it seems to be the very figure which provides us with a way of accessing this novel that challenges and reconfigures traditional conceptions of narrativity.

3.3.4 Computer Game Configurations

As a form the computer game is simultaneously the figure which interacts best with narrative, because there will often be narrative elements in a game, and also the most radical break with the causal sequence of a traditional, linear narrative, because it lets a player who acquires influence on the sequence into the narrative space. The novels that we have considered all employ the figure of the game in different ways, highlighting both kinship with narratives and the eerie strangeness of the logic of the game for a printed novel.

In November 2006 Nigel Andrews wrote in *FTmagazine* on the future of Hollywood films, analysing the recent success of *Pirates of the Caribbean 2*. He describes one of the reasons for its success in the following manner:

---

193 Ibid. p. 103.

The film has no concern with cogent storytelling, and neither do today's youngsters. For them fiction, like gaming, is an eternal present and plots a perpetuum mobile. The only narrative is the need to get to the next level. So while *Pirates 2* unspools for older people like a story whose reels have been muddled – a nightmare of botched narrative – for children and young adults up to, say 20, the film advances to higher things on stepping stones of incremental surrealism.[194]

Towards the end of the article he concludes:

To quote Richard Doherty, director of technology strategy at Microsoft: ›What is entertainment in the future? Is it necessarily a linear movie?‹ A work of art or cinema, like life, can be a multitude of stories. Is there a story in *Pirates 2*? Not really. There is none and there are a dozen. Is there a story in a computer game? No: there are step levels of interactive drama.[195]

The type of modern fiction which we have looked at has not been films, but novels.[196] However, the quotations indicate that our consideration of the way in which contemporary fiction negotiates narrativity and the influence of information technology on this negotiation can be interpreted in a broader cultural framework. Looking at the analyses conducted in this chapter in conjunction with Nigel Andrews' experience of *Pirates of the Caribbean 2*, containing more game than story, we see how the computer game points to ways in which information technology accentuates a perception and representation of human life and experience which facilitates a negotiation of narrativity articulated by other fictional forms. Computer games represent one possibility, the database and hyperlink others.

number9dream, *Im Krebsgang*, and *Le Décodeur* have shown us three different ways in which the figure of the computer game does not just occur as a motif in the novels, but also influences the way they organise information and represent experiences. These novels thereby establish themselves in a history of novels which have used the figure of the game in their negotiation of narrativity, as we saw in *ZT*. However, the notion of the game at work in these three novels presents itself as more concrete and more directly related to the act of playing than the more abstract notion of game found in *ZT*, which primarily deals with consciousness and language. The understanding of the figure of the game in the three novels we have looked at in this chapter thus appears to be situated in between Gadamer's notion of the game as a self-contained occupation and an artwork which

---

194 Andrews, p. 51.

195 Ibid. p. 53.

196 Although beyond the scope of the present study, it would be interesting to extend the present enquiry to include filmic fiction as well. We shall return to this prospect in the concluding remarks.

opens itself towards the viewer, thereby reflecting the triple significance which the computer game has acquired as aesthetic analogy, social event, *and* aesthetic object. By referring to the notion of game connected to the computer, the games alluded to in the three novels acquire connotations as actual physical events: Eiji's video games, Konrad's chatroom, and *Le Décodeur*'s interactive webpage are physically manifest undertakings in a different way than the »Längeres Gedankenspiel« of *ZT*. However, in the way in which the game works itself into the construction and negotiation of the narrative, we have seen that similar traits can be identified.

In the exploration of the game as a concrete material sign of information technology as a symbolic form – a figure which emphasises the sensation of immersion – we have focussed on examples that were all published in the twenty-first century. The issues dealt with in relation to the computer game and the sense of immersion it represents signify a third generation of occupancy in relation to the computer medium and information technology: the computer is no longer an office machine taking up entire rooms as it once did, neither is it merely a personal computer which we access only at our desk. Today digital technology is ubiquitous, dominating most areas of our everyday life from the mobile phone in our pocket, the wireless-internet access to be bought alongside a caffè latte in Starbucks, to the microchip imbedded in the neck of the cat making it possible to identify stray pets. Our immersion in digital environments is thus not limited to the hours we spend in front of the screen of our computer, and it can be argued that the novels we have discussed respond to this experience of pervasiveness by articulating issues of immersion through the figure of the computer game.

We have thus reached the end of our journey from the database to the hyperlink and the computer game. Each concrete material sign we have looked at carries significant qualities and connotations of information technology which all participate equally in conferring on it the status of a symbolic form in contemporary culture. Although a certain progression in the connotations can be identified from the database, to the hyperlink, and the computer game, reflected in the selection of texts in this study, it is important, before we move on to the concluding remarks, to emphasise that all these connotations are equally at play within the pervasiveness of information technology in contemporary culture.

4. Concluding remarks

The first wave of academic interest in the cultural and aesthetic effects of information technology was dominated by scholars from the field of literary studies, who took an interest in the computer medium and its aesthetic possibilities, especially in relation to poststructuralist theory and the aims and ambitions of the avant-garde movements.[1] However, as the medium developed from being primarily text-based to becoming increasingly visual, so academic interest shifted from literary studies to the visual arts. The artworks produced in and by the digital medium are no longer primarily text-based in the same way as the hypertext novels developed in the programs *Storyspace* and *Intermedia* in the 1990s were, but they increasingly take advantage of the medium's capacity to combine image, sound, text, and the surrounding environment, and this in turn affects the nature of the academic approaches taken and the methodologies employed. Studies of plot and narrative originally pursued by scholars such as George P. Landow have increasingly given way to analyses of issues dealt with in relation to the study of computer games or research into the development of interactive films, relocating these studies to the fields of film and media studies because these are the fields in which the main new artistic developments are occurring at the moment. Hypertext novels are no longer alone at the forefront of digital culture, and large resources are devoted to the development of computer games and the digital enhancement of films.

However, as I hope to have shown in this study, there is good reason for taking a renewed interest in the relationship between literature and information technology, both when it comes to understanding the impact of information technology on the conditions of literary fiction in an information age, *and* in order to understand fundamental mechanisms of human perception and representation embedded in narrative negotiations intrinsic to the novel genre. Digital technology has not brought about the end of the book, as theorists such as Sven Birkerts feared in the 1990s. Print novels remain an important cultural artefact in many people's lives, even if digital technology has helped accentuate the visual part of our culture and

---

1 See, for instance, the seminal texts Jay David Bolter's *Writing Space: the Computer, Hypertext and the History of Writing* (1991), *Hypermedia and Literary Studies* edited by Paul Dalany and George P. Landow (1991), or Margot Lovejoy's *Postmodern Currents. Art and Artists in the Age of Electronic Media* (1989).

by all accounts will continue emphasising issues of sensory perception, performance, interaction, and embodiment in the future.[2] In looking at printed fiction I do not attempt to argue that printed novels provide more or less insight into the cultural significance of information technology than other media. However, a focus on the novel genre allows us to place the impact of information technology on contemporary culture in a larger historical framework. In the present study we have thus focussed on how digital information structures are adopted, adapted, and tailored for the purpose of re-articulating narrative negotiations.[3]

Now, it would be going too far to say that literary studies has given up interest in information technology and completely handed the field over to art history, visual culture, media and game studies. Apart from the remarkable research being done on the ability of new media to facilitate research and teaching of printed texts, as well as their context and reception,[4] studies of the relationship between literature and information technology have been done by theorists with an interest in the intersection between science and literature. N. Katherine Hayles, for instance, has done intriguing work on the impact of information technology on contemporary culture, combining readings of printed literature, electronic literature, and visual arts.[5] However, these types of studies have mostly been done on American fiction with a slant towards science fiction – works by authors like Kurt Vonnegut, Thomas Pynchon, William Gibson, Douglas Coupland, Neal Stephenson, and Don Delillo. The reason for this is most probably that these are the novels which explicitly relate to computer technology and therefore call for such an approach. The aim in this study has been to go beyond the explicit thematization of the technology and regard information

---

2 Hansen.

3 In *Remediation. Understanding New Media* Bolter and Grusin work from Marchall McLuhan's thesis that the content of any medium is always another medium. In the development of their own concept of »remediation«, which they argue is a defining characteristic of new digital media, they look at how older media such as film and television try to incorporate digital media into their structure. However, they focus on visual media and do not enter into a discussion of the way in which printed literature incorporates digital media

4 See, for instance, Jerome McGann's *Radiant Textuality* (2003), which outlines his perspectives in the scholarly use of digital technology, drawing on his experiences from working on the hypertext project *The Rosetti Archive,* which facilitates the study of the painter, designer, writer, and translator Dante Gabriel Rossetti.

5 See also Joseph Tabbi's book *Cognitive Fictions* (2002) which maintains an interest in the specifically literary. Hayles' recent book *Electronic Literature: New Horizons for the Literary* (2008) deals mainly with electronic literature, but discusses also Jonathan Safran Foer's *Extremely Loud and Incredibly Close* (2005) and Mark Danielewski's *House of Leaves* (2000) in a concluding chapter on the mark of the digital on print novels. More recent publications on electronic literature such as David Ciccoricco's *Reading Network Fiction* (2007) also provide illuminating insights to this field and the future of the literary.

technology as a ubiquitous phenomenon which is not only present in the fictional world of the novel when explicitly manifest as a dominant entity. By regarding information technology as a symbolic form it becomes possible to approach the pervasiveness of digital technology and the more subtle ways in which it leaves its mark on fictional worlds. The novels we have looked at are therefore novels which do not necessarily feature the computer as a main thematic component, but have the logic of the concrete material signs of information technology visible in the narrative structures of the fictional worlds rendered. These novels are concerned with questions with which the novel genre has always battled; issues of how human existence should be understood and can be represented, and, as we have seen, information technology provides these novels with new ways of articulating this in a way that responds to the conditions of our present lifeworld and the methods of information processing to which we have become accustomed. The argument has thus been that information technology has come to bear such a significance that we might regard it as a symbolic form.

The concept of the symbolic form has assisted our understanding of the impact of information technology on contemporary culture by allowing us to approach the complexity of its cultural influence and break it down into units that can be analysed. From the introduction we might recall Cassirer's description of the three elements of which a symbolic form consists: a »konkretes sinnliches Zeichen«, a »geistiger Bedeutungsgehalt«, and an »Energie des Geistes« describing the way in which the other two are connected.[6] Translated into contemporary terms for our present purpose we can say that, through information technology as a symbolic form, a specific image of the cultural significance of information technology (»ein geistiger Bedeutungsgehalt«) is connected to specific material signs (»konkrete sinnliche Zeichen«). The concrete material signs we have identified in this study are the database, the hyperlink, and the computer game. In chapter 3 we examined the characteristics of each of these three concrete material signs. Furthermore, by looking at the way in which they are represented in contemporary fiction, it has become possible also to approach an understanding of the significance of these signs for contemporary culture, which shows itself not only in the application of these figures as motifs and metaphors, but also in the narrative structures of the selected texts. By applying the concept of the symbolic form when looking at evidence of the general impact of information technology on the cultural imagination of our

---

6 »Unter einer ›symbolischen Form‹ soll jede Energie des Geistes verstanden werden, durch welche ein geistiger Bedeutungsgehalt an ein konkretes sinnliches Zeichen geknüpft und diesem Zeichen innerlich zugeeignet wird.« (Cassirer, Der Begriff der symbolischen Form, p. 175).

time, it has thus become possible to scrutinize in a concrete way the implications of information technology for contemporary culture and show how narrative representations are influenced.

Due to the often commented-upon convergence between the modes of representation of the computer and poststructuralist theories, the concrete material signs of the database, the hyperlink, and the computer game, on which we have focussed in this study, are often identified as postmodernist iconography articulating issues of multilinearity, the death of the author, and an endless postponement of the signifier. While acknowledging that these figures can indeed be employed for such purposes, the aim of this study has been to emphasise a larger historical framework in which the database, the hyperlink, and the computer game can be placed, and thus identify the kinship between the archive and the database, the network and the hyperlink, the game and the computer game as well as the similarities in their usefulness for articulating issues of uneasiness with narrative representations of human existence. This approach has likewise become possible by applying the concept of the symbolic form. As a symbolic form, information technology is inextricable from the way in which we perceive the world, and it is consequently at the same time a dominant entity in our present time and closely linked to fundamental human ways of organising information which allow the characteristics of its concrete material signs to be considered in a historical framework.

The present study can be read chronologically. It starts in the early nineteenth century with *Wilhelm Meisters Wanderjahre* and the birth of a conception of the individual as interspersed between filling out a fixed role in society and being in a continuous process of becoming, which in the novel is represented by the simultaneously assembled and enlarged archive organised according to a principle of provenance. It then moves to the early twentieth century and Robert Musil's *Der Mann ohne Eigenschaften*, in which we see the early beginnings of the use of the figure of the network as a way of describing the social interactions within society, simultaneously reflecting Ulrich's discomfort with the disparateness of modern existence, the inadequacy of a narrative to articulate these conditions, and the form that the novel in the end finds for itself. Subsequently Arno Schmidt's postwar *Zettels Traum* presents itself as a vibrating play with words and connotations that aims to dissolve the boundaries between writing, speaking, and thinking. *Zettels Traum* shows us the mind of a consciousness trying to understand the world but failing to turn it into a consistent representation that can be narrated. Consciousness and the text alike thus come to resemble aggregations of discrete entities continuously shuffled and combined anew like a deck of playing cards. This brings us to chapter 3 and its three sections on the database, the hyperlink, and the computer game as concrete material signs of information technology as a symbolic form, which traces the connotations of information technology from the 1990s onwards. The database accentuates combinatorics and complexity management by displaying ways of organising information that are not dependent on causal or temporal sequences. The hyperlink emphasises navigation in an associative network and is bound up with the wish to let all the possible options of combinations flicker in sequenceless simultaneity. And in the computer game the combination of events is affected by the wish to immerse oneself in an unfamiliar environment and the need to get to the next level. The novels chosen as examples in these three sections each illustrate in different ways the implications that these figures may have for the contemporary novel and its approach to narration. They show us that the concepts and forms from the world of information technology do not just occur as motifs in the novels, but are used in the way the novels organise information and represent experiences. They provide us with examples of how narrative fiction reacts to and even incorporates these forms, which are increasingly prevalent in other areas of contemporary culture, but which also represent an ongoing negotiation of narrativity through their kinship with the figures of the archive, the network, and the game.

Another mode of reading which emphasises the correspondences between the figures we have traced is, however, also suggested by the structure of the present study: chapter 2.1 on the archive in *Wilhelm Meisters Wanderjahre* can be read in conjunction with chapter 3.1 on the database in *Rand*, *Nox*, and *Beginnlosigkeit*. Here we see the differences between an archive organised according to a principle of provenance and a digital database. However, we also see the similarities between the way in which this type of structure, which has to do with the *organisation* of information, helps facilitate an articulation of a negotiation of narrative through other ways of creating connections and making relations. In a similar manner, chapter 2.2 on the figure of the network in *Der Mann ohne Eigenschaften* can be read in conjunction with chapter 3.2 on the hyperlink in *Finder sted*, the Wergeland trilogy, and *Abtrünnig*, emphasising a structure which has to do with the *navigation* of information. Finally, chapter 2.3, which reads Arno Schmidt's *Zettels Traum* through the figure of the game, can be read together with chapter 3.3 on the computer game in *number9dream*, *Im Krebsgang*, and *Le Décodeur* as a reflection on a structure that has to do with the *experience* of information. This way of approaching the present study emphasizes the usefulness of the concept of the symbolic form as a framework for understanding the conditions of storytelling in an information age, being informed on the one hand by present media conditions and on the other hand by an ongoing challenge to the narrative mode of representation. By exploring the way in which the database, the hyperlink, and the computer game manifest themselves and are used in relation to the narrative constructions and the representation of human existence, we have uncovered ways in which the logic of digital technology provides the novel with figures to articulate an increasingly necessary negotiation of narrativity brought about by the growing amount of information that needs to be processed in our everyday world. We have also seen that these figures do not appear only with the advent of information technology, but are situated rather in a dialogue with negotiations of narrativity in previous periods found in the figure of the archive, the network, and the game, as seen in the works of Goethe, Musil, and Schmidt. In mapping out these relationships, the concept of the symbolic form has worked as a conceptual framework for the analyses through which the impact of information technology on these particular examples of contemporary fiction has been identified. But the analyses of these works of fiction simultaneously provide the evidence that information technology can indeed be regarded as a symbolic form that is particularly pervasive in art, theory, and culture today. As a symbolic form, information technology reveals itself in the figures of the database, the hyperlink, and the computer game, and by focussing on these we can begin to comprehend the ways in which cultural imagination is developing in the age of information technology. The fact that the types of narrative negotiations generated by the concrete material signs of information technology are in dialogue with a hybridity and a problematisation of narrative which is coextensive with the novel genre itself does not contradict the extent of the contemporary impact of information technology, which has caused us to approach it as a symbolic form. On the contrary, the description of information technology as a symbolic form aquires its validity precisely because it allows us to scrutinise the effect of information technology on the organisation, representation and experience of information in a historical framework that neither write the tendencies we see in recent fiction off as unremarkable, nor praise them as innovative without considering their antecedents.

Although beyond the scope of this book, the present enquiry can be taken further by turning to the wider implications of these issues for cultural fields other than the novel. Film has already been mentioned as an obvious area for further investigation. For example, films such as *Memento* (2000) could be read in relation to the database, *Sliding Doors* (1998) in relation to hypertext, and *Kill Bill* vol. 1-2 (2003-04) with reference to the computer game. Another area of investigation which might benefit from this type of approach is the artworks made in and for the computer medium, often displayed online. They clearly stand in a different relation to the principles of the database, the hyperlink, and the computer game, because they operate in the same medium from which these figures stem. But it should not be overlooked that these artworks are also engaged in a dialogue with the media and problematics that precede them. For instance, one could look at an artwork such as *A is for Apple* by David Clark (2002)[7] which explores the associations and connotations of the apple:

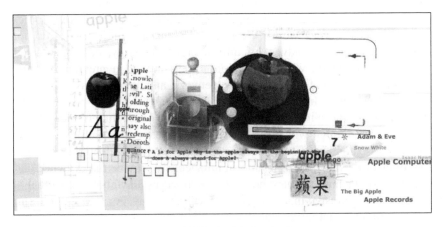

David Clark: *A is for Apple*

It does so by interlinking references from popular culture, religion, psychoanalysis and cryptography, thereby establishing a database of human existence, knowledge and perception. On the one hand, it presents itself as a database avoiding notions of sequence and acting subjects. Narrative plot is replaced by the random shuffling of a search engine. On the other hand, it creates a relation between a narrator and the viewer, thus re-establishing a notion of agency and a narrative framework which points to an unresolved relationship with narrative that might benefit from further scrutiny in the manner we have seen in this book.

What we have been dealing with in this book are novels that want to tell a story, but at the same time display an uneasiness towards the well-rounded narrative form – as if it works against them, prohibiting them from being able to say what they want to say. In the reading of these novels we have repeatedly returned to Galen Strawson's claim that there »are deeply non-Narrative people and there are good ways to live that are deeply non-Narrative«. In the introduction we saw how the oscillation between narrative and non-narrative modes of representation was embedded in the metonymic and metaphoric poles of language itself. In *Echo Objects. The Cognitive Work of Images* (2007) Barbara Maria Stafford takes this a step further

---

7 www.aisforapple.net by David Clark in collaboration with Rob Whynot, Randy Knott, and Ron Gervais.

by arguing that Strawson's thesis of an episodic self which does not string life into an ongoing story, but feels that what is remembered did not necessarily happen to the same self as that which is now present, is supported by neuroscientific research:

My argument is that an important neuroscientific as well as phenomenological fact about consciousness gets lost, when this *granular* inner sense gets subsumed under the blending structures of an ›ongoing story‹ we silently tell ourselves. One of the key insights of contemporary cognitive science is precisely that mental faculties can be decomposed, not just into multicomponent information processing systems, but into two different kinds of nervous systems. The specialized cells of one operate in parallel, unconsciously, with some autonomy. But there is another nervous system that is serial, internally consistent at any given moment rather than distributed, and strongly associated with consciousness.[8]

By employing the figures of the archive/database, the network/hyperlink, and the game/computer game the novels looked at in this study embody this duality within the nervous system. They articulate the simultaneity of a narrative and a non-narrative impetus in human perception. The quotation by Stafford suggests that, when identifying these figures in the novels, we are not merely looking at the products of cultural formations; rather we gain an insight into the way in which the duality of narrative and non-narrative are fundamentally linked to the faculty of our sensory perception and the workings of our brain. Stafford approaches this topic with her interest in the cognitive work of images in mind, not from a literary point of view, and she therefore relates the styles of the episodic authors suggested by Strawson (such as Michel de Montaigne, Novalis, Coleridge, and Beckett) to pictorial strategies:

Strawson's ›episodic‹ authors possess an interruptive style that resembles more the ›fretwork‹ imagism of Ezra Pound's poetry – tellingly modelled after enameling, damascening, or emblazoning pictorial strategies – than they do ›what led to what‹ causative fiction. Further, this emergent style of self-presentation is ultimately modeled, not on texts, but on ›patchy‹ artworks. Such paratactic visual compositions, favoring side-by-side connectivity, emphasize simultaneity and effortful co-construction. [...] If narrative turns the world into a plot, gapped configurations undercut automaticity, illusion, and the feeling that one is in the grips of remote control. They thus provide an insight into how we consciously struggle to make the weird details of the world hang together.[9]

The archive/database, the network/hyperlink, and the game/computer game are not images, they are modes of organising, navigating, and experiencing

---

8 Stafford, pp. 152-53.
9 Ibid. pp. 153-54.

information. However, in the characteristics of combinatorics, navigation, and emergence (which we have identified as characterising these figures) we can see pictorial strategies like the ones Stafford mentions, creating »side-by-side connectivity, simultaneity and effortful co-construction«. This allows us to understand the narrative negotiation we have been tracing as linked to the faculty of sensory perception and cognitive processing. The narrative negotiation finds its form in the cultural imagination of the novel, which sets out a narrative while at the same time displaying uneasiness about this form as an exhaustive mode of representing human existence.

We consequently arrive at a fuller understanding of why and how the concept of the symbolic form has proven useful for comprehending the impact of information technology upon contemporary culture and the conditions for literary fiction in a digital age. The notion of the symbolic form allows us to see this double significance of cultural formation linked to a specific period in time and to fundamental human capabilities. On the one hand information technology accentuates certain modes of representation which react to the increase in the amounts of information that need to be processed and the ubiquity of information technology in contemporary society and culture. This is what we have seen in the novels employing the concrete material signs of the database, the hyperlink, and the computer game in their narrative constructions. On the other hand, the notion of information technology as a symbolic form (rather than merely a particularly pervasive cultural metaphor connected to our present day and age) also points to the way in which the conditions of storytelling in an information age are part of a more fundamental questioning of the relationship between narrative and non-narrative in human perception. This has made it possible to trace the characteristics of the database, the hyperlink, and the computer game as an ongoing narrative negotiation in the genre of the novel which in contemporary fiction takes on a form unique to the challenges of the present cultural moment. The analysis of narrative negotiations in this book has thus aimed to show how information technology, interpreted as a symbolic form, makes apparent our way of perceiving our lives and our world in the conditions of the present day.

The concept of the symbolic form has helped us to articulate the nature of the narrative negotiation on a concrete level in the characteristics of the database, the hyperlink, and the computer game and their respective antecedents, highlighting how combinatorics, network structures, immersion and emergence work their way into narrative fiction. This has enabled us to approach the cultural significance of information technology in more specific terms and show how the uneasiness about narrativity as a mode of representation is renewed and accentuated by the concrete material signs of information technology. We consequently broaden our understanding of the interaction between story and information in contemporary literary fiction and begin to see that Susan Sontag's distinction between *stories*, which »have as their goal, an end, completeness, closure«, and *information*, which »is always, by definition, partial incomplete, fragmentary«, with which we began this study, should be regarded not as a strict line of demarcation, but as a fluctuating field of narrative negotiations which fuels the creative vitality of the novel and makes it respond to the cultural moment and conditions of information processing in which it was conceived.

Bibliography

1.1 Primary Literature

Goethe, Johann Wolfgang von: Wilhelm Meisters Wanderjahre oder Die Entsagenden, Bahr, Erhard (ed.), Stuttgart 1982.

Grass, Günter: Im Krebsgang, Göttingen 2002.

Hettche, Thomas: Nox, Berlin 2004 [1995].

Jirgl, Reinhard: Abtrünnig. Roman aus der nervösen Zeit, München 2005.

Kjærstad, Jan: Der Entdecker, Trans. Schmidt-Henkel, Hinrich, Berlin 2006.

–: Der Eroberer, Trans. Gundlach, Angelika, Köln 2002.

–: Der Verführer, Trans. Gundlach, Angelika, Berlin 2005.

–: Erobreren, Oslo 1996.

–: Forføreren, Oslo 1993.

–: Oppdageren, Oslo 1999.

–: Rand, Oslo 1990.

–: Rand, Trans. Gundlach, Angelika, München 2003.

Madsen, Svend Åge: Finder sted, Copenhagen 1998.

Mitchell, David: number9dream, London 2001.

Musil, Robert: Der Mann ohne Eigenschaften, Gesammelte Werke, Frisé, Adolph (ed.), 1-5 vols, Reinbek bei Hamburg 1981.

Schmidt, Arno: Zettels Traum, Frankfurt 2004 [1970].

Strauß, Botho: Beginnlosigkeit. Reflexionen über Fleck und Linie, München 1997 [1992].

Tournaye, Guy: Le Décodeur, Paris 2005.

1.2 Secondary Literature

Aarseth, Espen: Cybertext. Perspectives on Ergodic Literature, Baltimore 1997.

–: Quest Games as Post-Narrative Discourse, in: Ryan, Marie-Laure (ed.), Narrative across Media. The Languages of Storytelling, Lincoln 2004, pp. 361-77.

Abbott, H. Porter: The Cambridge Introduction to Narrative, Cambridge 2002.

Adorno, Theodor W.: Standort des Erzählers im zeitgenössischen Roman, in: Noten zur Literatur I, Frankfurt am Main 1958, pp. 61-72.

Agamben, Giorgio: Remnants of Auschwitz. The Witness and the Archive, New York 1999.

Andersen, Frits: Realismens Metode, Aarhus 1994.

Andrews, Nigel: The Guess Men. FTmagazine 11-12 November 2006, pp. 50-53.

Aristotle: Ethics, New York 1976.

Austin, John Langshaw: How to do Things with Words, Oxford 1962.

Avedon, Elliott M. / Sutton-Smith, Brian (eds.): The Study of Games, New York 1971.

Bahr, Ehrhard: The Novel as Archive. The Genesis, Reception, and Criticism of Goethe's *Wilhelm Meisters Wanderjahre*, Columbia 1998.

Bakthin, Mikael M.: The Dialogic Imagination. Four Essays by M. M. Bakthin, Trans. Emerson, Caryl / Holquist, Michael, Austin 1981.

Banzhaf, Hajo: Tarot and the Journey of the Hero, York Beach 2000.

Bayer, Thora Ilin: Cassirer's Metaphysics of Symbolic Forms, New Haven 2001.

Benjamin, Walter: Der Erzähler. Betrachtungen zum Werk Nikolai Lesskows, in: Tiedemann, Rolf / Schweppenhäuser, Hermann (eds.), Gesammelte Schriften, Bd. II, 2, Frankfurt am Main 1977, pp. 438-465.

–: Krisis des Romans. Zu Döblins *Berlin Alexanderplatz*, in: Tiedemann-Bartels, Hella (ed.), Gesammelte Schriften, Bd. III, Frankfurt am Main 1972, pp. 230-36.

Birkerts, Sven: The Gutenberg Elegies. The Fate of Reading in an Electronic Age, Boston 1994.

Blessin, Stefan: Goethes Romane. Aufbruch in die Moderne, Paderborn 1996.

Blok, Rasmus: Fortælling og Litteratur i en Digital Æra, in: Fibiger, Johannes / Lütken, Gerd / Mölgaard, Niels (eds.), Litteraturens Tilgange. Metodiske Angrebsvinkler, Copenhagen 2001, pp. 407-23.

Blumenbach, Ulrich: Das Werk auf den Schultern vergänglicher Riesen. Arno Schmidt an den Grenzen der Speicherbarkeit kulturellen Wissens, in: Zettelkasten 14 (1995), pp. 187-218.

Bock, Hans Michael: Über Arno Schmidt. Rezensionen vom *Leviathan* bis zur *Julia*, Zürich 1984.

Bolter, J. David: Writing Space. The Computer, Hypertext, and the History of Writing, Hillsdale 1991.

Bolter, J. David / Grusin, Richard: Remediation. Understanding New Media, Cambridge Mass. 1999.

Bonacchi, Silvia: Die Gestalt der Dichtung. Der Einfluss der Gestalttheorie auf das Werk Robert Musils, Bern 1998.

Broch, Hermann: James Joyce und die Gegenwart. Rede zu Joyces 50.Geburtstag, in: Dichten und Erkennen. Essays, VI, Zürich 1955, pp. 183-210.

Brueggemann, Aminia: Identity Construction and Computers in Thomas Hettche's novel *Nox*, in: The German Quarterly Vol. 72, No. 4 (1999), pp. 340-48.

Burke, Ruth E.: The Games of Poetics. Ludic Criticism and Postmodern Fiction, New York 1994.

Bush, Vannevar: As We May Think, in: The Atlantic Monthly 176, 1 (1945), pp. 101-08.

Buytendijk, Frederik Jacobus Johannes: Wesen und Sinn des Spiels. Das Spielen des Menschen und der Tiere als Erscheinungsform der Lebenstriebe, New York 1976 [1933].

Böhme, Hartmut: Netzwerke. Zur Theorie und Geschichte einer Konstruktion, in: Barkhoff, Jürgen / Böhme, Harmut / Riou, Jeanne (eds.), Netzwerke. Eine Kulturtechnik der Moderne, Köln 2004, pp. 17-37.

–: Theoretische Problem der Interpretation von Robert Musils Roman *Der Mann oh-ne Eigenschaften*, in: Heydebrand, Renate von (ed.), Robert Musil, Darmstadt 1982, pp. 120-60.

Caillois, Roger: Les Jeux et les Hommes. Le Masque et le Vertige, Paris 1991 [1967].

Cassirer, Ernst: Der Begriff der symbolischen Form im Aufbau der Geisteswissenschaften, in: Wesen und Wirkung des Symbolbegriffs, Darmstadt 1977 [1956], pp. 169-201.

–: An Essay on Man. An Introduction to a Philosophy of Human Culture, New Haven 1944.

–: Philosophie der symbolischen Formen, 3 vols, Darmstadt 1973-75.

–: Symbol, Technik, Sprache. Aufsätze aus den Jahren 1927-1933, Hamburg 1995.

Castells, Manuel: The Rise of the Network Society, Oxford 1996.

Ciccoricco, David: Reading Network Fiction, Alabama 2007.

Clark, David: A is for Apple, 2002, www.aisforapple.net

Cunningham, David / Mapp, Nigel (eds.): Adorno and Literature, London 2006.

De Certeau, Michel: The Practice of Everyday Life, Berkeley 1988.

De Winde, Arne: Das Erschaffen von »eigen-Sinn«. Notate zu Reinhard Jirgls Schrift-Bildlichkeitsexperimenten, in: Clarke, David / De Winde, Arne (eds.), Reinhard Jirgl. Perspektiven, Lesarten, Kontexte, Amsterdam 2007, pp. 111-51.

Deleuze, G. / Guattari, F.: A Thousand Plateaus. Capitalism and Schizophrenia, Minneapolis 1987.

Derrida, Jacques: Archive Fever. A Freudian Impression, Chicago 1996.

–: De la Grammatologie, Paris 1967.

Douglas, Yellowless J.: The End of Books or Books Without End. Reading Interactive Narratives, Ann Arbor 2000.

Dovey, Jon / Kennedy, Helen W.: Game Cultures. Computer Games as New Media, Maidenhead 2006.

Eco, Umberto: The Role of the Reader. Explorations in the Semiotics of Texts, London 1981.

Eisele, Ulf: Ulrichs Mutter ist doch ein Tintenfass. Zur Literaturproblematik in Musils *Der Mann ohne Eigenschaften*, in: von Heydebrand, Renate (ed.), Robert Musil, Darmstadt 1982, pp. 160-204.

Emden, Christian: Netz, in: Konersmann, Ralf (ed.), Wörterbuch der philosophischen Metaphern, Darmstadt 2006, pp. 248-61.

Erlandsson, Alf: The Principle of Provenance and the Concept of Records Creator and Record, in: Abukhanfusa, Kerstin / Sydbeck, Jan (eds.), The Principle of Provenance. Report from the First Stockholm Conference on Archival Theory and the Principle of Provenance, 2-3 September 1993, Stockholm 1994, pp. 33-51.

Eskelinen, Markku: Towards Computer Game Studies, in: Wardrip-Fruin, Noah / Harrigan, Pat (eds.), First Person. New Media as Story, Performance, and Game, Cambridge Mass. 2004, pp. 36-45.

Eubanks, Victoria: The Mythography of the »New« Frontier, MIT Communications Forums, 1999, http://web.mit.edu/comm-forum/papers.html

Foucault, Michel: The Archaeology of Knowledge, London 1972.

–: Une Histoire restée muette, in: Defert, Daniel / Ewald, François (eds.), Dits et écrits, 1, Paris 1994 [1966], pp. 545-49.

Freudenthal, Gideon: The Missing Core of Cassirer's Philosophy. Homo Faber in Thin Air, in: Hamlin, Cyrus / Krois, John Michael (eds.), Symbolic Forms and Cultural Studies. Ernst Cassirer's Theory of Culture, New Haven 2004, pp. 203-27.

Fues, Wolfram Malte: *Wanderjahre* im Hypertext, in: Gutjahr, Ortrud / Segeberg, Harro (eds.), Klassik und Anti-Klassik. Goethe und seine Epoche, Würzburg 2001, pp. 137-57.

Funck, Gisa: Die Rache des freien Mitarbeiters. Berlin ist doch Weimar. Reinhard Jirgls wütende Romanpredigt, Frankfurter Allgemeine Zeitung 31 October 2005, p. 36, www.faz.net/s/Rub79A33397BE834406A5D2BFA87FD1391 3/Doc~E2-AE656314CB84F10B3BAB024BE2AC37E~ATpl~Ecommon~Scontent.html

–: Wutschnaubend und düster. Reinhard Jirgs Roman *Abtrünnig*, DeutschlandRadio-Online Deutschlandfunk Büchermarkt 13 November 2005, www.dradio.de/dlf/-sendungen/buechermarkt/438021/.

Gadamer, Hans-Georg: Wahrheit und Methode. Grundzüge einer philosophischen Hermeneutik, Tübingen 1975.

Genette, Gérard: Narrative Discourse. An Essay in Method, Ithaca 1988.

Grangeray, Emilie: Et Guy Tournaye inventa le résau littéraire infini, Le Monde 03 June 2005, p. III

Grimm, Erk: Fathoming the Archive. German Poetry and the Culture of Memory, in: New German Critique 88 (2003), pp. 107-40.

Gründer, Karlfried: Cassirer und Heidegger in Davos 1929, in: Braun, Hans-Jürg / Holzhey, Helmut / Orth, Ernst Wolfgang (eds.), Über Ernst Cassirers Philosophie der symbolischen Formen, Frankfurt am Main 1988, pp. 290-302.

Gränström, Claes: The Janus Syndrome, in: Abukhanfusa, Kerstin / Sydbeck, Jan (eds.), The Principle of Provenance. Report from the First Stockholm Conference on Archival Theory and the Principle of Provenance, 2-3 September 1993, Stockholm 1994, pp. 11-25.

Günzel, Stephan: Nietzsches Schreibmaschinentexte. Interpretationsansätze und Vorstellung der Edition, in: Kopij, Marta / Kunicki, Wojciech (eds.), Nietzsche und Schopenhauer. Rezeptionsphänomene der Wendezeit, Leipzig 2006, pp. 413-29.

Halliwell, Stephen: The Poetics of Aristotle. Translation and Commentary, London 1987.

Hamsun, Knut: Hunger, Edinburgh 1996 [1890].

Hansen, Mark: New Philosophy for New Media, Cambridge Mass. 2006.

Haraway, Donna: A Cyborg Manifesto. Science, Technology, and Socialist-Feminism in the Late Twentieth Century, in: Wardrip-Fruin, Noah / Montfort, Nick (eds.), The New Media Reader, Cambridge Mass. 2003, pp. 515-43.

Haugan, Jørgen: Solgudens fall. Knut Hamsun – en litterær biografi, Oslo 2004.

Hautzinger, Nina: Vom Buch zum Internet? Eine Analyse der Auswirkungen hypertextueller Strukturen auf Text und Literatur, St. Ingbert 1999.

Hayles, N. Katherine: Electronic Literature. New Horizons for the Literary, Notre Dame 2008.

–: Flesh and Metal. Reconfiguring the Mindbody in Virtual Environments, in: Configurations 10 2 (Spring 2002), pp. 297-320.

–: How We Became Posthuman. Virtual Bodies in Cybernetics, Literature, and Informatics, Chicago 1999.

–: My Mother was a Computer, Chicago 2005.

–: Narrating Bits. Encounters between Humans and Intelligent Machines, in: Comparative Critical Studies 2 2 (2005), pp. 165-91.

Hayman, David: Some writers in the wake of the *Wake*, in: Hayman, David / Anderson, Elliot (eds.), In the Wake of the *Wake*, Madison 1978, pp. 3-39.

Hettche, Thomas: Es gibt keine Kriterien für Texte - außer ihren Gelingen, in: Pütz, Eric / Lenz, Daniel (eds.), LebensBeschreibungen. Zwanzig Gespräche mit Schriftstellern, München 2000, pp. 207-17.

Hink, Wolfgang: Der Ausflug ins Innere der eigenen Persöhnlichkeit. Zur Funktion der Zitate im Werk Arno Schmidts, Heidelberg 1989.

Hoffmann, Christoph: Der Dichter am Apparat. Medientechnik, Experimentalpsychologie und Texte Robert Musils 1899-1942, München 1997.

Holland, John H.: Emergence. From Chaos to Order, Oxford 1998.

Horsman, Peter: Taming the Elephant. An Orthodox Approach to the Principle of Provenance, in: Abukhanfusa, Kerstin / Sydbeck, Jan (eds.), The Principle of Provenance. Report from the First Stockholm Conference on Archival Theory and the Principle of Provenance, 2-3 September 1993, Stockholm 1994, pp. 51-63.

Huizinga, Johan: Homo Ludens. A Study of the Play-element in Culture, Boston 1950 [1938].

Hutchinson, Peter: Games Authors Play, London 1983.

Iser, Wolfgang: Das Fiktive und das Imaginäre. Perspektiven literarischer Anthropologie, Frankfurt am Main 1991.

–: Die Appellstruktur der Texte, in: Warning, Rainer (ed.), Rezeptionsästhetik. Theorie und Praxis, München 1975, pp. 228-53.

Jakobson, Roman: Two Aspects of Language and Two Types of Aphasic Disturbances, in: Jakobson, Roman / Halle, Moris (eds.), Fundamentals of Language, Hague 1980, pp. 69-96.

Jirgl, Reinhard: Das obszöne Gebet. Totenbuch, Frankfurt 1993.

–: Das poetische Vermögen des alphanumerischen Codes in der Prosa, in: Gewitterlicht, Hannover 2003, pp. 51-83.

John, Johannes: Aphoristik und Romankunst. Eine Studie zu Goethes Romanwerk, Rheinfelden 1987.

Johnson, Steven: Interface Culture. How new technology transforms the way we create and communicate, San Francisco 1997.

Joyce, Michael: Afternoon. A Story, Cambridge Mass., 1999 [1989]. Eastgate Systems.

JP: Unvorstellbarer Autor der allumfassenden Finsternis, Die Welt 26 November 2005, www.welt.de/data/2005/11/26/808798.html

Jung, Carl Gustav: Memories, Dreams, Reflections, London 1963.

Juul, Jesper: En Kamp mellem Spil og Fortælling. Om Interaktiv Fiktion, in: KRITIK 135 (1998), pp. 60-67.

–: Games Telling Stories. A brief note on games and narratives, Game Studies 25 September 2007 2001, www.gamestudies.org/0101/juul-gts/

–: Half-real. Video Games between Real Rules and Fictional Worlds, Cambridge Mass. 2005.

–: Hvad spillet betyder. Om Grand Theft Auto 3, in: Engholm, Ida / Klastrup, Lisbeth (eds.), Digitale Verdener. De nye Mediers Æstetik og Design, Copenhagen 2004, pp. 181-95.

–: The Open and the Closed. Games of Emergence and Games of Progression, in: Mäyrä, Frans (ed.), Computer Game and Digital Cultures. Conference Proceedings, Tampere 2002, pp. 323-29.

Kant, Immanuel: Kritik der Urteilskraft, Hamburg 1974.

Kerby, Anthony Paul: Narrative and the Self, Bloomington 1991.

Kern, Stephen: A Cultural History of Causality. Science, Murder Novels, and Systems of Thought, Princeton 2004.

Kittler, Friedrich A.: Aufschreibesysteme 1800-1900, München 2003.

–: Grammophon, Film, Typewriter, Berlin 1986.

–: Literature, Media, Information Systems. Essays, Johnston, John (ed.), Amsterdam 1997.

Kjærstad, Jan: Litteraturens mulighet. Romanen og nettet, in: Menneskets Felt, Oslo 1997, pp. 234-62.

–: Menneskets Nett, in: Menneskets Nett, Oslo 2004, pp. 45-69.

Kocher, Manuela / Böhler, Michael: Über den ästhetischen Begriff des Spiels als Link zwischen traditioneller Texthermeneutik, Hyperfiction und Computerspielen, in: Braungart, Georg / Eibl, Karl / Jannidis, Fotis (eds.), Jahrbuch für Computerphilologie 3, 2001, pp. 81-107.

Kontje, Todd (ed.): A Companion to German Realism 1848-1900, New York 2002.

Krois, John Michael: Cassirer. Symbolic Forms and History, New Haven 1987.

Kundera, Milan: The Curtain, New York 2006.

Kühne, Jörg: Das Gleichnis. Studien zur inneren Form von Robert Musils Roman *Der Mann ohne Eigenschaften*, Tübingen 1968.

Kümmel, Albert: Das MoE-Programm. Eine Studie über geistige Organisation, München 2001.

Landow, George P.: Hypertext 2.0, Baltimore 1997.

–: Hypertext. The Convergence of Contemporary Critical Theory and Technology, Baltimore 1992.

Landow, George P. (ed.): Hyper/Text/Theory, Baltimore 1994.

Landow, George P. / Delany, Paul (eds.): Hypermedia and Literary Studies, Cambridge Mass. 1991.

Langbehn, Volker Max: Arno Schmidt's *Zettel's Traum*. An Analysis, New York 2003.

Langner, Beatrix: Wortmacht. Abtrünnig. Reinhard Jirgl über die »inneren Arbeitslosen«, Neue Zürcher Zeitung 24 November 2005, http://nzz.ch/2005/11/24/fe/-articleDBPK3.html

Lennon, Brian: Two Novels by Arno Schmidt, in: The Iowa Review 29 Spring (1999), pp. 170-76.

Lodge, David: The Modes of Modern Writing. Metaphor, Metonymy, and the Typology of Modern Literature, London 1977.

Lovejoy, Margot: Postmodern Currents. Art and Artists in the Age of Electronic Media, Ann Arbor 1989.

Luhmann, Niklas: Soziale Systeme. Grundriss einer allgemeinen Theorie, Frankfurt am Main 1987.

Lukács, Georg: The Theory of the Novel. A Historico-philosophical Essay on the Forms of Great Epic Literature, London 1971.

Löser, Philipp: Mediensimulation als Schreibstrategie. Film, Mündlichkeit und Hypertext in Postmoderner Literatur, Göttingen 1999.

MacFarlane, Robert: When Blade Runner meets Jack Kerouac, The Observer 11 March 2001, http://books.guardian.co.uk/reviews/generalfiction/0,1270217,00.-html

Manovich, Lev: Datavisualisation as New Abstraction and Anti-Sublime, 2002, www.manovich.net/DOCS/data_art_2.doc

–: The Language of New Media, Cambridge Mass. 2001.

Markussen, Bjarne: Romanens Optikk. Komposisjon og Persepsjon i Jan Kjæstads Rand og Svein Jarvolls En Australiareise, Kristiansand 2003.

Martin, James: Computer Data-Base Organization, New Jersey 1975.

Maturana, Humberto R. / Varela, Francisco J.: Autopoiesis and Cognition. The Realization of the Living, Dordrecht 1980.

Matuschek, Stefan: Literarische Spieltheorie. Von Petrarca bis zu den Brüdern Schlegel, Heidelberg 1998.

Matussek, Peter: Die memoria erschüttern. Zur Aktualität der Gedächtnisteater, in: Schramm, Helmar / Herrmann, Hans-Christian von (eds.), Bühnen des Wissens. Interferenzen zwischen Wissenschaft und Kunst, Berlin 2002, pp. 214-25.

Maunsell, Boyd Jerome: Dream time in Tokyo, Evening Standard 23 April 2001, www.highbeam.com/doc/1P2-5314943.html

McAllister, Ken S.: Game Work. Language, Power, and Computer Game Culture, Tuscaloosa 2004.

McGann, Jerome: Radiant Textuality. Literature after the World Wide Web, New York 2001.

Mehigan, Timothy J.: The Critical Response to Robert Musil's The Man without Qualities, New York 2003.

Meister, Martina: Sterbenwollen, Lebenmüssen. Reinhard Jirgls Roman hat eine Sprache für die Trostlosigkeit, Frankfurter Rundschau 19 October 2005, www.fr-aktuell.de/in_und_ausland/kultur_und_medien/literatur/?em_cnt=742847&sid=6471b7f336eb630c3ca856d4de2d57d6

Merewether, Charles (ed.): The Archive, Cambridge Mass. 2006.

Miall, David S.: Reading Hypertext. Theoretical Ambitions and Empirical Studies, in: Braungart, Georg / Eibl, Karl / Jannidis, Fotis (eds.), Jahrbuch für Computerphilologie 5, 2003, pp. 161-79.

Midgley, David R. (ed.): The German Novel in the Twentieth Century. Beyond Realism, Edinburgh 1993.

–: Günter Grass, Im Krebsgang. Memory, Medium, and Message, in: Seminar. A Journal of Germanic Studies 41 1 (February 2005), pp. 55-67.

Minden, Michael: Arno Schmidt. A Critical Study of his Prose, Cambridge 1982.

Mogensen, Tine Engel: Den gode historie. Opslag i Jan Kjærstads Forføreren, Erobreren og Opdageren, Odense 2002.

Mohr, Peter: Die verglühten, aschigen Individuen, Titel Magazin. Literatur und mehr, 6 November 2005, www.titel-forum.de/modules.php?op=modload &name=News &file=article&sid=4005

Moretti, Franco: The Way of the World. The Bildungsroman in European Culture, London 2000 [1987].

Moser, Walter: Diskursexperimente im Romantext. Zu Musils *Der Mann ohne Eigenschaften*, in: Baur, Uwe / Castex, Elisabeth (eds.), Robert Musil. Untersuchungen, Königstein 1980, pp. 170-98.

Motte, Warren: Playtexts. Ludics in Contemporary Literature, Lincoln 1995.

Moulthrop, Stuart: Rhizome and Resistance. Hypertext and the Dreams of a New Culture, in: Landow, George P. (ed.), Hyper/Text/Theory, Baltimore 1994, pp. 299-319.

Murray, Janet H.: From Game-Story to Cyberdrama, in: Wardrip-Fruin, Noah / Harrigan, Pat (eds.), First Person. New Media as Story, Performance, and Game, Cambridge Mass. 2004, pp. 2-11.

–: Hamlet on the Holodeck. The Future of Narrative in Cyberspace, Cambridge Mass. 1998.

Musil, Robert: Briefe-Nachlese. Dialog mit dem Kritiker Walther Petry, Frisé, Adolph (ed.), Saarbrücken 1994.

–: Briefe 1901-1942, Frisé, Adolph (ed.), Hamburg 1981.

Müller, Lothar: Der Dämon und seine Meinung, Süddeutsche Zeitung 18 October 2005, http://sz-mediathek.sueddeutsche.de/mediathek/shop/catalog/ShowMedia-Detail VP.do;jsessionid=1CDA5C8E7251496FB0586F063E7 1DDE8.kafka: 9009?pid=755713&extraInformationShortModus=false

Naumann, Barbara: Philosophie und Poetik des Symbols. Cassirer und Goethe, München 1998.

Neuhaus, Volker: Die Archivfiktion in *Wilhelm Meisters Wanderjahre*, in: Euphorion 62 (1968), pp. 13-28.

Nord, Cristina: Suche in der Düsternis, Die Tageszeitung 14 December 2005, p. 23 www.taz.de/pt/2005/12/24/a0271.1/text

Nusser, Peter: Musils Romantheorie, Hague 1967.

Ortmann, Sabrina: Netz Literaturprojekt. Entwicklung einer neuen Literaturform von 1960 bis heute, 2001.

Ovid: Metamorphoses, Trans. Miller, Frank Justus, London 1916.

Panofsky, Erwin: Perspective as Symbolic Form, New York 1991 [1924-25].

Paul, Christiane: The Database as System and Cultural Form. Anatomies of Cultural Narratives, in: Vesna, Victoria (ed.), Database Aesthetics. Art in the Age of Information Overflow, Minneapolis 2007.

Pfeiffer, Peter C.: Aphorismus und Romanstruktur. Zu Robert Musils *Der Mann ohne Eigenschaften*, Bonn 1990.

Podak, Klaus / Vollmann, Rolf: Das Bilderbuch, in: Bock, Hans Michael / Schreiber, Thomas (eds.), Über Arno Schmidt. Rezensionen vom *Leviathan* bis zur *Julia*, Zürich 1984, pp. 217-20.

Radisch, Iris: Das Glück, allein zu sein, Die Zeit 1 December 2005, www.zeit.de/2005/49/L-Jirgl?page=1.

Rasch, Wolfdietrich: Über Robert Musils Roman *Der Mann ohne Eigenschaften*, Göttingen 1967.

Ricœur, Paul: Temps et Récit. La Configuration dans le Recit de Fiction (vol.2), Paris 1984.

Riha, Karl: Cross-reading und Cross-talking. Zitat-Collagen als poetische und satirische Technik, Stuttgart 1971.

Ryan, Marie-Laure: Avatars of Story, Minneapolis 2006.

– (ed.): Narrative across Media. The Languages of Storytelling, Lincoln 2004.

–: Narrative as Virtual Reality. Immersion and Interactivity in Literature and Electronic Media, Baltimore 2001.

Saussure, Ferdinand: Course in General Linguistics, Trans. Harris, Roy, London 1983 [1916].

Schiller, Friedrich: On the Aesthetic Education of Man. In a Series of Letters (English and German facing), Wilkinson, Elizabeth M. / Willougsby, L. A. (eds.), Oxford 1967.

Schmidt, Arno: Aus dem Leben eines Fauns. Kurzroman, Frankfurt am Main 1982 [1953].

–: Rosen & Porree, Karlsruhe 1959.

–: Sitara und der Weg dorthin. Eine Studie über Wesen, Werk & Wirkung Karl Mays, Karlsruhe 1963.

Schoeller, Wilfried F.: Laudatio zur Verleihung des Bremer Literaturpreis an Reinhard Jirgl für den Roman *Abtrünnig* im Bremer Rathaus am 26. Januar, 2006, www.stadtbibliothek-bremen.de/dateien/Laudatio_JIRGL(c2c) .doc

Schwamborn, Claudia: Individualität in Goethes *Wanderjahren*, Paderborn 1997.

Schößler, Franziska: Mythos als Kritik. Zu Thomas Hettches Wenderoman *Nox*, in: Literatur für Leser 3, 22 (1999), pp. 171-82.

Sdun, Nora: Mächtig tranig, Textem, 2005, www.textem.de/847.0.html

Sebastian, Thomas: The Intersection of Science and Literature in Musil's *The Man without Qualities*, New York 2005.

Simanowski, Roberto: Interfictions. Vom Schreiben im Netz, Frankfurt am Main 2002.

Sontag, Susan: At the Same Time. The Novelist and Moral Reasoning, in: Dilonardo, Paolo / Jump, Anne (eds.), At the Same Time. Essays and Speeches, New York 2007, pp. 210-33.

Spariosu, Mihai: Literature, Mimesis and Play. Essays in Literary Theory, Tübingen 1982.

Stafford, Barbara Maria: Echo Objects. The Cognitive Work of Images, Chicago 2007.

Stephenson, R. H.: »Eine zarte Differenz«. Cassirer on Goethe on the Symbol, in: Hamlin, Cyrus / Krois, John Michael (eds.), Symbolic Forms and Cultural Studies, New Haven 2004, pp. 157-85.

Stolz, Dieter: »Das Aufbrechen der verpanzerten Wahrnehmung«. Reinhard Jirgls Roman *Abtrünnig* – ein (un)vermeidbarer Amoklauf, in: Clarke, David / De Winde, Arne (eds.), Reinhard Jirgl. Perspektiven, Lesarten, Kontexte, Amsterdam 2007, pp. 235-53.

Storkerson, Peter / Wong, Janine: Hypertekst and the Art of Memory, in: Visible Language 31 2 (1997), pp. 126-57.

Strauß, Botho: Paare, Passanten, München 1981.

Strawson, Galen: Against Narrativity, in: Ratio 17 4 (2004), pp. 428-52.

Sutton-Smith, Brian: The Ambiguity of Play, Cambridge Mass. 1997.

Tabbi, Joseph: Cognitive Fictions, Minneapolis 2002.

Taylor, Mark C.: The Moment of Complexity. Emerging Network Culture, Chicago 2001.

Thurah, Thomas: Så hvad er et Menneske? Tre Kapitler om P.O. Enquist, Peer Hultberg og Jan Kjærstad, Copenhagen 2003.

Tronstad, Ragnhild: Semiotic and Non-Semiotic MUD Performance, COSIGN, 11 September 2001, www.cosignconference.org/downloads/papers/ tronstad_cosign_2001.pdf

Turkle, Sherry: The Second Self. Computers and the Human Spirit, New York 1984.

Turner, Mark: The Literary Mind. The Origins of Thought and Language, Oxford 1996.

Tygstrup, Frederik: Den demiurgiske romanhelt. Nogle bemærkninger til Jan Kjærstads Forføreren, in: KRITIK 111 (1994), pp. 25-35.

Ueding, Gert: Die gelehrte Traumwelt des Arno Schmidt, in: Bock, Hans-Michael/ Schreiber, Thomas (eds.), Über Arno Schmidt. Rezensionen vom Leviathan bis zur Julia, Zürich 1984, pp. 226-33.

Veel, Kristin: Once upon a time there was a Database. Narrative and Database from a Cognitive point of View, in: Refresh! First International Conference on the Histories of Media Art, Science and Technology, Banff, Canada, 2005, www.banffcentre.ca/bnmi/programs/archives/2005/refresh /conference_docs.asp

–: Virtual Memory in Günter Grass' Im Krebsgang, in: German Life and Letters LVII 2 (April 2004), pp. 206-19.

Vesna, V.: Introduction, in: Database Aesthetics. Issues of Organization and Category in Online Art in: AI & Society. Journal of Human Centred & Machine Intelligence 14, 2 (2000).

Vogler, Heinrich: Riesenwell der Empörung, Der Bund 15 December 2005, p. 13 http://194.209.226.170/pdfarchiv/bund/2005/12/15/29313Kultur20051215_1.pdf

Voigt, Stefan: In der Auflösung begriffen. Erkenntnismodelle in Arno Schmidts Spätwerk, Bielefeld 1999.

Wardrip-Fruin, Noah / Montfort, Nick (eds.): The New Media Reader, Cambridge Mass. 2003.

Weidermann, Volker: Der abwesende Herr Strauß. Ein Treffen mit dem unbekannten Schriftsteller der deutschen Literatur, Frankfurter Allgemeine Sonntagszeitung 14 March 2004, p. 23.

Yates, Frances A.: The Art of Memory, London 2001 [1966].

Zalewski, Daniel: Zombie Spawn Descend to Earth, The New York Times 24 March 2002, http://query.nytimes.com/gst/fullpage.html?res=9504E3D91 039F937A15-750C0A9649C8B63&sec=&spon=&pagewanted=1

Zymner, Rüdiger: Manerismus. Zur Poetischen Artistik bei Johann Fischart, Jean Paul und Arno Schmidt, Paderborn 1995.

Index

I thank Rebecca Linford for her help in compiling this index.

Note: Page numbers followed by *n* indicate note numbers.

Palaestra

Untersuchungen zur europäischen Literatur

V&R

329: Aura Maria Heydenreich

Wachstafel und Weltformel

Erinnerungspoetik und Wissenschafts-
kritik in Günter Eichs »Maulwürfen«

2007. 436 Seiten, gebunden
ISBN 978-3-525-20602-7

Lange Zeit galten Günter Eichs »Maulwürfe« als resignative Unsinnspoesie.
Dieses Fehlurteil wird hier Zug um Zug
revidiert, das Buch führt auf überra-
schend neues Terrain: Es widmet sich
dem Verhältnis von Gedächtnispoetik
und Intertextualität im Spätwerk
Günter Eichs. Es verortet dessen Spätwerk zwischen Poetik und Naturwis-
senschaften, deren bisher ungeahnte
hohe Relevanz für Eichs Poetologie
erstmals aufgezeigt wird. Ein neues
und überraschendes Licht fällt auf
Eichs »Maulwürfe«.

328: Christoph Jürgensen

»Der Rahmen arbeitet«

Paratextuelle Strategien der Lektüre-
lenkung im Werk Arno Schmidts

2007. 274 Seiten mit 6 Abb., gebunden
ISBN 978-3-525-20598-3

Die Arbeit zeigt anhand ausgewählter
Werke Arno Schmidts beispielhaft, auf
welche Weise Paratexte die Rezeption
›ihrer‹ Texte lenken.

327: Sandra Poppe

Visualität in Literatur und Film

Eine medienkomparatistische
Untersuchung moderner Erzähltexte und
ihrer Verfilmungen

2007. 334 Seiten, gebunden
ISBN 978-3-525-20600-3

Die Arbeit erläutert die Phänomene
literarischer und filmischer Visualität
und unternimmt einen ausführlichen
Vergleich dreier bedeutender Werke der
Weltliteratur (Proust, Kafka, Conrad)
und ihrer Verfilmungen. Ein abschlie-
ßendes Fazit zeigt, inwiefern die Visualität nicht nur als Schnittpunkt von
Literatur und Film, sondern auch als
Brücke zwischen anderen Künsten und
Medien steht.

326: Markus Neumann

Die »englische Komponente«

Zu Genese, Formen und Funktionen
des Traditionsverhaltens im Werk
Rudolf Borchardts

2007. 318 Seiten Mit 9 Abb., gebunden
ISBN 978-3-525-20601-0

Die komparatistisch ausgerichtete Studie
erschließt die Entstehungsbedingungen,
Gestaltungszüge und Funktionsweisen
der Bezugnahme auf die »großen Englän-
der« des 19. Jahrhunderts im Werk.

Vandenhoeck & Ruprecht